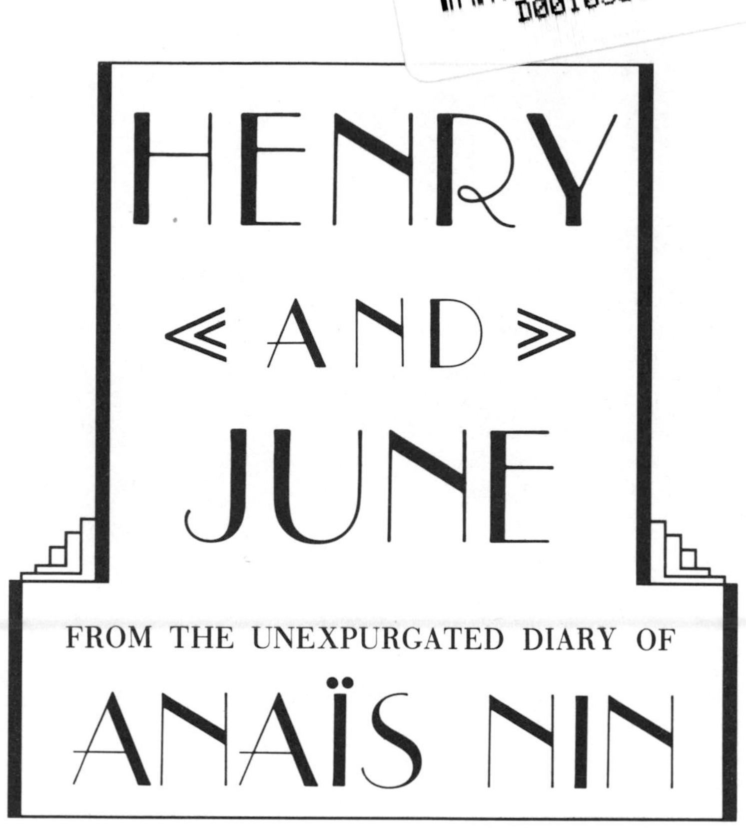


HARCOURT BRACE JOVANOVICH, PUBLISHERS
SAN DIEGO NEW YORK LONDON

HBJ



Library of Congress Cataloging-in-Publication Data

Nin, Anaïs, 1903–1977.
Henry and June.

Selections from: Diary of Anaïs Nin. 1931–1934.
1. Nin, Anaïs, 1903–1977—Diaries. 2. Authors, American—20th century—Diaries. 3. Miller, Henry, 1891–     —Friends and associates. I. Title.
PS3527.I865Z4642 1986 818′.5203 [B] 86-4754
ISBN 0-15-140003-2

Designed by Dalia Hartman

Printed in the United States of America

First edition

A B C D E

## EDITOR'S PREFACE

Anaïs Nin knew very early that she would be a writer. At age seven she signed her stories "Anaïs Nin, Member of the French Academy." In her schoolgirl French she wrote numerous stories and plays that seemed to spring spontaneously from a most dramatic imagination, heightened by Anaïs's need to control her two younger brothers. This, she discovered, could only be accomplished by telling them endless stories and casting them in her theatrical productions.

In 1914, when she was eleven, she began the now-famous diary as a series of letters to her father, who had abandoned the family. She treated the diary as a confidante and wrote in it almost daily throughout her life—in French, until 1920; after that, in English. (The handwritten journals, comprising some 35,000 pages, are now in the Special Collections Department of U.C.L.A.) The discipline of daily writing without readers or censorship gave Anaïs, over the years, an ability to describe her emotions of the moment, an ability not fully realized until the period of *Henry and June*, which began in 1931.

She wrote continuously, both fiction and her diary, for another forty-five years. Anaïs the diarist and Anaïs the novelist carried on an uneasy relationship. She wrote in the diary in 1933: "My book [a novel] and my journal step on each other's feet constantly. I can neither divorce nor reconcile them. I play the traitor to both. I am more loyal to my journal, however. I will put pages of my journal into the book but never pages of the book into the journal, showing a human faithfulness to the human authenticity of the journal."

In the late twenties John Erskine told Anaïs that her diary contained her best writing, and she began to work on an idea that would allow her to publish "many pages" of it. At this time it could have been published complete; she had nothing to conceal. Thereafter she would devise a number of plans for publication: transforming the diary into fiction, doing it in diary form with fictitious names, or doing it in diary form with both fictitious and real names. But from 1932 on, when she began with Henry Miller what became a lifelong search for the perfect love, she realized she could never publish the diary as she wrote it without hurting her husband, Hugh Guiler, as well as others. She turned, instead, to publishing fiction.

By the mid-fifties, after her stories and novels has failed to bring her more than underground recognition, she thought of another, more workable method of publishing the diary without risk of injury to others. She decided to use real names and to simply edit out her personal life, her husband, and her lovers. After reading *Henry and June*, anyone familiar with the first published diary (1966) will realize what an ingenious accomplishment this was. Anaïs the diarist would probably have begun that initial diary at its actual beginning in 1914. But Anaïs the novelist, always dominant, chose to begin in 1931, her most interesting and dramatic period, when she had just met Henry and June Miller.

The present volume reexamines that period from a new perspective, releasing material deleted from the original diary and never before published. It was Anaïs's wish to have the full story told.

The text is taken from journals thirty-two through thirty-six, titled "June," "The Possessed," "Henry," "Apotheosis and Downfall," and "Journal of a Possessed," written from October 1931 to October 1932. It has been edited to focus on the story of Anaïs, Henry, and June. Material that appeared in *The Diary of Anaïs Nin, 1931–1934* has been deleted, for the most part, but some of it has been repeated here for the sake of giving a coherent account.

Anaïs's diary writing was at its most prolific during this period. In 1932 alone she completed six journals. These include her first experiments in erotic writing. The puritanical Catholic girl who could not bring herself to describe to her diary her salacious (to her innocent mind) experiences as a model was now faced with recording her awakening to passion. She was influenced, of course, by Henry Miller's style and vocabulary. Ultimately her own unique voice prevails, and her writing reflects her emotional and physical frenzy during this momentous year. She is never to be quite this wild again, although her sexual odyssey will continue for many years to come.

Rupert Pole
Executor, The Anaïs Nin Trust

Los Angeles, California
February, 1986

# HENRY ≪ AND ≫ JUNE

## *PARIS. OCTOBER 1931*

My cousin Eduardo came to Louveciennes yesterday. We talked for six hours. He reached the conclusion I had come to also: that I need an older mind, a father, a man stronger than me, a lover who will lead me in love, because all the rest is too much a self-created thing. The impetus to grow and live intensely is so powerful in me I cannot resist it. I will work, I will love my husband, but I will fulfill myself.

As we were talking, Eduardo suddenly began to tremble, and he took my hand. He said that I belonged to him from the very beginning; that an obstacle stood between us: his fear of impotence because at first I had aroused ideal love in him. He has suffered from the realization that we are both seeking an experience which we might have given to each other. It has seemed strange to me, too. The men

I have wanted, I couldn't have. But I am determined to have an experience when it comes my way.

"Sensuality is a secret power in my body," I said to Eduardo. "Someday it will show, healthy and ample. Wait a while."

Or is this not the secret of the obstacle between us?—that his type is the large, buxom woman, heavy on the earth, while I will always be the virgin-prostitute, the perverse angel, the two-faced sinister and saintly woman.

For a whole week Hugo has come home very late, and I kept cheerful and unconcerned, as I had promised myself. Then on Friday he got worried and said, "Do you realize it is twenty minutes to eight, that I'm very late? Say something about it." And we both burst out laughing. He did not like my indifference.

On the other hand, our quarrels, when they come, seem harder and more emotional. Are all our emotions stronger now that we give vent to them? There is a desperation in our reconciliations, a new violence both in anger and in love. The problem of jealousy alone remains. It is the one obstacle to our complete freedom. I cannot even talk of my wish to go to a cabaret where we could dance with professional dancers.

I now call Hugo my "little magnate." He has a new private office the size of a studio. The entire bank building is magnificent and inspiring. I often wait for him in the conference room, where there are murals of New York as seen from an aeroplane, and I feel the power of New York reaching way over here. I do not criticize his work any more because such conflict kills him. We have both accepted the genius-banker as a reality, and the artist as a very vague possibility. However, psychology, being scientific thinking, has become a successful bridge between his banking and my writing. Such a bridge he can cross without much jolting.

It is true, as Hugo says, that I do my thinking and speculation in my journal and that he is only aware of the pain I can cause him when an incident happens. However, I am *his* journal. He can only think aloud with or through me. So Sunday morning he began to think aloud about the same things I had written in my journal, the need of orgies, of fulfillment in other directions. His need came to him in the middle of his own talk. He was wishing he could go to the Quatz Art Ball. He was just as overwhelmed with surprise at himself as I was by the sudden alteration of his expression, the loosening of his mouth, the rising of instincts he had never before entirely brought to the surface.

Intellectually I expected this, but I crumbled. I felt an acute conflict between helping him to accept his own nature and preserving our love. While I asked his forgiveness for my weakness I sobbed. He was tender and desperately sorry—made wild promises which I did not accept. When I had exhausted my pain, we went out in the garden.

I offered him all kinds of solutions: one, to let me go away to Zurich to study and give him temporary freedom. We fully realized we could not bear to meet our new experiences under each other's eyes. Another, to let him live in Paris for a while, and I would stay at Louveciennes and tell Mother he was traveling. All I asked for was time and distance between us to help me face the life we were throwing ourselves into.

He refused. He said he could not bear my absence just now. We had simply made a mistake; we had progressed too quickly. We had aroused problems we were not physically able to face. He was worn out, almost ill, and so was I.

We want to enjoy our new closeness for a while, live entirely in the present, postpone the other issues. We only ask each other for time to become reasonable again, to accept ourselves and the new conditions.

I asked Eduardo, "Is the desire for orgies one of those experiences one must live through? And once lived, can one pass on, without return of the same desires?"

"No," he said. "The life of freed instincts is composed of layers. The first layer leads to the second, the second to the third and so on. It leads ultimately to abnormal pleasures." How Hugo and I could preserve our love in this freeing of the instincts he did not know. Physical experiences, lacking the joys of love, depend on twists and perversions for pleasure. Abnormal pleasures kill the taste for normal ones.

All this, Hugo and I knew. Last night when we talked he swore that he desired no one but me. I am in love with him, too, and so we let the issue lie in the background. Yet the menace of those wayward instincts is there, inside of our very love.

## *NOVEMBER*

We have never been as happy or as miserable. Our quarrels are portentous, tremendous, violent. We are both wrathful to the point of madness; we desire death. My face is ravaged by tears, the veins on my temple swell. Hugo's mouth trembles. One cry from me brings him suddenly into my arms, sobbing. And then he desires me physically. We cry and kiss and come at the same moment. And the next moment we analyze and talk rationally. It is like the life of the Russians in *The Idiot*. It is hysteria. In cooler moments I wonder at the extravagance of our feelings. Dullness and peace are forever over.

We asked ourselves yesterday, in the middle of a quarrel, "What is happening to us? We never said such terrible things to each other?" And then Hugo said: "This is our honeymoon, and we are keyed up."

"Are you sure?" I asked incredulously.

"It may not seem like one," he said, laughing, "but it is. We are just overflowing with feelings. We can't keep our balance."

A seven-year-late, mature honeymoon, full of the fear of life. In between our quarrels we are acutely happy. Hell and heaven all at once. We are at once free and enslaved.

At times it seems as if we know that the only tie which can bind us together now is one of white-heat living, the same kind of intensity one finds in lovers and mistresses. We have unconsciously created a highly effervescent relationship within the security and peace of marriage. We are widening the circle of our sorrows and pleasures within the circle of our home and our two selves. It is our defense against the intruder, the unknown.

### *DECEMBER*

I've met Henry Miller.

He came to lunch with Richard Osborn, a lawyer I had

to consult on the contract for my D. H. Lawrence book.

When he first stepped out of the car and walked towards the door where I stood waiting, I saw a man I liked. In his writing he is flamboyant, virile, animal, magnificent. He's a man whom life makes drunk, I thought. He is like me.

In the middle of lunch, when we were seriously discussing books, and Richard had sailed off on a long tirade, Henry began to laugh. He said, "I'm not laughing at you, Richard, but I just can't help myself. I don't care a bit, not a bit who's right. I'm too happy. I'm just so happy right this moment with all the colors around me, the wine. The whole moment is so wonderful, so wonderful." He was laughing almost to tears. He was drunk. I was drunk, too, quite. I felt warm and dizzy and happy.

We talked for hours. Henry said the truest and deepest things, and he has a way of saying "hmmm" while trailing off on his own introspective journey.

Before I met Henry I was intent on my D. H. Lawrence book. It is being published by Edward Titus, and I am working with his assistant, Lawrence Drake.

"Where are you from?" he asks me at our first meeting.

"I'm half Spanish, half French. But I was raised in America."

"You've certainly survived the transplantation." He appears to be sneering as he talks. But I know better.

He takes up the work with tremendous enthusiasm and speed. I'm grateful. He calls me a romantic. I get angry. "I'm sick of my own romanticism!"

He has an interesting head—vivid, strong accents of black eyes, black hair, olive skin, sensual nostrils and mouth, a good profile. He looks like a Spaniard, but he is Jewish—Russian, he tells me. He is puzzling to me. He looks raw, easily hurt. I talk warily.

When he takes me to his place to go over the proofs, he tells me I interest him. I can't see why—he seems to have had a lot of experience; why does he bother about a beginner? We talk, fencingly. We work, not so very well. I don't trust him. When he says nice things to me, I think he is playing on my inexperience. When he puts his arms around me, I think he is amusing himself with an overintense and ridiculous little woman. When he gets more intense, I turn my face away from the new experience of his mustache. My hands are cold and moist. I tell him frankly, "You shouldn't flirt with a woman who doesn't know how to flirt."

It amuses him, my seriousness. He says, "Perhaps you are the kind of woman who doesn't hurt a man." He has been humiliated. When he thinks I have said, "You annoy me," he jumps away as if I had bitten him. I don't say that sort of thing. He is very impetuous, very strong, but he doesn't annoy me. I answer his fourth or fifth kiss. I begin to feel drunk. So I get up and say incoherently, "I'm going now—for me it can't be without love." He teases me. He bites my ears and kisses me, and I like his fierceness. He throws me on the couch for a moment, but somehow I escape. I am aware of his desire. I like his mouth and the knowing force of his arms, but his desire frightens me, repulses me. I think, it's because I don't love him. He's stirred me but I don't love him, I don't want him. As soon as I know this (his desire, pointing at me, is like a sword between us), I free myself, and I leave, without hurting him in any way.

I think, well, I just wanted the pleasure without feeling. But something holds me back. There is in me something untouched, unstirred, which commands me. *That* will have to be moved if I am to move wholly. I think of this in the Métro, and I get lost.

A few days later I met Henry. I was waiting to meet him, as if that would solve something, and it did. When I saw him, I thought, here is a man I could love. And I was not afraid.

Then I read Drake's novel, and I discover an unsuspected Drake—foreign, uprooted, fantastic, erratic. A realist, exasperated by reality.

Immediately his desire ceases to repulse me. A little link has been formed between two strangenesses. I respond to his imagination with mine. His novel conceals a few of his own feelings. How do I know? They are not consistent with the story, not quite. They are there because they are natural to him. The name Lawrence Drake is put on, too.

There are two ways to reach me: by way of kisses or by way of the imagination. But there is a hierarchy: the kisses alone don't work. I wondered at this last night as I closed Drake's book. I knew it would take me years to forget John [Erskine], because it was he who first stirred the secret source of my life.

There is nothing of Drake himself in the book, I am convinced. He hates the parts I like. It was all written objectively, consciously, and even the fantasy was carefully planned. We settle this at the beginning of my next visit. Very good. I am beginning to see things more clearly. I know now why I did not trust him the first day. His actions are devoid of either feeling or imagination. They are motivated by sheer habits of living and grabbing and analyzing. He's a grasshopper. He has now hopped into my life. My feeling of dislike becomes intensified. When he tries to kiss me, I evade him.

At the same time I concede to myself that he knows the technique of kissing better than anyone I've met. His gestures never miss their aim, no kiss ever goes astray. His hands are deft. My curiosity for sensuality is stirred. I have always been tempted by unknown pleasures. He has, like me, a sense of smell. I let him inhale me, then I slip away. Finally I lie still on the couch, but when his desire grows, I try to escape. Too late. Then I tell him the truth: woman's trouble. That does not seem to deter him. "You don't think I want that mechanical way—there are other ways." He sits up and uncovers his penis. I don't understand what he wants. He makes me get down on my knees. He offers it to my mouth. I get up as if struck by a whip.

He is furious. I say to him, "I told you we have different ways of doing things. I warned you I was inexperienced."

"I never believed it. I don't yet believe it. You can't be, with your sophisticated face and your passionateness. You're playing a trick on me."

I listen to him; the analyst in me is uppermost, still on the job. He pours out stories to show me that I don't appreciate what other women do.

In my head I answer, "*You* don't know what sensuality is. Hugo and I do. It's in us, not in your devious practices; it's in feeling, in passion, in love."

He goes on talking. I watch him with my "sophisticated face." He does not hate me because, however repulsed, however angry I am, I have a facility for forgiveness. When I see that I have let him be aroused, it seems natural to let him release his desire between my legs. I just let him, out of pity. That, he senses. Other women, he says, would have insulted him. He understands my pity for his ridiculous, humiliating physical necessity.

I owed him that; he had revealed a new world to me. I had understood for the first time the abnormal experiences Eduardo had warned me against. Exoticism and sensuality now had another meaning for me.

Nothing was spared my eyes, so that I might always remember: Drake looking down at his wet handkerchief, offering me a towel, heating water on the gas stove.

I tell Hugo the story partially, leaving out my activity, extracting the meaning for him and for me. As something forever finished, he accepts it. We efface an hour by passionate love, without twists, without aftertaste. When it is finished, it is not finished, we lie still in each other's arms, lulled by our love, by tenderness—sensuality in which the whole being can participate.

Henry has imagination, an animal feeling for life, the greatest power of expression, and the truest genius I have ever known. "Our age has need of violence," he writes. And he is violence.

Hugo admires him. At the same time he worries. He says justly, "You fall in love with people's minds. I'm going to lose you to Henry."

"No, no, you won't lose me." I know how incendiary my imagination is. I am already devoted to Henry's work, but I separate my body from my mind. I enjoy his strength, his ugly, destructive, fearless, cathartic strength. I could write a book this minute about his genius. Almost every other word he utters causes an electric charge: on Buñuel's

*Age d'Or*, on Salavin, on Waldo Frank, on Proust, on the film *Blue Angel*, on people, on animalism, on Paris, on French prostitutes, on American women, on America. He is even walking ahead of Joyce. He repudiates form. He writes as we think, on various levels at once, with seeming irrelevance, seeming chaos.

I have finished my new book, minus polishing. Hugo read it Sunday and was transported. It is surrealistic, lyrical. Henry says I write like a man, with tremendous clearness and conciseness. He was surprised by my book on Lawrence, although he does not like Lawrence. "So intelligent a book." It is enough. He knows I have outgrown Lawrence. I have already another book in my head.

I have transposed Drake's sexuality into another kind of interest. Men need other things besides a sexual recipient. They have to be soothed, lulled, understood, helped, encouraged, and listened to. By doing all of this tenderly and warmly—well, he lit his pipe and let me alone. I watched him as if he were a bull.

Besides, being intelligent, he understands that my type can't be "made" without the illusion. He cannot bother with illusions. O.K. He is a little angry, but . . . he'll make a story of it. He is amused because I tell him I know he doesn't love me. He thought I might really be childish enough to believe that he did. "Bright kid," he says. And he tells me all his troubles.

Again the question: Do we want parties, orgies? Hugo says definitely no. He won't take chances. It would be forcing our temperament. We don't enjoy parties, we don't enjoy drinking, we don't envy Henry his life. But I protest:

One doesn't do those things lucidly, one gets drunk. Hugo doesn't want to get drunk. Neither do I. Anyway, we won't go and seek the whore or the man. If she or he comes our way, inevitably, then we'll live out what we want.

Meanwhile we live satisfied with our less intense life, because, of course, the intensity has died down—after the quickening of Hugo's passion because of my entanglement with John. He has also been jealous of Henry and of Drake—he was miserable—but I have reassured him. He sees that I am wiser, that in fact I never again intend to run into a blank wall.

I really believe that if I were not a writer, not a creator, not an experimenter, I might have been a very faithful wife. I think highly of faithfulness. But my temperament belongs to the writer, not to the woman. Such a separation may seem childish, but it is possible. Subtract the overintensity, the sizzling of ideas, and you get a woman who loves perfection. And faithfulness is one of the perfections. It seems stupid and unintelligent to me now because I have bigger plans in mind. Perfection is static, and I am in full progress. The faithful wife is only one phase, one moment, one metamorphosis, one condition.

I might have found a husband who loved me less exclusively, but it would not be Hugo, and whatever is Hugo, whatever Hugo is composed of, I love. We deal in different values. For his faithfulness, I give him my imagination—even my talent, if you will. I have never been satisfied with our accounts. But they must stand.

He will come home tonight and I will watch him. Finer than any man I know, the nearly perfect man. Touchingly perfect.

---

The hours I have spent in cafés are the only ones I call living, apart from writing. My resentment grows because of the stupidity of Hugo's bank life. When I go home, I know I go back to the banker. He smells of it. I abhor it. Poor Hugo.

Everything is made right by a talk with Henry all afternoon—that mixture of intellect and emotionalism which I like. He can be swept away completely. We talked without noticing the time until Hugo came home, and we had dinner together. Henry remarked on the green fat-bellied bottle of wine and the hissing of the slightly damp log in the fire.

He thinks I must know about life because I posed for painters. The extent of my innocence would be incredible to him. How late I have awakened and with what furor! What does it matter what Henry thinks of me? He'll know soon enough exactly what I am. He has a caricatural mind. I'll see myself in caricature.

Hugo says rightly that it takes great hate to make a caricature. Henry and my friend Natasha [Troubetskoi] have great hates. I do not. Everything with me is either worship and passion or pity and understanding. I hate rarely, though when I hate, I hate murderously. For example now, I hate the bank and everything connected with it. I also hate Dutch paintings, penis-sucking, parties, and cold rainy weather. But I am more preoccupied with loving.

I am absorbed by Henry, who is uncertain, self-critical, sincere. I get a tremendous and selfish pleasure out of our gift of money to him. What do I think of when I sit by the fire? To get a bunch of railroad tickets for Henry; to buy him *Albertine disparue*. Henry wants to read *Albertine disparue*? Quick, I won't be happy until he has the book. I am an ass. Nobody likes to have these things done for them, nobody but Eduardo, and even he, in certain moods, prefers utter indifference. I would like to give Henry a home, marvelous food, an income. If I were rich, I would not be rich very long.

Drake no longer interests me in the least. I was relieved he did not come today. Henry interests me, but not physically. Is it possible I might at last be satisfied with Hugo? It hurt me when he left for Holland today. I felt old, detached.

A startlingly white face, burning eyes. June Mansfield, Henry's wife. As she came towards me from the darkness of my garden into the light of the doorway I saw for the first time the most beautiful woman on earth.

Years ago, when I tried to imagine a true beauty, I had created an image in my mind of just that woman. I had even imagined she would be Jewish. I knew long ago the color of her skin, her profile, her teeth.

Her beauty drowned me. As I sat in front of her I felt that I would do anything mad for her, anything she asked of me. Henry faded. She was color, brilliance, strangeness.

Her role in life alone preoccupies her. I knew the reasons: her beauty brings dramas and events to her. Ideas mean little. I saw in her a caricature of the theatrical and dramatic personage. Costume, attitudes, talk. She is a superb actress. No more. I could not grasp her core. Everything Henry had said about her was true.

By the end of the evening I was like a man, terribly in love with her face and body, which promised so much, and I hated the self created in her by others. Others feel because of her; and because of her, others write poetry; because of her, others hate; others, like Henry, love her in spite of themselves.

June. At night I dreamed of her, as if she were very small, very frail, and I loved her. I loved a smallness which had appeared to me in her talk: the disproportionate pride, a hurt pride. She lacks the core of sureness, she craves admiration insatiably. She lives on reflections of herself in others' eyes. She does not dare to be herself. There is no June Mansfield. She knows it. The more she is loved, the more she knows it. She knows there is a very beautiful woman who took her cue last night from my inexperience and tried to lose her depth of knowledge.

A startlingly white face retreating into the darkness of the garden. She poses for me as she leaves. I want to run out and kiss her fantastic beauty, kiss it and say, "You carry away with you a reflection of me, a part of me. I dreamed you, I wished for your existence. You will always be part of my life. If I love you, it must be because we have shared at some time the same imaginings, the same madness, the same stage.

"The only power which keeps you together is your love for Henry, and for that, you love him. He hurts you, but he keeps your body and soul together. He integrates you. He lashes and whips you into occasional wholeness. I have Hugo."

I wanted to see her again. I thought Hugo would love her. It seemed so natural to me that everybody should love her. I talked to Hugo about her. I felt no jealousy.

When she came out of the dark again, she seemed even more beautiful to me than before. Also she seemed more sincere. I said to myself, "People are always more sincere with Hugo." I also thought it was because she was more at ease. I could not tell what Hugo was thinking. She was going upstairs to our bedroom to leave her coat. She stood for a second halfway up the stairs where the light set her off against the turquoise green wall. Blond hair, pallid face, demoniac peaked eyebrows, a cruel smile with a disarming dimple. Perfidious, infinitely desirable, drawing me to her as towards death.

Downstairs, Henry and June formed an alliance. They were telling us about their quarrels, breakdowns, wars against each other. Hugo, who is uneasy in the presence of emotions, tried to laugh off the jagged corners, to smooth out the discord, the ugly, the fearful, to lighten their confidences. Like a Frenchman, suave and reasonable, he dissolved all possibility of drama. There might have been a fierce, inhuman, horrible scene between June and Henry, but Hugo kept us from knowing.

Afterwards I pointed out to him how he had prevented all of us from living, how he had caused a living moment to pass him by. I was ashamed of his optimism, his trying to smooth things out. He understood. He promised to remember. Without me he would be entirely shut out by his habit of conventionality.

We had a cheerful dinner together. Henry and June were both famished. Then we went to the Grand Guignol. In the car June and I sat together and talked in accord.

"When Henry described you to me," she said, "he left out the most important parts. He did not get you at all." She knew that immediately; she and I had understood each other, every detail and nuance of each other.

In the theatre. How difficult to notice Henry while she sits resplendent with a masklike face. Intermission. She and I want to smoke, Henry and Hugo don't. Walking out together, what a stir we create. I say to her, "You are the only woman who ever answered the demands of my imagination." She answers, "It is a good thing that I am going away. You would soon unmask me. I am powerless before a woman. I do not know how to deal with a woman."

Is she telling the truth? No. In the car she had been telling me about her friend Jean, the sculptress and poetess. "Jean had the most beautiful face," and then she adds hastily, "I am not speaking of an ordinary woman. Jean's face, her beauty was more like that of a man." She stops. "Jean's hands were so very lovely, so very supple because she had handled clay a lot. The fingers tapered." What anger stirs in me at June's praise of Jean's hands? Jealousy? And her insistence that her life has been full of men, that she does not know how to act before a woman. Liar!

She says, staring intently, "I thought your eyes were blue. They are strange and beautiful, gray and gold, with those long black lashes. You are the most graceful woman I have ever seen. You glide when you walk." We talk about the colors we love. She always wears black and purple.

We return to our seats. She turns constantly to me instead of to Hugo. Coming out of the theatre I take her arm. Then she slips her hand over mine; we lock them. She says, "The other night at Montparnasse I was hurt to hear your name mentioned. I don't want to see cheap men crawl into your life. I feel rather . . . protective."

In the café I see ashes under the skin of her face. Disintegration. What terrible anxiety I feel. I want to put my arms around her. I feel her receding into death and I am willing to enter death to follow her, to embrace her. She is dying before my eyes. Her tantalizing, somber beauty is dying. Her strange, manlike strength.

I do not make any sense out of her words. I am fascinated by her eyes and mouth, her discolored mouth, badly rouged. Does she know I feel immobile and fixed, lost in her?

She shivers with cold under her light velvet cape.

"Will you have lunch with me before you leave?" I ask.

She is glad to be leaving. Henry loves her imperfectly and brutally. He has hurt her pride by desiring her opposite: ugly, common, passive women. He cannot endure her positivism, her strength. I hate Henry now, heartily. I hate men who are afraid of women's strength. Probably Jean loved her strength, her destructive power. For June is destruction.

My strength, as Hugo tells me later when I discover he hates June, is soft, indirect, delicate, insinuating, creative, tender, womanly. Hers is like that of a man. Hugo tells me she has a mannish neck, a mannish voice, and coarse hands. Don't I see? No, I do not see, or if I see, I don't care. Hugo admits he is jealous. From the very first minute they hated each other.

"Does she think that with her woman's sensibility and subtlety she can love anything in you that I have not loved?"

It is true. Hugo has been infinitely tender with me, but while he talks of June I think of our hands locked together. She does not reach the same sexual center of my being that man reaches; she does not touch that. What, then, has she moved in me? I have wanted to possess her as if I were a man, but I have also wanted her to love me with the eyes, the hands, the senses that only women have. It is a soft and subtle penetration.

I hate Henry for daring to injure her enormous and shallow pride in herself. June's superiority arouses his hatred, even a feeling of revenge. He eyes my gentle, homely maid, Emilia. His offense makes me love June.

I love her for what she has dared to be, for her hardness, her cruelty, her egoism, her perverseness, her demoniac destructiveness. She would crush me to ashes without hesitation. She is a personality created to the limit. I worship her courage to hurt, and I am willing to be sacrificed to it. She will add the sum of me to her. She will be June plus all that I contain.

## *JANUARY 1932*

We met, June and I, at American Express. I knew she would be late, and I did not mind. I was there before the hour, almost ill with tenseness. I would see her, in full daylight, advance out of the crowd. Could it be possible? I was afraid that I would stand there exactly as I had stood in other places, watching a crowd and knowing no June would ever appear because June was a product of my imagination. I could hardly believe she would arrive by those streets, cross such a boulevard, emerge out of a handful of dark, faceless people, walk into that place. What a joy to watch that crowd scurrying and then to see her striding, resplendent, incredible, towards me. I hold her warm hand. She is going for mail. Doesn't the man at American Express see the wonder of her? Nobody like her ever called for mail. Did any woman ever wear shabby shoes, a shabby black dress, a shabby dark blue cape, and an old violet hat as she wears them?

I cannot eat in her presence. But I am calm outwardly, with that Oriental placidity of bearing that is so deceptive. She drinks and smokes. She is quite mad, in a sense, subject to fears and manias. Her talk, mostly unconscious, would be revealing to an analyst, but I cannot analyze it. It is mostly lies. The contents of her imagination are realities to her. But what is she building so carefully? An aggrandizement of her personality, a fortifying and glorifying of it. In the obvious and enveloping warmth of my admiration she expands. She seems at once destructive and helpless. I want to protect her. What a joke! I, protect her whose power is infinite. Her power is so strong that I actually believe it when she tells me her destructiveness is unintentional. Has she tried to destroy me? No, she walked into my house and I was willing to endure any pain from her hands. If there is any calculation in her, it comes only afterwards, when she becomes aware of her power and wonders how she should use it. I do not think her evil potency is directed. Even she is baffled by it.

I have her in myself now as one to be pitied and protected. She is involved in perversities and tragedies she cannot live up to. I have at last caught her weakness. Her life is full of fantasies. I want to force her into reality. I want to do violence to her. I, who am sunk in dreams, in half-lived acts, see myself possessed by a furious intention: I want to grasp June's evasive hands, oh, with what strength, take her to a hotel room and realize her dream and mine, a dream she has evaded facing all her life.

I went to see Eduardo, tense and shattered by my three hours with June. He saw the weakness in her and urged me to act out my strength.

I could hardly think clearly because in the taxi she had pressed my hand. I was not ashamed of my adoration, my humility. Her gesture was not sincere. I do not believe she could love.

She says she wants to keep the rose dress I wore the first night she saw me. When I tell her I want to give her a going-away present, she says she wants some of that perfume she smelled in my house, to evoke memories. And she needs shoes, stockings, gloves, underwear. Sentimentality? Romanticism? If she *really* means it . . . Why do I doubt her? Perhaps she is just very sensitive, and hypersensitive people are false when others doubt them; they waver. And one thinks them insincere. Yet I want to believe her. At the same time it does not seem so very important that she should love me. It is not her role. I am so filled with my love of her. And at the same time I feel that I am dying. Our love would be death. The embrace of imaginings.

When I tell Hugo the stories June has told me, he says they are simply very cheap. I don't know.

Then Eduardo spends two days here, the demoniac analyst, making me realize the crisis I am passing through. I want to see June. I want to see June's body. I have not dared to look at her body. I know it is beautiful.

Eduardo's questions madden me. Relentlessly, he observes how I have humbled myself. I have not dwelt on the successes which could glorify me. He makes me remember that my father beat me, that my first remembrance of him is a humiliation. He had said I was ugly after having typhoid fever. I had lost weight and my curls.

What has made me ill now? June. June and her sinister appeal. She has taken drugs; she loved a woman; she talks the cops' language when she tells stories. And yet she has kept that incredible, out-of-date, uncallous sentimentalism: "Give me the perfume I smelled in your house. Walking up the hill to your house, in the dark, I was in ecstasy."

I ask Eduardo, "Do you really think I am a lesbian? Do you take this seriously? Or is it just a reaction against my experience with Drake?" He is not sure.

Hugo takes a definite stand and says he considers

everything outside of our love extraneous—phases, passionate curiosities. He wants a security to live by. I rejoice in his finding it. I tell him he is right.

Finally Eduardo says I am not a lesbian, because I do not hate men—on the contrary. In my dream last night I desired Eduardo, not June. The night before, when I dreamed of June, I was at the top of a skyscraper and expected to walk down the façade of it on a very narrow fire ladder. I was terrified. I could not do it.

She came to Louveciennes Monday. I asked her cruelly, just as Henry had, "Are you a lesbian? Have you faced your impulses in your own mind?"

She answered me so quietly. "Jean was too masculine. I have faced my feelings, I am fully aware of them, but I have never found anyone I wanted to live them out with, so far." And she turned the conversation evasively. "What a lovely way you have of dressing. This dress—its rose color, its old-fashioned fullness at the bottom, the little black velvet jacket, the lace collar, the lacing over the breasts—how perfect, absolutely perfect. I like the way you cover yourself, too. There is very little nudity, just your neck, really. I love your turquoise ring, and the coral."

Her hands were shaking; she was trembling. I was ashamed of my brutality. I was intensely nervous. She told me how at the restaurant she had wanted to see my feet and how she could not bring herself to stare. I told her how I was afraid to look at her body. We talked brokenly. She looked at my feet, in sandals, and thought them lovely.

I said, "Do you like these sandals?" She answered that she had always loved sandals and worn them until she had become too poor to have them. I said, "Come up to my room and try the other pair I have."

She tried them on, sitting on my bed. They were too small for her. I saw she wore cotton stockings, and it hurt me to see June in cotton stockings. I showed her my black cape, which she thought beautiful. I made her try it on, and then I saw the beauty of her body, its fullness and heaviness, and it overwhelmed me.

I could not understand why she was so ill-at-ease, so timid, so frightened. I told her I would make her a cape like mine. Once I touched her arm. She moved it away. Had I frightened her? Could there be someone more sensitive and more afraid than I? I couldn't believe it. I was not afraid at that moment. I wanted desperately to touch her.

When she sat on the couch downstairs, the opening of her dress showed the beginning of her breasts, and I wanted to kiss her there. I was acutely upset and trembling. I was becoming aware of her sensitiveness and fear of her own feelings. She talked, but now I knew she talked to evade a deeper inner talk—the things we could not say.

We met the next day at American Express. She came in her tailored suit because I had said I liked it.

She had said she wanted nothing from me but the perfume I wore and my wine-colored handkerchief. But I insisted that she had promised to let me buy her sandals.

First I made her go to the ladies' room. I opened my bag and pulled out a pair of sheer stockings. "Put them on," I pleaded. She obeyed. Meanwhile I opened a bottle of perfume. "Put some on." The attendant was there, staring, waiting for her tip. I did not care about her. June had a hole in her sleeve.

I was terribly happy. June was exultant. We talked simultaneously. "I wanted to call you last night. I wanted to send you a telegram," June said. She had wanted to tell me she was very unhappy on the train, regretting her awkwardness, her nervousness, her pointless talk. There had been so much, so much she wanted to say.

Our fears of displeasing each other, of disappointing each other were the same. She had gone to the café in the evening as if drugged, full of thoughts of me. People's voices reached her from afar. She was elated. She could not sleep. What had I done to her? She had always been poised, she could always talk well, people never overwhelmed her.

When I realized what she was revealing to me, I almost went mad with joy. She loved me, then? June! She sat beside me in the restaurant, small, timid, unworldly, panic-stricken. She would say something and then beg forgiveness for its stupidity. I could not bear it. I told her, "We have both lost ourselves, but sometimes we reveal the most when we are least like ourselves. I am not trying to think any more. I can't think when I am with you. You are like me, wishing for a perfect moment, but nothing too long imagined can be perfect in a worldly way. Neither one of us can say just the right thing. We are overwhelmed. Let us be overwhelmed. It is so lovely, so lovely. I love you, June."

And not knowing what else to say I spread on the bench between us the wine-colored handkerchief she wanted, my coral earrings, my turquoise ring, which Hugo had given me and which it hurt me to give, but it was blood I wanted to lay before June's beauty and before June's incredible humility.

We went to the sandal shop. In the shop the ugly woman who waited on us hated us and our visible happiness. I held June's hand firmly. I commandeered the shop. I was the man. I was firm, hard, willful with the shopkeepers. When they mentioned the broadness of June's feet, I scolded them.

June could not understand their French, but she could see they were nasty. I said to her, "When people are nasty to you I feel like getting down on my knees before you."

We chose the sandals. She refused anything else, anything that was not symbolical or representative of me. Everything I wore she would wear, although she had never wanted to imitate anyone else before.

When we walked together through the streets, bodies close together, arm in arm, hands locked, I could not talk. We were walking over the world, over reality, into ecstasy. When she smelled my handkerchief, she inhaled me. When I clothed her beauty, I possessed her.

She said, "There are so many things I would love to do with you. With you I would take opium." June, who does not accept a gift which has no symbolical significance; June, who washes laundry to buy herself a bit of perfume; June, who is not afraid of poverty and drabness and who is untouched by it, untouched by the drunkenness of her friends; June, who judges, selects, discards people with severity, who knows, when she is telling her endless anecdotes, that they are ways of escape, keeping herself all the more secret behind that profuse talk. Secretly mine.

Hugo begins to understand. Reality exists only between him and me, in our love. All the rest, dreams. Our love is solved. I can be faithful. I was terrifyingly happy during the night.

But I must kiss her, I must kiss her.

If she had wanted to, yesterday I would have sat on the floor, with my head against her knees. But she would not have it. Yet at the station while we wait for the train she begs for my hand. I call out her name. We stand pressed together, faces almost touching. I smile at her while the train leaves. I turn away.

The stationmaster wants to sell me some charity tickets. I buy them and give them to him, wishing him luck at the lottery. He gets the benefit of my wanting to give to June, to whom one cannot give anything.

What a secret language we talk, undertones, overtones, nuances, abstractions, symbols. Then we return to Hugo and to Henry, filled with an incandescence which frightens them both. Henry is uneasy. Hugo is sad. What is this powerful magical thing we give ourselves to, June and I, when we are together? Wonder! Wonder! It comes with her.

Last night, after June, filled with June, I could not bear Hugo reading the newspapers and talking about trusts and a successful day. He understood—he does understand—but he couldn't share, he could not grasp the incandescent. He teased me. He was humorous. He was immensely lovable and warm. But I could not come back.

So I lay on the couch, smoking, and thinking of June. At the station, I had fainted.

The intensity is shattering us both. She is glad to be leaving. She is less yielding than I am. She really wants to escape from that which is giving her life. She does not like my power, whereas I take joy in submitting to her.

When we met for half an hour today to discuss Henry's future, she asked me to take care of him, and then she gave me her silver bracelet with a cat's-eye stone, when she has so few possessions. I refused at first, and then the joy of wearing her bracelet, a part of her, filled me. I carry it like a symbol. It is precious to me.

Hugo noticed it and hated it. He wanted to take it from

me, to tease me. I clung to it with all my strength while he crushed my hands, letting him hurt me.

June was afraid that Henry would turn me against her. What does she fear? I said to her, "There is a fantastic secret between us. I only know about you through my own knowledge. Faith. What is Henry's knowledge to me?"

Then I met Henry accidentally at the bank. I saw that he hated me, and I was startled. June had said that he was uneasy and restless, because he is more jealous of women than of men. June, inevitably, sows madness. Henry, who thought me a "rare" person, now hates me. Hugo, who rarely hates, hates her.

Today she said that when she talked to Henry about me she tried to be very natural and direct so as not to imply anything unusual. She told him, "Anaïs was just bored with her life, so she took us up." That seemed crude to me. It was the only ugly thing I have heard her say.

Hugo and I yield entirely to each other. We cannot be without each other, we cannot endure discord, war, estrangement, we cannot take walks alone, we do not like to travel without each other. We have yielded in spite of our individualism, our hatred of intimacy. We have absorbed our egocentric selves into our love. Our love *is* our ego.

I do not think June and Henry have achieved that, because both their individualities are too strong. So they are at war; love is a conflict; they must lie to each other, mistrust each other.

June wants to go back to New York and do something well, be lovely for me, satisfy me. She is afraid of disappointing me.

We had lunch together in a softly lighted place which

surrounded us with velvety closeness. We took off our hats. We drank champagne. June refused all sweet or tasteless food. She could live on grapefruit, oysters, and champagne.

We talked in half-spoken abstractions, clear to us alone. She made me realize how she eluded all of Henry's attempts to grasp her logically, to reach a knowledge of her.

She sat there filled with champagne. She talked about hashish and its effects. I said, "I have known such states without hashish. I do not need drugs. I carry all that in myself." At this she was a little angry. She did not realize that I achieved those states without destroying my mind. My mind must not die, because I am a writer. I am the poet who must see. I am not just the poet who can get drunk on June's beauty.

It was her fault that I began to notice discrepancies in her stories, childish lies. Her lack of coordination and logic left loopholes, and when I put the pieces together, I formed a judgment, a judgment which she fears always, which she wants to run away from. She lives without logic. As soon as one tries to coordinate June, June is lost. She must have seen it happen many times. She is like a man who is drunk and gives himself away.

We were talking about perfumes, their substance, their mixtures, their meaning. She said casually, "Saturday, when I left you, I bought some perfume for Ray." (Ray is a girl she has told me about.) At the moment I did not think. I retained the name of the perfume, which was very expensive.

We went on talking. She is as affected by my eyes as I am by her face. I told her how her bracelet clutched my wrist like her very fingers, holding me in barbaric slavery. She wants my cape around her body.

After lunch we walked. She had to buy her ticket for New York. First we went in a taxi to her hotel. She brought out a marionette, Count Bruga, made by Jean. He had violet hair and violet eyelids, a prostitute's eyes, a Pulcinella nose, a loose, depraved mouth, consumptive cheeks, a mean, aggressive chin, murderer's hands, wooden legs, a Spanish sombrero, a black velvet jacket. He had been on the stage.

June sat him on the floor of the taxi, in front of us. I laughed at him.

We walked into several steamship agencies. June did not have enough money for even a third-class passage and she was trying to get a reduction. I saw her lean over the counter, her face in her hands, appealing, so that the men behind the counter devoured her with their eyes, boldly. And she so soft, persuasive, alluring, smiling up in a secret way at them. I was watching her begging. Count Bruga leered at me. I was only conscious of my jealousy of those men, not of her humiliation.

We walked out. I told June I would give her the money she needed, which was more than I could afford to give, much more.

We went into another steamship agency, with June barely finishing some mad fairy tale before she stated her errand. I saw the man at the counter taken out of himself, transfixed by her face and her soft, yielding way of talking to him, of paying and signing. I stood by and watched him ask her, "Will you have a cocktail with me tomorrow?" June was shaking hands with him. "Three o'clock?" "No. At six." She smiled at him as she does at me. Then as we left she explained herself hurriedly. "He was very useful to me, very helpful. He is going to do a lot for me. I couldn't say no. I don't intend to go, but I couldn't say no."

"You must go, now that you said yes," I said angrily, and then the literalness and stupidity of this statement nauseated me. I took June's arm and said almost in a sob, "I can't bear it, I can't bear it." I was angry at some undefinable thing. I thought of the prostitute, honest because in exchange for money she gives her body. June would never give her body. But she would beg as I would never beg, promise as I would not promise unless I were to give.

June! There was such a tear in my dream. She knew it. So she took my hand against her warm breast and we walked, I feeling her breast. She was always naked under her dress. She did it perhaps unconsciously, as if to soothe an angry child. And she talked about things that were not to the point. "Would you rather I had said no, brutally, to the man? I am sometimes brutal, you know, but I couldn't be in front of you. I didn't want to hurt his feelings. He had been very helpful." And as I did not know what angered me, I said nothing. It was not a question of accepting or refusing a cocktail. One had to go back to the root of why she should need the help of that man. A statement of hers came back to me: "However bad things are for me I always find someone who will buy me champagne." Of course. She was a woman accumulating huge debts which she never intended to pay, for afterwards she boasted of her sexual inviolability. A gold digger. Pride in the possession of her own body but not too proud to humiliate herself with prostitute eyes over the counter of a steamship company.

She was telling me that she and Henry had quarreled over buying butter. They had no money and . . . "No money?" I said. "But Saturday I gave you 400 francs, for you and Henry to eat with. And today is Monday."

"We had things to pay up that we owed. . . ."

I thought she meant the hotel room. Then suddenly I remembered the perfume, which cost 200 francs. Why didn't she say to me, "I bought perfume and gloves and stockings Saturday." She did not look at me when she intimated they had the rent to pay. Then I remembered another thing she had said. "People say to me that if I had a fortune, I could spent it in a day, and no one would ever know how. I can never account for the way I spend money."

This was the other face of June's fantasy. We walked the streets, and all the softness of her breast could not lull the pain.

I went home and was very heavy in Hugo's arms. I said to him, "I have come back." And he was very happy.

But yesterday at four, when I was waiting for her at American Express, the doorman said to me, "Your friend was here this morning and she said good-bye to me as if she were not coming back." "But we had agreed to meet here." If I were never again to see June walking towards me—impossible. It was like dying. What did it matter, all I thought the day before. She was unethical, irresponsible—it was her nature. I would not tamper with her nature. My pride about money matters was aristocratic. I was too scrupulous and proud. I would not change anything in June which was basic and at the root of her fantastic being. She alone was without fetters. I was a fettered, ethical being, in spite of my amoral intellect. I could not have let Henry go hungry. I accepted her entirely. I would not fight her. If only she would come and meet me for that last hour.

I had dressed ritually for her, in the very costume which created a void between me and other people, a costume which was a symbol of my individualism and which she alone would understand. Black turban, old rose dress with black lace bodice and collar, old rose coat with Medici collar. I had created a stir as I walked, and I was lonelier than ever because the reaction was partly hostile, mocking.

Then June came, all in black velvet, black cape and plumed hat, paler and more incandescent than ever, and carrying Count Bruga, as I had asked her to do. The wonder of her face and smile, her smileless eyes . . .

I took her to a Russian tearoom. The Russians sang as we felt. June wondered if they were really burning, as it seemed from their voices and intense playing. Probably they were not burning as June and I were.

Champagne and caviar with June. It is the only time one knows what champagne is and what caviar is. They are June, Russian voices and June.

Ugly, unimaginative, dead people surround us. We are blind to them. I look at June, in black velvet. June rushing towards death. Henry cannot rush on with her because he fights for life. But June and I together do not hold back. I follow her. And it is an acute joy to go along, giving in to the dissolution of the imagination, to her knowledge of strange experiences, to our games with Count Bruga, who bows to the world with the weeping willowness of his purple hair.

It is all over. In the street, June says regretfully, "I had wanted to hold you and caress you." I put her in a taxi. She sits there about to leave me and I stand by in torment. "I want to kiss you," I say. "I want to kiss you," says June, and she offers her mouth, which I kiss for a long time.

When she left, I just wanted to sleep for many days, but I still had something to face, my relationship with Henry.

We asked him to come to Louveciennes. I wanted to offer him peace and a soothing house, but of course I knew we would talk about June.

We walked off our restlessness, and we talked. There is in both of us an obsession to grasp June. He has no jealousy of me, because he said I brought out wonderful things in June, that it was the first time June had ever attached herself to a woman of value. He seemed to expect I would have power over her life.

When he saw that I understood June and was ready to be truthful with him, we talked freely. Yet once I paused, hesitant, wondering at my faithlessness to June. Then Henry observed that although truth, in June's case, had to be disregarded, it could be the only basis of any exchange between us.

We both felt the need of allying our two minds, our two different logics, in understanding the problem of June. Henry loves her and always her. He also wants to possess June the character, the powerful, fictionlike personage. In his love for her he has had to endure so many torments that the lover has taken refuge in the writer. He has written a ferocious and resplendent book about June and Jean.

He was questioning the lesbianism. When he heard me say certain things he had heard June say, he was startled, because he believes me. I said, "After all, if there is an explanation of the mystery it is this: The love between women is a refuge and an escape into harmony. In the love between man and woman there is resistance and conflict. Two women do not judge each other, brutalize each other, or find anything to ridicule. They surrender to sentimentality, mutual understanding, romanticism. Such love is death, I'll admit."

Last night I sat up until one o'clock reading Henry's novel, *Moloch*, while he read mine. His was overwhelming, the work of a giant. I was at a loss to tell him how it affected me. And this giant sat there quietly and read my slight book with such comprehension, such enthusiasm, talking about the deftness of it, the subtlety, the voluptuousness, shouting at certain passages, criticizing, too. What a force he is!

I gave him the one thing June cannot give him: honesty. I am so ready to admit what a supremely developed ego would not admit: that June is a terrifying and inspiring character who makes every other woman insipid, that I would live her life except for my compassion and my conscience, that she may destroy Henry the man, but Henry the writer is more enriched by ordeals than by peace. I, on the other hand, cannot destroy Hugo, because he has nothing else. But like June, I have a capacity for delicate perversions. The love of only one man or one woman is an enclosure.

My conflict is going to be greater than June's, because she has no mind watching her life. Others do it for her, and she denies all they say or write. I have a mind which is bigger than all the rest of me, an inexorable conscience.

Eduardo says, "Go and be psychoanalyzed." But that seems too simple. I want to make my own discoveries.

I do not need drugs, artificial stimulation. Yet I want to experience those very things with June, to penetrate the evil which attracts me. I seek life, and the experiences I want are denied me because I carry in me a force which neutralizes them. I meet June, the near-prostitute, and she becomes pure. A purity which maddens Henry, a purity of face and being which is awesome, just as I saw her one afternoon in the corner of the divan, transparent, supernatural.

Henry speaks to me of her extreme vulgarity. I know her lack of pride. Vulgarity gives the joy of desecrating. But June is not a demon. Life is the demon, possessing her, and their coition is violent because her voraciousness for life is enormous, a tasting of its bitterest flavors.

After Henry's visit I began to tiger-pace the house and to say to Hugo I had to go away. There were outcries. "You are not really sick—just tired." But Hugo, as usual, understood, consented. The house suffocated me. I couldn't see people, I couldn't write, I couldn't rest either.

Sunday Hugo took me out for a walk. We found some very large, deep rabbit holes. He playfully incited our dog Banquo to stick his nose in them, to dig. I felt a terrifying oppression, as if I had crawled into a hole and were stifling. I remembered many dreams I have had of being forced to crawl on my stomach, like a snake, through tunnels and apertures that were too small for me, the last one always smaller than all the others, where the anxiety grew so strong that it awakened me. I stood before the rabbit hole and shouted angrily at Hugo to stop. My anger baffled him. It was only a game, and with the dog.

Now that the feeling of suffocation was so crystallized, I was determined to go away. At night, in Hugo's arms, my decision wavered. But I made all the preparations, careless ones, unlike my usual self. I didn't care about my appearance, clothes. I left hurriedly. To find myself. To find Hugo in myself.

Sonloup, Switzerland. To Hugo I write: "Believe me, when I talk about living out all instincts, it is only steam. There are a lot of instincts that should not be lived out because they are decayed and putrid. Henry is wrong to despise D. H. Lawrence for refusing to plunge into unnecessary misery. The first thing June and Henry would do would be to initiate us into poverty, starvation, drabness just to share their sufferings. That is the weakest way of enjoying life: to let it whip you. By conquering misery we are creating a future independence of being such as they will never know. When you retire from the bank, darling, we will know a freedom they have never known. I'm a bit sick of this Russian wallowing in pain. Pain is something to master, not to wallow in.

"I came here to seek my strength, and I find it. I'm fighting. This morning I saw young, tall, thick silhouettes of skiers, with heavy boots, and their slow, conquering walk was like a gust of power. Defeat is only a phase for me. I must conquer, live. Forgive me for the suffering I inflict on you. At least it will never be useless suffering."

I lie in bed, half-asleep, playing possum. This fortress of calm which I erect against the invasion of ideas, against fever, is like down. I sleep in the down, and the ideas press in on me, insistently. I want to understand slowly. And I begin: June, you have destroyed reality. Your lies are not lies to you; they are conditions you want to live out. You have made greater efforts than any of us to live out illusions. When you told your husband that your mother had died, that you never knew your father, that you were a bastard, you wanted to begin nowhere, to begin without roots, to plunge into invention. . . .

I seek to illumine June's chaos not with man's direct mind but with all the deftness and circumlocution known to woman.

Henry said, "June had tears in her eyes when she spoke of your generosity." And I could see he loved her for that.

In his novel it is clear that June's generosity did not go out to him—she constantly tortured him—but to Jean, because she was obsessed with Jean. And what does she do to Henry? She humiliates him, she starves him, she breaks his health, she torments him—and he thrives; he writes his book.

To hurt and to be aware of hurting, and to know its ultimate necessity, that is intolerable to me. I do not have June's courage. I struggle to spare Hugo every humiliation. I do not ride over his feelings. Only twice in my life has passion been stronger than pity.

An aunt of mine taught our cook how to make a soufflé of carrots, and the cook taught our maid Emilia. Emilia serves it for every festive meal. She served it to Henry and June. They were already hypnotized by the oddness of Louveciennes, the coloring, the strangeness of my dressing, my foreignness, the smell of jasmine, the open fires in which I burned not logs but tree roots, which look like monsters. The soufflé looked like an exotic dish, and they ate it as one eats caviar. They also ate purée of potatoes which had been made airy with a beaten egg. Henry, who is thoroughly bourgeois, began to feel uncomfortable, as if he had not been properly fed. His steak was real and juicy, but cut neatly round, and I am sure he did not recognize it. June was in ecstasy. When Henry knew us better, he ventured to ask if we always ate like that, expressing concern for our health. Then we told him about the origin of the soufflé and laughed. June would have wrapped it in mystery forever.

One morning when Henry was staying with us, after all his starvation, sloppy meals, café-counter slobbery, I tried to give him a beautiful breakfast. I came down and lit the fire in the fireplace. Emilia brought, on a green tray, hot coffee, steaming milk, soft-boiled eggs, good bread and biscuits, and the freshest butter. Henry sat by the fire at the lacquered table. All he could say was that he longed for the bistro around the corner, the zinc counter, the dull greenish coffee and milk full of skin.

I was not offended. I thought that he lacked a certain capacity for enjoying the uncommon, that is all. I might be down in the dumps a hundred times, but each time I would clamber out again to good coffee on a lacquered tray beside an open fire. Each time I would clamber out to silk stockings and perfume. Luxury is not a necessity to me, but beautiful and good things are.

June is a storyteller. She is constantly telling stories about her life that are inconsequential. I tried at first to connect them into a whole, but then I surrendered to her chaos. I didn't know at the time that, like Albertine's stories, to Proust, each one was a secret key to some happening in her life which it is impossible to clarify. A lot of these stories are in Henry's novel. She does not hesitate to repeat herself. She is drugged with her own romances. I stand humbly before this fantastic child and give up my mind.

In the hotel last night a baby's feverish crying kept me awake, and my thinking was like a high-powered machine. It wore me out. In the morning a monstrously ugly *femme de chambre* came in to open the shutters. A man who had red hair standing in a bush around his face was sweeping the hall carpets. I telephoned Hugo, begging him to come sooner than he had promised. His letters had been soft and sad. But over the telephone he was reasonable. "I'll come immediately *if* you are ill." I said, "Never mind. I'll come home Thursday. I can't stay any longer." Fifteen minutes later he called, now fully aware of my distress, to say he would be here Friday instead of Saturday morning. I was in despair over the sudden and terrifying need of Hugo. It would have led me to commit any act. I sat in bed, shaking. I am definitely ill, I thought. My mind is not altogether in power.

I made a tremendous effort to write Hugo a steady, clear letter, to reassure him. I had made the same effort to steady myself when I came here to Switzerland. Hugo understood. He had written to me: ". . . how well I know with what burning intensity you live. You have experienced many lives already, including several you have shared with me—full rich lives from birth to death, and you will just have to have these rest periods in between.

"Do you realize what a live force you are, just to speak of you in the abstract? I feel like a machine that has lost its motor. You represent everything that is vital, live, moving, rising, flying, soaring. . . ."

June objects strongly to Henry's frank sensualism. Hers is so much more intricate. Besides, he represents goodness to her. She clings desperately to it. She is afraid he will be spoiled. All Henry's instincts are good, not in the nauseating Christian sense but in the simple human sense. Even the ferocity of his writing is not monstrous or intellectual but human. But June is nonhuman. She has only two strong human feelings: her love of Henry and her tremendous selfless generosity. The rest is fantastic, perverse, pitiless.

What demoniac accounts she manages to keep, so that Henry and I look with awe on her monstrosity, which enriches us more than the pity of others, the measured love of others, the selflessness of others. I will not tear her to pieces as Henry has done. I will love her. I will enrich her. I will immortalize her.

Henry sends a desperate letter from Dijon. Dostoevsky in Siberia, only Siberia was far more interesting, from what poor Henry says. I send him a telegram: "Resign and come home to Versailles." And I send him money. I think about him most of the day.

But I would never let Henry touch me. I struggle to find the exact reason, and I can only find it in his own language. "I don't want just to be pissed on."

Do you do such things, June, do you? Or does Henry caricature your desires? Are you half sunk in such sophisticated, such obscure, such tremendous feelings that Henry's bordellos seem almost laughable? He counts on me to understand, because, like him, I am a writer. I must know. It must be clear to me. To his surprise I tell him just what you say: "It is not the same thing." There is one world forever closed to him—the world which contains our abstract talks, our kiss, our ecstasies.

He senses uneasily that there is a certain side of you he has not grasped, everything that is left out of his novel. You slip between his fingers!

The richness of Hugo. His power to love, to forgive, to give, to understand. God, but I am a blessed woman.

I will be home tomorrow night. I am finished with hotel life and solitude at night.

## *FEBRUARY*

Louveciennes. I came home to a soft and ardent lover. I carry about rich, heavy letters from Henry. Avalanches. I have tacked up on the wall of my writing room Henry's two big pages of words, culled here and there, and a panoramic map of his life, intended for an unwritten novel. I will cover the walls with words. It will be *la chambre des mots*.

Hugo found my journals on John Erskine and read them while I was away, with a last pang of curiosity. There was nothing in them he did not know, but he suffered. I would live through it again, yes, and Hugo knows it.

Also while I was away, he found my black lace underwear, kissed it, found the odor of me, and inhaled it with such joy.

There was an amusing incident on the train, going to Switzerland. To reassure Hugo, I had not painted my eyes, barely powdered, barely rouged my lips, and had not touched my nails. I was so happy in my negligence. I had dressed carelessly in an old black velvet dress I love, which is torn at the elbows. I felt like June. My dog Ruby sat at my side, and so my black coat and velvet jacket were covered with his white hair. An Italian who had tried all during the trip to catch my attention finally, in desperation, came up and offered me a brush. This amused me, and I laughed. When I was through brushing (and his brush was full of white hairs), I thanked him. He said very nervously, "Will you come and have coffee with me?" I said no, as I thought, what would it have been like if I had painted my eyes?

Hugo says my letter to Henry is the slipperiest thing he has ever seen. I begin so honestly and frankly. I seem to be June's opposite, but in the end I am just as slippery. He thinks I will disturb Henry and upset his style for a while—his raw strength, his "pisses and fucks," in which he was so secure.

When I wrote to Henry, I was so grateful for his fullness and richness that I wanted to give him everything that was in my mind. I began with great impetus, I was frank, but as I approached the final gift, the gift of *my* June and my thoughts about her, I felt reticent. I employed much craft and elusiveness to interest him, while keeping what was precious to me.

I sit down before a letter or my journal with a desire for honesty, but perhaps in the end I am the biggest liar of them all, bigger than June, bigger than Albertine, because of the semblance of sincerity.

His real name was Heinrich—how I prefer that. He is German. To me he seems like a Slav, but he has the German sentimentality and romanticism about women. Sex is *love* to him. His morbid imagination is German. He has a love of ugliness. He doesn't mind the smell of urine and of cabbage. He loves cursing, and slang, prostitutes, apache quarters, squalor, toughness.

He writes his letters to me on the back of discarded "Notes"—fifty ways of saying "drunk," information on poisons, names of books, bits of conversation. Or lists like this: "Visit Café des Mariniers on river bank near Exposition

Bridge off Champs Elysées—sort of boarding house for fishermen. Eat 'Bouillabaisse,' Caveau des Oubliettes Rouges. Le Paradis, rue Pigalle—rough point, pickpockets, apaches, etc. Fred Payne's Bar, 14 rue Pigalle (see the Art Galerie downstairs, rendezvous of English and American show girls). Café de la Régence, 261 rue St. Honoré (Napoleon and Robespierre played chess here. See their table)."

Henry's letters give me the feeling of plentitude I get so rarely. I take great joy in answering them, but the bulk of them overwhelm me. I have barely answered one when he writes another. Comments on Proust, descriptions, moods, his own life, his indefatigable sexuality, the way he immediately gets tangled in action. Too much action, to my mind. Undigested. No wonder he marvels at Proust. No wonder I watch his life with a realization that my life will never resemble his, for mine is slowed up by thought.

To Henry: "Last night I read your novel. There were some passages in it which were *éblouissants*, staggeringly beautiful. Particularly the description of a dream you had, the description of the jazzy night with Valeska, the whole of the last part when the life with Blanche comes to a climax. . . . Other things are flat, lifeless, vulgarly realistic, photographic. Still other things—the older mistress, Cora, even Naomi, are not *born* yet. There is a slapdash, careless rushing by. You have come a long way from that. Your writing has had to keep pace with your living, and because of your animal vitality you have lived too much. . . .

"I have a strange sureness that I know just what should be left out, exactly as you knew what should be left out of my book. I think the novel is worth weeding out. Would you let me?"

To Henry: "Please understand, Henry, that I'm in full rebellion against my own mind, that when I live, I live by impulse, by emotion, by white heat. June understood that. My mind didn't exist when we walked insanely through Paris, oblivious to people, to time, to place, to others. It didn't exist when I first read Dostoevsky in my hotel room and laughed and cried together and couldn't sleep, and didn't know where I was. But afterwards, understand me, I make the tremendous effort to rise again, not to wallow any more, not to go on just suffering or burning. Why should I make such an effort? Because I have a fear of being like June *exactly*. I have a feeling against complete chaos. I want to be able to live with June in utter madness, but I also want to be able to understand afterwards, to grasp what I've lived through.

"You ask contradictory and impossible things. You want to know what dreams, what impulses, what desires June has. You'll never know, not from her. No, she couldn't tell you. But do you realize what joy I took in my telling her what our feelings were, in that special language? Because I am not always just living, just following all my fantasies; I come up for air, for understanding. I dazzled June because when we sat down together the wonder of the moment didn't just make me drunk; I lived it with the consciousness of the poet, not the consciousness of the dead-formula-making psychoanalysts. We went to the edge, with our two imaginations. And you beat your head against the wall of our world, and you want me to tear all the veils. You want to force delicate, profound, vague, obscure, voluptuous sensations into something you can seize on. You do not ask it of Dostoevsky. You thank God for the living chaos. Why, then, do you want to know more about June?"

June has no ideas, no fantasies of her own. They are given to her by others, who are inspired by her being. Hugo says angrily that she is an empty box and that I am the full box. But who wants the ideas, the fantasies, the contents, if the box is beautiful and inspiring? I am inspired by June the empty box. To think of her in the middle of the day lifts me out of ordinary living. The world has never been as empty for me since I have known her. June supplies the beautiful incandescent flesh, the fulgurant voice, the abysmal eyes, the drugged gestures, the presence, the body, the incarnate image of our imaginings. What are we? Only the creators. She *is*.

I get letters from Henry every other day. I answer him immediately. I gave him my typewriter, and I write by hand. I think of him day and night.

I dream of an extraordinary extra life I am going to lead someday, which may even fill another and special diary. Last night, after reading Henry's novel, I couldn't sleep. It was midnight. Hugo was sleeping. I wanted to get up and go to my writing room and write Henry about his first novel. But I would have awakened Hugo. There are two doors to open, and they creak. Hugo was so exhausted when he went to bed. I lay very still and forced myself to sleep, with phrases rushing through my head like a cyclone. I thought that I would remember them in the morning. But I couldn't remember, not even half. If Hugo did not have to go to work, I could have awakened him, and he could have slept on the next morning. Our whole life is spoiled by his work in the bank. I must get him out of it. And that makes me work on my novel, rewriting, which I hate, for a new book is boiling in my head—June's book.

The conflict between my being "possessed" and my devotion to Hugo is becoming unbearable. I will love him with all my strength but in my own way. Is it impossible for me to grow in only one direction?

Tonight I am full of joy because Henry is here again. The impression is always the same: one is filled with the weight and lashing of his writing, and then he comes upon you so softly—soft voice, trailing off, soft gestures, soft, fine white hands—and one surrenders to his indefatigable curiosity and his romanticism towards women.

Henry's description of the Henry Street joint (where June brought Jean to live with them):

Bed unmade all day; climbing into it with shoes on frequently; sheets a mess. Using soiled shirts for towels. Laundry seldom gotten out. Sinks stopped up from too much garbage. Washing dishes in bathtub, which was greasy and black-rimmed. Bathroom always cold as an icebox. Breaking up furniture to throw into fire. Shades always down, windows never washed, atmosphere sepulchral. Floor constantly strewn with plaster of Paris, tools, paints, books, cigarette butts, garbage, soiled dishes, pots. Jean running around all day in overalls. June, always half naked and complaining of the cold.

What is all that to me? A side of June I will never know. And the other side, which belongs to me, is full of magic and dazzling with beauty and fineness. These details only show me the two-sideness of all things, my own two-sideness, now craving abject living, animality.

To Henry: "You say, 'Gide has mind, Dostoevsky has the other thing, and it is what Dostoevsky has that really matters.' For you and for me the highest moment, the keenest joy, is not when our minds dominate but when we lose our minds, and you and I both lose it in the same way, through love. We have lost our minds to June. . . .

"Tell me something. You have a feeling for the macabre. Your imagination is attracted by certain grim images. Did you tell Bertha that living with June was like carrying a corpse about? Do you really mind June's neuroses and illness, or are you merely cursing at what enslaves you?"

I have an acute struggle to keep Henry, whom I don't want to give up, and to keep the relationship between June and me a precious secret.

Yesterday at the café he tore bits of our story from me. It hurt and maddened me. I came home and wrote him a long, feverish letter. If he showed this letter to June, I would lose her. Henry cannot make me love her less, but he can torment me by making her appear more unreal, more selfless, by proving that there is no June, only an image, invented by us, by Henry's mind, and my poetry. He talked about influences on her. The influence of Jean, the woman in New York. This was torture to me.

And then he said, "You mystify me." And I said nothing. Is he going to hate me? When we first met he was so warm and so responsive to my presence. His whole body was aware of me. We leaned over eagerly to look at the book I had brought him. We were both exultant. He forgot to drink his coffee.

I am trapped, between the beauty of June and the genius of Henry. In a different way, I am devoted to both, a part of me goes out to each of them. But I love June madly, unreasonably. Henry gives me life, June gives me death. I must choose, and I cannot. For me to give Henry all the feelings I have had about June is exactly like giving my body and soul to him.

To Henry: "Perhaps you didn't realize it, but for the first time today you shocked and startled me out of a dream. All your notes, your stories of June never hurt me. Nothing hurt me until you touched on the source of my terror: June and the influence of Jean. What terror I have when I remember her talk and sense through it how loaded she is with the riches of others, all the others who love her beauty. Even Count Bruga was Jean's creation. When we were together June said, 'You will invent what we will do together.' I was ready to give her everything I have ever invented and created, from my house, my costumes, my jewelry to my writing, my imaginings, my life. I would have worked for her alone.

"Understand me. I worship her. I accept everything she is, but she must *be*. I only revolt if there is no June (as I wrote the first night I met her). Don't tell me that there is no June except the physical June. Don't tell me, because you must know. You have lived with her.

"I never feared, until today, what our two minds would discover together. But what a poison you distilled, perhaps the very poison which is in you. Is that your terror, too? Do you feel haunted and yet deluded, as by a creation of your own brain? Is it fear of an illusion you fight with crude words? Tell me she is not just a beautiful image. Sometimes when we talk I feel that we are trying to grasp her reality. She is unreal even to us, even to you who have possessed her, and to me, whom she has kissed."

Hugo reads one of my old journals, the John Erskine period, Boulevard Suchet, and almost sobs with pity for me, realizing that I was living in The House of the Dead. I did not succeed in resuscitating him until he almost lost me to John and to suicide.

More letters from Henry, parts of his book as he writes it, quotations, notes while listening to Debussy and Ravel, on the back of menus of small restaurants in shabby quarters. A torrent of realism. Too much of it in proportion to imagination, which is growing smaller. He will not sacrifice a moment of life to his work. He is always rushing and writing about work and in the end never really tackling it, writing more letters than books, doing more investigating than actual creation. Yet the form of his last book, discursive, a chain of associations, reminiscences is very good. He has assimilated his Proust, minus the poetry and the music.

I have dipped into obscenity, dirt, and his world of "shit, cunt, prick, bastard, crotch, bitch" and am on the way up again. The symphonic concert today confirmed my mood of detachment. Again and again I have traversed the regions of realism and found them arid. And again I return to poetry. I write to June. It is almost impossible. I can't find words. I make such a violent effort of the imagination to reach out to her, to my image of her. And when I come home, Emilia says, "There is a letter for the Señorita." I run upstairs, hoping it is a letter from Henry.

I want to be a strong poet, as strong as Henry and John are in their realism. I want to combat them, to invade and annihilate them. What baffles me about Henry and what attracts me are the flashes of imagination, the flashes of insight, and the flashes of dreams. Fugitive. And the depths. Rub off the German realist, the man who "stands for shit," as Wambly Bald says to him, and you get a lusty imagist. At moments he can say the most delicate or profound things. But his softness is dangerous, because when he writes he does not write with love, he writes to caricature, to attack, to ridicule, to destroy, to rebel. He is always against something. Anger incites him. I am always for something. Anger poisons me. I love, I love, I love.

Then at certain moments I remember one of his words and I suddenly feel the sensual woman flaring up, as if violently caressed. I say the word to myself, with joy. It is at such a moment that my true body lives.

I spent a tense, harrowing day yesterday with Eduardo, who resuscitates the past. He was the first man I loved. He was weak, sexually. I suffered from his weakness, I know now. That pain was buried. It was newly aroused when we met again two years ago. It was buried again.

I have had masculine elements in me always, knowing exactly what I want, but not until John Erskine did I love strong men; I loved weak or timorous, overfine men. Eduardo's vagueness, indecision, ethereal love, and Hugo's frightened love caused me torment and bewilderment. I acted delicately and yet as a man. It would have been more feminine to have been satisfied with the passion of other admirers, but I insisted on my own selection, on a fineness of nature which I found in a man weaker than I was. I suffered deeply from my own forwardness as a woman. As a man, I would have been glad to have what I desired.

Now Hugo is strong, but I am afraid it is too late. The masculine in me has made too much progress. Now even if Eduardo wanted to live with me (and yesterday he was tormented by an impotent jealousy), we couldn't do so because creatively I am stronger than he is, and he couldn't bear it. I have discovered the joy of a masculine direction of my life by my courting of June. Also I have discovered the terrible joy of dying, of disintegrating.

Sitting by the fire with Hugo last night, I began to cry, the woman sundered again into a woman-man, begging that by a miracle, by the great human strength of poets, she might be saved. But the animal strength which satisfies woman lies in brutal men, in the realists like Henry, and from him I do not want love. I prefer to move forward and choose my June, freely, like a man. But my body will die, because I have a sensual body, a living body, and there is no life in the love between women.

Hugo alone holds me, still, with his idolatry, his warm human love, his maturity, for he is the oldest among all of us.

I want to write so wonderfully to June that I can't write to her at all. What a pathetically inadequate letter:

"I cannot believe that you will not come again towards me from the darkness of the garden. I wait sometimes where we used to meet, expecting to feel again the joy of seeing you walk towards me out of a crowd—you, so distinct and unique.

"After you went away the house suffocated me. I wanted to be alone with my image of you. . . .

"I have taken a studio in Paris, a small, shaky place, and attempt to run away only for a few hours a day, at least. But what is this other life I want to lead without you? I have to imagine that you are there, June, sometimes. I have a feeling that I want to be you. I have never wanted to be anyone but myself before. Now I want to melt into you, to be so terribly close to you that my own self disappears. I am happiest in my black velvet dress because it is old and is torn at the elbows.

"When I look at your face, I want to let go and share your madness, which I carry inside of me like a secret and cannot conceal any more. I am full of an acute, awesome joy. It is the joy one feels when one has accepted death and disintegration, a joy more terrible and more profound than the joy of living, of creating."

*MARCH*

Yesterday at the Café de la Rotonde Henry told me he had written me a letter which he had torn up. Because it was a crazy letter. A love letter. I received this silently, without surprise. I had sensed it. There is so much warmth between us. But I am unmoved. Deep down. I am afraid of this man, as if in him I had to face all the realities which terrify me. His sensual being affects me. His ferocity, enveloped in tenderness, his sudden seriousness, the heavy, rich mind. I am a bit hypnotized. I observe his fine soft white hands, his head, which looks too heavy for his body, the forehead about to burst, a shaking head, harboring so much that I love and hate, that I want and fear. My love of June paralyzes me. I feel warmth towards this man, who can be two separate beings. He wants to take my hand and I appear not to notice. I make a swift gesture of flight.

I want his love to die. What I have been dreaming of, just such a man's desire of me, now I reject. The moment has come to sink in sensuality, without love or drama, and I cannot do it.

He misunderstands so much: my smile when he talks about June at first fighting off all his ideas violently and later absorbing them and expressing them as if they were her own. "It happens to all of us," he says, looking at me aggressively, as if my smile had been one of disdain. I believe he wants to fight. After the violence, the bitterness, the brutality, the ruthlessness he has known, my state of mellowness annoys him. He finds that, like a chameleon, I change color in the café, and perhaps lose the color I have in my own home. I do not fit into his life.

His life—the underworld, Carco, violence, ruthlessness, monstrosity, gold digging, debauch. I read his notes avidly and with horror. For a year, in semisolitude, my imagination has had time to grow beyond measure. At night, in a fever, Henry's words press in on me. His violent, aggressive manhood pursues me. I taste that violence with my mouth, with my womb. Crushed against the earth with the man over me, possessed until I want to cry out.

At the Café Viking, Henry talks about discovering my real nature one evening when I danced the rumba for a few minutes alone. He still remembers a passage in my novel, wants to have the manuscript, to be able to read it over. He says it is the most beautiful writing he has read lately. Talks about the fantastic possibilities in me: his first impression of me standing on the doorstep—"so lovely"—

and then sitting in the big black armchair "like a queen." He wants to destroy the "illusion" of my great honesty.

I read him what I wrote on the effect of his notes. He said I could only write like that, with imaginative intensity, because I had not lived out what I was writing about, that the living-out kills the imagination and the intensity, as happens to him.

Note to Henry in purple ink on silver paper: "The woman will sit eternally in the tall black armchair. I will be the one woman you will never have. Excessive living weighs down the imagination. We will not live, we will only write and talk to swell the sails."

Writers make love to whatever they need. Henry conforms to my image and tries to be more subtle, becomes poetic. He said he could very well imagine June saying to him, "I would not mind your loving Anaïs because it is Anaïs."

I affect their imaginations. It is the strongest power.

I have seen romanticism outlast the realistic. I have seen men forget the beautiful women they have possessed, forget the prostitutes, and remember the first woman they idolized, the woman they never could have. The woman who aroused them romantically holds them. I see the tenacious yearning in Eduardo. Hugo will never be healed of me. Henry can never really love again after loving June.

When I talk about her, Henry says, "What a lovely way you have of putting things."

"Perhaps it is an evasion of facts."

He says to me exactly what I wrote some time ago: I submit to life and then I find beautiful explanations for my act. I make the piece fit into the creative weaving.

"You and June wanted to embalm me," I say.

"Because you seem so utterly fragile."

I dream of a new faithfulness, with stimulation from others, imaginative living, and my body only for Hugo.

I lie. That day in the café, sitting with Henry, seeing his hand tremble, hearing his words, I was moved. It was madness to read him my notes, but he incited me; it was madness to drink and to answer his questions while staring into his face, as I have never dared to look at any man. We did not touch each other. We were both leaning over the abyss.

He spoke of "Hugo's great kindness, but he is a boy, a boy." Henry's older mind, of course. I, too, am always waiting for Hugo, but leaping ahead, sometimes perfidiously, with the older mind. I try to leave my body out of it. But I have been caught. And so when I come home I extricate myself and write him that note.

And meanwhile I read his love letter over ten or fifteen times, and even if I do not believe in his love, or in mine, the nightmare of the other night holds me. I am possessed.

"Beware," said Hugo, "of being trapped in your own imaginings. You instill sparks in others, you charge them with your illusions, and when they burst forth into illuminations, you are taken in."

We walk in the forest. He plays with Banquo. He reads by my side. His intuition tells him: be kind, be sweet, be blind. With me, it is the craftiest and cleverest method. It is the way to torture me, to win me. And I think of Henry every moment, chaotically, fearing his second letter.

I meet Henry in the dim, cavernous Viking. He has not received my note. He has brought me another love letter. He almost cries out, "You are veiled now. Be real! Your words, your writing, the other day. You were real." I deny it. Then he says humbly, "Oh, I knew it, I knew I was too presumptuous to aspire to you. I'm a peasant, Anaïs. Only whores can appreciate me." That brings out the words he wants to hear. Feebly, we argue. We recall the beginning: we began with the mind. "Did we, but did we?" says Henry, trembling. And suddenly he leans over and engulfs me in an endless kiss. I do not want the kiss to end. He says, "Come to my room."

How stifling the veil about me, which Henry struggles to tear, my fear of reality. We are walking to his room, and I do not feel the ground, but I feel his body against mine. He says, "Look at the carpet on the stairs, it is worn," and I do not see, I only feel the ascension. My note is in his hands. "Read it," I say, at the bottom of the stairs, "and I'll leave you." But I follow him. His room, I do not see. When he takes me in his arms, my body melts. The tenderness of his hands, the unexpected penetration, to the core of me but without violence. What strange, gentle power.

He, too, cries out, "It is all so unreal, so swift."

And I see another Henry, or perhaps the same Henry who walked that day into my house. We talk as I wished we would talk, so easily, so truly. I lie on his bed covered by his coat. He watches me.

"You expected—more brutality?"

His mountains of words, of notes, of quotations are sundered. I am surprised. I did not know this man. We were not in love with each other's writing. But what are we in love with now? I cannot bear the picture of June's face on the mantelpiece. Even in the photograph, it is uncanny, she possesses us both.

I write crazy notes to Henry. We cannot meet today. The day is empty. I am caught. And he? What does he feel? I am invaded, I lose everything, my mind vacillates, I am only aware of sensations.

There are moments in the day when I do not believe in Henry's love, when I feel June dominating both of us, when I say to myself, "This morning he will awake and realize he loves no one but June." Moments when I believe, madly, that we are going to live something new, Henry and I, outside of June's world.

How has he imposed truth on me? I was about to take flight from the prison of my imaginings, but he takes me to his room and there we live a dream, not a reality. He places me where he wants to place me. Incense. Worship. Illusion. And all the rest of his life is effaced. He comes with a new soul to this hour. It is the sleeping potion of fairy tales. I lie with a burning womb and he scarcely notices it. Our gestures are human, but there is a curse on the room. It is June's face. I remember, with great pain, one of his notes: "life's wildest moment—June, kneeling on the street." Is it June or Henry I am jealous of?

He asks to see me again. When I wait in the armchair in his room, and he kneels to kiss me, he is stranger than all my thoughts. With his experience he dominates me. He dominates with his mind, too, and I am silenced. He whispers to me what my body must do. I obey, and new instincts rise in me. He has seized me. A man so human; and I, suddenly brazenly natural. I am amazed at my lying there in his iron bed, with my black underwear vanquished and trampled. And the tight secrecy of me broken for a moment, by a man who calls himself "the last man on earth."

Writing is not, for us, an art, but breathing. After our first encounter I breathed some notes, accents of recognition, human admissions. Henry was still stunned, and I was breathing off the unbearable, willing joy. But the second time, there were no words. My joy was impalpable and terrifying. It swelled within me as I walked the streets.

It transpires, it blazes. I cannot conceal it. I am woman. A man has made me submit. Oh, the joy when a woman finds a man she can submit to, the joy of her femaleness expanding in strong arms.

Hugo looks at me as we sit by the fire. I am talking drunkenly, brilliantly. He says, "I've never seen you look so beautiful. I have never felt your power so strongly. What is the new confidence in you?"

He desires me, just as he did that other time, after John's visit. My conscience dies at that moment. Hugo bears down on me, and I instinctively obey Henry's whispered words. I close my legs about Hugo, and he exclaims in ecstasy, "Darling, darling, what are you doing? You're driving me wild. I've never felt such joy before!"

I cheat him, I deceive him, yet the world does not sink in sulphur-colored mists. Madness conquers. I can no longer put my mosaics together. I just cry and laugh.

After a concert, Hugo and I left together, like lovers, he said. That was the day after Henry and I acknowledged certain feelings at the Viking. Hugo was so attentive, so tender. It was a holiday for him. We were having dinner in a restaurant in Montparnasse. I had invented a pretext to call at a friend's for Henry's first love letter. It was in my pocketbook. I was thinking of it while Hugo asked me, "Do you want oysters? Take oysters tonight. It's a special night. Every time I go out with you I feel as if I were taking my mistress out. You are my mistress. I love you more than ever."

I want to read Henry's letter. I excuse myself. I go to the washroom. I read the letter there. It is not very eloquent, and I am touched by the fact. I don't know what else I feel. I return to the table, dizzy. This was where we met Henry when he returned from Dijon and where I realized I was happy he had returned.

On another occasion Hugo and I go to the theatre. I am thinking of Henry. Hugo knows, and he shows the same old tender uneasiness, the desire to believe, and I reassure him. He himself had given me a message that I should call Henry at eight-thirty.

So before the play we go to a café, and Hugo helps me to find the number of Henry's office. I joke about what he is going to hear. Henry and I do not say very much: "Did you get my letter?" "Yes." "Did you get my note?" "No."

I have a bad night after the play. Hugo gets up in the early morning to bring me medicine, a sleeping pill. "What is the matter?" he asks. "What do you feel?" He offers the refuge of his arms.

The first time I come back from Henry's room, stunned, I find difficulty in talking in my usual lively way.

Hugo sits down, takes up his diary book and writes wildly about me and "art" and how everything I do is right. While he reads this to me, I bleed to death. Before the end he begins to sob. He doesn't know why. I get on my knees before him. "What is it, darling, what is it?" And I say this terrible thing: "Do you have an intuition?"—which, because of his faith and his slow senses, he cannot understand. He believes Henry only stimulates me imaginatively, as a writer. And it is because he believes this that he sits down to write also, to woo me with writing.

I want to cry out, "That is so young of you; it's like the faith of a child." God, I'm old, I'm the last *woman* on earth. I am aware of a monstrous paradox: By giving myself I learn to love Hugo more. By living as I do I am preserving our love from bitterness and death.

The truth is that this is the only way I can live: in two directions. I need two lives. I am two beings. When I return to Hugo in the evening, to the peace and warmth of the house, I return with a deep contentment, as if this were the only condition for me. I bring home to Hugo a whole woman, freed of all "possessed" fevers, cured of the poison of restlessness and curiosity which used to threaten our marriage, cured through action. Our love lives, because I live. I sustain and feed it. I am loyal to it, in my own way, which cannot be his way. If he ever reads these lines, he must believe me. I am writing calmly, lucidly while waiting for him to come home, as one waits for the chosen lover, the eternal one.

Henry makes notes on me. He registers all I say. We are both registering, each with different sensors. The life of writers is another life.

I sit on his bed, with my rose dress spread around me, smoking, and as he observes me, he says he will never take me into his life, to the places he has told me about, that for me all the trappings of Louveciennes are right and fitting, that I must have them. "You couldn't live otherwise."

I contemplate his sordid room and exclaim, "I think it is true. If you put me in this room, poor, I would start all over again."

The next day I write him one of the most human notes he has ever received: no intellect, just words about his voice, his laughter, his hands.

And he writes me: "Anaïs, I was stunned when I got your note this evening. Nothing I can ever say will match these words. To you the victory—you have silenced me—I mean so far as expressing these things in writing goes. You don't know how I marvel at your ability to absorb quickly and then turn about, rain down the spears, nail it, penetrate it, envelop it with your intellect. The experience dumbed me; I felt a singular exaltation, a surge of vitality, then of lassitude, of blankness, of wonder, of incredulity, everything, everything. Coming home I kept remarking about the Spring wind—everything had grown soft and balmy, the air licked my face, I couldn't gulp down enough of it. And until I got your note I was in a panic. I was afraid you would disavow everything. But as I read—I read very slowly because each word was a revelation to me—I thought back to your smiling face, to your sort of innocent gayety, something I had always sought for in you but never quite realized. There were times when you began this way, at Louveciennes, and then the mind crashed through and I would see the grave, round eyes and the set purse of your lips, which used almost to frighten me, or at any rate, always intimidated me.

"You make me tremendously happy to hold me undivided—to let me be the artist, as it were, and yet not forego the man, the animal, the hungry, insatiable lover. No woman has ever granted me all the privileges I need—

and you, why you sing out so blithely, so boldly, with a laugh even—yes, you invite me to go ahead, be myself, venture anything. I adore you for that. That is where you are truly regal, a woman extraordinary. What a woman you are! I laugh to myself now when I think of you—I have no fear of your femaleness. And that you burned. Then I remember vividly your dress, the color and texture of it, the voluptuous, airy spaciousness of it—precisely what I would have begged you to wear had I been able to anticipate the moment.

"Note how you were anticipating what I wrote today—I refer to your words about caricature, hate, etc.

"I could stay here all night writing you. I see you before me constantly, with your head down and your long lashes lying on your cheeks. And I feel very humble. I don't know why you should single me out—it puzzles me. It seems to me that from the very moment when you opened the door and held out your hand, smiling, I was taken in, I was yours. June felt it, too. She said immediately that you were in love with me, or else I with you. But I didn't know myself that it was love. I spoke about you glowingly, without reserve. And then June met you and she fell in love with you."

Henry is playing with the idea of saintliness. I am thinking of the organ tones of voice and the expressions and admissions I get from him. And I am thinking of his capacity to be awed, which means to sense divinity. When I have been most natural, most womanly, rising from bed to get him a cigarette, to serve him champagne, to comb my hair, to dress, he still says, "I do not feel natural with you yet."

He lives rather quietly, almost coldly at moments. He

is absent from the present. Afterwards, when he is writing, he warms up, begins to dramatize and to burn.

Our bouts: he in his language, I in mine. I never use his words. I think my registering is more unconscious, more instinctive. It does not appear on the surface, and yet, I don't know, for he was aware of it, of the weight of my eyes. The slipperiness of my mind against his relentless dissection. My belief in wonder against his heavy, realistic notes. The joy, when he does seize upon wonder: "Your eyes seem to be expecting miracles." Will he perform them?

Does he make such notes as: "Anaïs: green comb with black hair on it. Indelible rouge. Barbaric necklace. Breakable. Fragile."

That second afternoon, he waited for me in the café and I waited for him in his room, through a misunderstanding. The *garçon* was cleaning his room. He asked me to wait in the other room across the hall, a very small drab one. I sat on a plain, homely chair. The *garçon* came with another chair covered in red plush velvet. "It will be better for you," he said. I was touched. It seemed to me that Henry was offering me velvet-covered chairs. I was happy as I waited. Then I got a little tired and went to sit in Henry's room. I opened a folder entitled "Notes from Dijon." The first page was a copy of a letter to me which I had not yet received. Then he came in, and when I said, "I do not believe in our love," he silenced me.

I felt humble that day, before his strength. Flesh as strong or stronger than the mind. His victory. He held me with a kind of fear. "You seem so breakable. I am afraid I'll kill you." And I did feel small in his bed, naked, with my barbaric jewelry tinkling. But he felt the strength of the core of me, which burns at his touch.

Think of that, Henry, when you hold my too-fragile body in your arms, a body you scarcely feel because you are so used to billowing flesh, but you feel the movements of its joy like the undulations of a symphony, not the static clay heaviness, but the dancing of it in your arms. You will not break me. You are molding me like a sculptor. The faun is to be made woman.

"Henry, I swear to you, I find joy in telling you the truth. Someday, after another one of your victories, I'll answer any question you put to me."

"Yes, I know that," said Henry, "I am sure of it. I wait quite patiently. I can wait."

What I could have found ridiculous only touched me with its humanness: Henry crawling to find my black silk garters, which had fallen behind the bed. His awe on seeing my twelve-franc necklace: "It is such a fine, rare thing you wear."

When I saw him naked, he appeared defenseless to me, and my tenderness welled up.

Afterwards he was languid, and I was gay. We even talked about our craft: "I like," said Henry, "to have my desk in order before I begin, only notes around me, a great many notes."

"Do you do that?" I said excitedly, as if it were a most interesting statement. Our craft. Delight in talk of techniques.

I guess, Henry, that you are suffering from the effort at complete revelations about yourself and June, inexorable frankness but painfully obtained. You have moments of reserve, of feeling you are violating sacred intimacies, the secret life of your own being as well as of others.

At moments I am willing to help you because of our common objective passion for truth. But it hurts, Henry, it hurts. I am trying to be honest in my journal, day to day.

You are right, in one sense, when you speak of my honesty. An effort, anyway, with the usual human or feminine retractions. To retreat is not feminine, male, or trickery. It is a terror before utter destruction. What we analyze inexorably, will it die? Will June die? Will our love die, suddenly, instantaneously if you should make a caricature of it? Henry, there is a danger in too much knowledge. You have a passion for absolute knowledge. That is why people will hate you.

And sometimes I believe your relentless analysis of June leaves something out, which is your feeling for her beyond knowledge, or in spite of knowledge. I often see how you sob over what you destroy, how you want to stop and just worship; and you do stop, and then a moment later you are at it again with a knife, like a surgeon.

What will you do after you have revealed all there is to know about June? Truth. What ferocity in your quest of it. You destroy and you suffer. In some strange way I am not with you, I am against you. We are destined to hold two truths. I love you and I fight you. And you, the same. We will be stronger for it, each of us, stronger with our love and our hate. When you caricature and nail down and tear apart, I hate you. I want to answer you, not with weak or stupid poetry but with a wonder as strong as your reality. I want to fight your surgical knife with all the occult and magic forces of the world.

I want to both combat you and submit to you, because

as a woman I adore your courage, I adore the pain it engenders, I adore the struggle you carry in yourself, which I alone fully realize, I adore your terrifying sincerity, I adore your strength. You are right. The world is to be caricatured, but I know, too, how much you can love what you caricature. How much passion there is in you! It is that I feel in you. I do not feel the savant, the revealer, the observer. When I am with you, it is the blood I sense.

This time you are not going to awake from the ecstasies of our encounters to reveal only the ridiculous moments. No. You won't do it this time, because while we live together, while you examine my indelible rouge effacing the design of my mouth, spreading like blood after an operation (you kissed my mouth and it was gone, the design of it was lost as in a watercolor, the colors ran); while you do that, I seize upon the wonder that is brushing by (the wonder, oh, the wonder of my lying under you), and I bring it to you, I breathe it around you. Take it. I feel prodigal with my feelings when you love me, feelings so unblunted, so new, Henry, not lost in resemblance to other moments, so much ours, yours, mine, you and I together, not any man or any woman together.

What is more touchingly real than your room. The iron bed, the hard pillow, the single glass. And all sparkling like a Fourth of July illumination because of my joy, the soft billowing joy of the womb you inflamed. The room is full of the incandescence you poured into me. The room will explode when I sit at the side of your bed and you talk to me. I don't hear your words: your voice reverberates against my body like another kind of caress, another kind of penetration. I have no power over your voice. It comes straight from you into me. I could stuff my ears and it would find its way into my blood and make it rise.

I am impervious to the flat visual attack of things. I see your khaki shirt hung up on a peg. It is your shirt and I could see you in it—you, wearing a color I detest. But I see you, not the khaki shirt. Something stirs in me as I look at it, and it is certainly the human you. It is a vision of the human you revealing an amazing delicacy to me. It is your khaki shirt and you are the man who is the axis of my world now. I revolve around your richness of being.

"Come close to me, come closer. I promise you it will be beautiful."

You keep your promise.

Listen, I do not believe that I alone feel we are living something new because it is new to me. I do not see in your writing any of the feelings you have shown me or any of the phrases you have used. When I read your writing, I wondered, What episode are we going to repeat?

You carry your vision, and I mine, and they have mingled. If at moments I see the world as you see it (because they are Henry's whores I love them), you will sometimes see it as I do.

To Henry the investigator I offer enigmatic replies.

When I was dressing, I was laughingly commenting on my underwear, which June had liked, June who is always naked under her dress. "It is Spanish," I said.

Henry said, "What comes to my mind when you say this is how did June know that you wore such underclothing?"

I said, "Don't you think I am trying to make it all more innocent than it was, but at the same time, don't go so directly at ideas like that or you'll never quite get the truth."

He overlooks the voluptuousness of half-knowledge, half-possession, of leaning over the edge dangerously, for no specific climax.

Both Henry and June have destroyed the logic and unity of my life. It is good, for a pattern is not living. Now I am living. I am not making patterns.

What eludes me forever is the reality of being a man. When the imagination and emotions of a woman overstep normal boundaries, occasionally she is possessed by feelings she cannot express. I want to possess June. I identify myself with the men who can penetrate her. But I am powerless. I can give her the pleasure of my love, but not the supreme coition. What a torment!

And Henry's letters: ". . . terribly, terribly alive, pained, and feeling absolutely that I need you . . . But I must see you: I see you bright and wonderful and at the same time I have been writing to June and all torn apart, but you will understand: you must understand. Anaïs, stand by me. You're all around me like a bright flame. Anaïs, by Christ, if you knew what I am feeling now.

"I want to get more familiar with you. I love you. I loved you when you came and sat on the bed—all that second afternoon was like warm mist—and I hear again the way you say my name—with that queer accent of yours. You arouse in me such a mixture of feelings, I don't know how to approach you. Only come to me—get closer and closer to me. It will be beautiful, I promise you. I like so much your frankness—a humility almost. I could never hurt that. I had a thought tonight that it was to a woman like you I should have been married. Or is it that love, in the beginning, always inspires such thoughts? I don't have a fear that you will want to hurt me. I see that you have a strength too—of a different order, more elusive. No you won't break. I talked a lot of nonsense—about your frailty. I have been a little embarrassed always. But less so the last time. It will all disappear. You have such a delicious sense of humor—I adore that in you. I want always to see you laughing. It belongs to you. I have been thinking of places we ought to go to together—little obscure places, here and there, in Paris. Just to say—here I went with Anaïs—here we ate or danced or got drunk together. Ah, to see you really drunk sometime, that would be a treat! I am almost afraid to suggest it—but Anaïs, when I think of how you press against me, how eagerly you open your legs and how wet you are, God, it drives me mad to think what you would be like when everything falls away.

"Yesterday I thought of you, of your pressing your legs against me standing up, of the room tottering, of falling on you in darkness and knowing nothing. And I shivered and groaned with delight. I am thinking that if the weekend must pass without seeing you it will be unbearable.

"If needs be I will come to Versailles Sunday—anything—but I must see you. Don't be afraid to treat me coolly. It will be enough to stand near you, to look at you admiringly. I love you, that's all."

Hugo and I are in the car, driving to an elegant evening. I sing until it seems my singing is driving the car. I swell my chest and imitate the *roucoulement* of the pigeons. My French *rrrrrrrrrr* roll. Hugo laughs. Later, with a marquis and a marquise, we come out of the theatre, and whores press in around us, very close. The marquise tightens her mouth. I think, they are Henry's whores, and I feel warmly towards them, friendly.

One evening I suggest to Hugo that we go to an "exhibition" together, just to see. "Do you want to?" I say, although in my mind I am ready to live, not to see. He is curious, elated. "Yes, yes." We call up Henry to ask for information. He suggests 32 rue Blondel.

On the way over, Hugo hesitates, but I am laughing at his side, and I urge him on. The taxi drops us in a narrow little street. We had forgotten the number. But I see "32" in red over one of the doorways. I feel that we have stood on a diving board and have plunged. And now we are in a play. We are different.

I push a swinging door. I was to go ahead to barter over the price. But when I see it is not a house but a café full of people and naked women, I come back to call Hugo, and we walk in.

Noise. Blinding lights. Many women surrounding us, calling us, trying to attract our attention. The *patronne* leads us to a table. Still the women are shouting and signaling. We must choose. Hugo smiles, bewildered. I glance over them. I choose a very vivid, fat, coarse Spanish-looking woman, and then I turn away from the shouting group to the end of the line and call a woman who had made no effort to attract my attention, small, feminine, almost timid. Now they sit before us.

The small woman is sweet and pliant. We talk, oh, so politely. We discuss each other's nails. They comment on the unusualness of my nacreous nail polish. I ask Hugo to look carefully to see if I have chosen well. He does and says I could not have done better. We watch the women dancing. I see only in spots, intensely. Certain places are utter blanks to me. I see big hips, buttocks, and sagging breasts, so many bodies, all at once. We had expected there would be a man for the exhibition. "No," says the *patronne*, "but the two girls will amuse you. You will see everything." It would not be Hugo's night, then, but he accepts everything. We barter over the price. The women smile. They assume it is my evening because I have asked them if they will show me lesbian poses.

Everything is strange to me and familiar to them. I only feel at ease because they are people who need things, whom one can do things for. I give away all my cigarettes. I wish I had a hundred packets. I wish I had a lot of money. We are going upstairs. I enjoy looking at the women's naked walk.

The room is softly lighted and the bed low and ample. The women are cheerful, and they wash themselves. How the taste for things must wear down with so much automatism. We watch the big woman tie a penis on herself, a rosy thing, a caricature. And they take poses, nonchalantly, professionally. Arabian, Spanish, Parisienne, love when one does not have the price of a hotel room, love in a taxi, love when one of the partners is sleepy . . .

Hugo and I look on, laughing a little at their sallies. We learn nothing new. It is all unreal, until I ask for the lesbian poses.

The little woman loves it, loves it better than the man's approach. The big woman reveals to me a secret place in the woman's body, a source of a new joy, which I had sometimes sensed but never definitely—that small core at the opening of the woman's lips, just what the man passes by. There, the big woman works with the flicking of her tongue. The little woman closes her eyes, moans, and trembles in ecstasy. Hugo and I lean over them, taken by that moment of loveliness in the little woman, who offers to our eyes her conquered, quivering body. Hugo is in turmoil. I am no longer woman; I am man. I am touching the core of June's being.

I become aware of Hugo's feelings and say, "Do you want the woman? Take her. I swear to you I won't mind, darling."

"I could come with anybody just now," he answers.

The little woman is lying still. Then they are up and joking and the moment passes. Do I want . . . ? They unfasten my jacket; I say no, I don't want anything.

I couldn't have touched them. Only a minute of beauty—the small woman's heaving, her hands caressing the other woman's head. That moment alone stirred my blood with another desire. If we had been a little madder . . . But the room seemed dirty to us. We walked out. Dizzy. Joyous. Elated.

We went to dance at the Bal Nègre. One fear was over. Hugo was liberated. We had understood each other's feelings. Together. Arm in arm. A mutual generosity.

I was not jealous of the little woman Hugo had desired. But Hugo thought, "What if there had been a man . . ." So we don't know yet. All we know is that the evening was beautifully carried off. I had been able to give Hugo a portion of the joy that filled me.

And when we returned home, he adored my body because it was lovelier than what he had seen and we sank into sensuality together with new realization. We are killing phantoms.

---

I went to the Viking to meet Eduardo. We have been confiding to each other: he, about a woman in his pension; I, about Henry. We sat in the mellow light. Eduardo is afraid to be left out of my life. "No," I said, "there is plenty of room. I love Hugo, better than ever, I love Henry and June, and you, too, if you wish." He smiled.

"I'll read you Henry's letters," I said, because he was worrying about my "imagination" (Perhaps Henry is nothing, he was thinking). And as I read to him, he stopped me. He couldn't bear it.

He talks to me about psychoanalysis, which reveals how he loves me, how he sees me now. Henry's love creates an aureole around me. I sit so securely before Eduardo's timidity. I watch him approaching me, seeking closeness, a touch of my hand, of my knee. I watch him becoming human. For this moment, a long time ago, I would have given so much, but I have left it all far behind.

"Before we leave," he says, "I want . . ." And he begins to kiss me. "It is Eduardo," I murmur, pliant. The kiss is lovely. I am half-moved, half-taken. But he does not pursue the desire. He had wanted a half-measure. Here it was. We leave the place. We take a taxi. He is overwhelmed with the joy of touching me. "Impossible," he cries out. "At last! But it means more to me than to you." It is true. I am moved only because I have become accustomed to desiring that very beautiful mouth.

Look what I have done! Look at the spectacle of Eduardo's torment. My beautiful Eduardo, Keats and Shelley, poems and crocuses—so many hours of looking into his limpid green eyes and seeing the reflections of men and whores. For thirteen years his face, his mind, his imagination turned towards me, but his body was dead. His body is alive now. He moans my name. "When will I see you? I must see you tomorrow." Kisses, on the eyes, on the neck. The world seems to have turned upside down. Tomorrow it will die, I thought.

But tomorrow, because I sit expecting nothing, Eduardo's madness returns, and I feel, for the first time, *destiny*, an imperative need of a psychological resolution. We walk in full sunshine to a hotel he knows, we climb stairs, gaily, we enter a yellow room. I ask him to close the curtains. We are weary of dreams, of imaginings, of tragedy, of literature.

Downstairs he pays for the room. I say to the woman, "Thirty francs is too much for us. Next time can't you let it for less?"

And in the street we burst out laughing: the next time!

The miracle is accomplished. We walk, expanded. We are very hungry. We go to the Viking and eat four big sandwiches (there was a time when I couldn't swallow in Eduardo's presence).

"How much I owe you!" he cries. And in my heart I answer, "How much you owe Henry."

I cannot help feeling today that some part of me stands aside watching me live and marveling. Thrown into life without experience, naïve, I feel that something has saved me. I feel equal to life. It is like the scenes of an exceptional play. Henry guided me. No. He waited. He watched me. *I* moved, *I* acted. I did unexpected things, surprising to myself—that moment, Henry mentions, when I sat on the edge of the bed. I had been standing before the mirror combing my hair. He lay in the bed and said, "I do not feel at ease with you yet." Impulsively, swiftly, I went to the bed, sat near him, put my face very near his. My coat slipped off, and the straps of my chemise, too, and in the whole gesture, in what I said, there was something so naturally giving, pliant, human that he couldn't talk.

I feel that when Henry talks or writes to me he seeks another language. I feel him evading the word which comes easiest to his lips, grasping another, a more subtle one. Sometimes I feel that I have taken him into an intricate world, a new country, and he does not walk like John, trampling, but with an awareness I sensed in him from the very first day. He walks inside of Proust's symphonies, of Gide's insinuations, of Cocteau's opium enigmas, of Valéry's silences; he walks into suggestivity, into spaces; into the illuminations of Rimbaud. And I walk with him. Tonight I love him, for the beautiful way he has given me the earth.

As I go along I cannot and must not tear down. I will not ask Hugo even for one free evening. Because of that I bring out new and profound feelings in Henry.

"Are you glad," asks Eduardo, "that he wants to write, work, that he is exalted rather than destroyed?"

"Yes."

"The real test will come when you begin to want to use your power over men destructively and cruelly."

Will that time come?

I tell Hugo about my *imaginary* journal of a possessed woman, which fortifies him in his attitude that everything is make-believe except our love.

"But how do you know there is not really such a journal? How do you know I'm not lying to you?"

"You may be," he said.

"You've got a really supple mind now."

"Give me realities to fight," he has said to me. "My imagination makes it worse." I let him read my letter to June, and he found relief in knowing. The best of lies are half-truths. I tell him half-truths.

Sunday. Hugo goes to play golf. I dress ritually and compare the joy of dressing for Henry to my sorrow at dressing for idiotic bankers and telephone kings.

Later, a small, dark room, so shabby, like a deep-set alcove. Immediately, the richness of Henry's voice and mouth. The feeling of sinking into warm blood. And he, overcome with my warmth and moisture. Slow penetration, with pauses and with twists, making me gasp with pleasure. I have no words for it; it is all new to me.

The first time Henry made love to me, I realized a terrible fact—that Hugo was sexually too large for me, so that my pleasure has not been unmixed, always somewhat painful. Has that been the secret of my dissatisfaction? I tremble as I write it. I don't want to dwell on it, on its effect on my life, on my hunger. My hunger is not abnormal. With Henry I am content. We come to a climax, we talk, we eat and drink, and before I leave he floods me again. I have never known such plenitude. It is no longer Henry; and I am just woman. I lose the sense of separate beings.

I come back to Hugo appeased and so joyous; it is communicated to him. And he says: "I have never been so happy with you." It is as if I had ceased devouring him, demanding from him. It is no wonder I am humble before my giant, Henry. And he is humble before me. "You see, Anaïs, I have never before loved a woman with a mind. All the other women were inferior to me. I consider you my equal." And he, too, seems to be full of a great joy, a joy he has not known with June.

That last afternoon in Henry's hotel room was for me like a white-hot furnace. Before, I had only white heat of the mind and of the imagination; now it is of the blood. Sacred completeness. I come out dazed in the mellow spring evening and I think, now I would not mind dying.

Henry has aroused my real instincts, so that I am no longer ill-at-ease, famished, incongruous in my world. I have found where I fit. I love him, and yet I am not blind to the elements in us which clash and out of which, later, will spring our divorce. I can only feel the now. The now is so rich and so tremendous. As Henry says, "Everything is good, good."

It is ten-thirty. Hugo has gone to a banquet, and I am waiting for him. He reassures himself by appealing to my mind. He thinks my mind is always in control. He does not know what madness I am capable of. I am going to keep this story for when he is older, when he, too, has freed his instincts. Telling the truth about myself now would only kill him. His development is naturally slower. At forty he will know what I know today. He will sense and absorb things without pain meanwhile.

I am always concerned over Hugo, as if he were my child. It is because I love him best. I wish he were ten years older.

Henry asked me, last time, "Have I been less brutal, less passionate than you expected? Did my writing perhaps lead you to expect more?"

I was amazed. I reminded him how almost the first

words I wrote him after our meeting were, "The mountain of words has sundered, literature has fallen away." I meant that real feelings had begun, and that the intense sensualism of his writing was one thing, and our sensuality together was another, a real thing.

Even Henry, with his adventurous life, does not altogether have confidence. No wonder Eduardo and I, over-tender, lacked it to a tragic degree. It was that delicate confidence we nurtured at our last meeting, Eduardo and I, trying to mend the harm we did each other unwillingly, trying to perfect and heal the course of a strange destiny. We only lay together because it was that we should have done at the beginning.

My friend Natasha rails at me by the hour on my idiotic attitude. What of Henry's curtains? Why shoes for June? "And you? And you?" She doesn't understand how spoiled I am. Henry gives me the world. June gave me madness. God, how grateful I am to find two beings I can love, who are generous to me in a way I cannot explain to Natasha. Can I explain to her that Henry gives me his watercolors and June her only bracelet? And more.

At the Viking, I tell Eduardo delicately, with moth words, that we should not continue, that I feel the experience was not meant to be continued; it was only a tampering of the past. It was wonderful, but there is no blood polarity between us.

Eduardo is pained. His fundamental terror of not being able to hold me is now realized. Why didn't we wait until he was entirely healed? Healed? What does that mean? Maturity, virility, wholeness, the power to conquer me?

Already I know he cannot conquer me, ever. I keep it a secret from him. Oh, the pity that stirs in me to see his beautiful head bowed down, his torment. The knowledge of Henry now stands between us. He begs me, "Come to our room, once more, just to be alone together. Believe in my feelings." I say, "We must not. Let us preserve the moment we had."

I had no desire to go. Premonitions. But he wants to bring the issue into clarity.

Our room was gray today, and cold. It was raining. I fought off the desolateness which invaded me. If ever I acted in my life, it was today. I was not stirred, but I did not admit it. Then he sensed the dissatisfaction, and we lived through pages out of Lawrence's books. For the first time I understood them, better perhaps than Lawrence did, because he described only the man's feelings.

And what does Eduardo feel? He feels more for me than for any woman; he has had his nearest taste of wholeness, of manhood.

I couldn't crush him. I went on with soft words: "Don't force life. Let things grow slowly. Don't suffer."

But he knows now.

This was all like a nightmare to me. My being clamored for Henry. I saw him today. He was with his friend Fred Perlès, the soft, delicate man with poetic eyes. I like Fred, and yet I felt closer to Henry, so close I couldn't bear to look at him. We were sitting in the kitchen of their new apartment in Clichy. Henry glowed. When I said I had to go, after we talked a long time, Henry took me to his room and began kissing me, and with Fred so very near, Fred the aristocrat and sensitive man, probably hurt. "I can't let you go," said Henry. "We'll close the door." I gave myself to that moment with frenzy. I think I am losing my mind, for the feelings it aroused in me haunt me, possess me every moment, and I crave more and more of Henry.

I come home. Hugo reads the paper. The tenderness, the smallness, the colorlessness of it all. But I have Henry, and I think of what he said, wildly, while he was coming. I think how I have never been as natural as I am now, have never lived out my true instincts. I didn't care today that Fred saw my madness. I wanted to face the world, shout to the world: "I love Henry."

I don't know why I trust him so much, why I want to give him everything tonight—truth, my journal, my life. I even wished that June might suddenly announce her arrival so as to feel the pain the loss of Henry would give me.

I went to have a massage. The masseuse was small and pretty. She wore a bathing suit. I saw her breasts when she leaned over me, small but full. I felt her hands over my body, her mouth near mine. One moment my head was near her legs. I could easily have kissed them. I was stirred madly. Immediately I was aware of the frustration of my desire. What I could do did not seem satisfying enough. Would I kiss her? I felt she was not a lesbian. I sensed that she would humiliate me. The moment passed. But what a half hour of exquisite torture! What torture to want to be man! I was amazed at myself, aware of the nature of my feelings for June. And only yesterday I was criticizing the vice of what Hugo and I call collective sexuality, depersonalized, unselective, which I now understand.

To Henry: "Persecutions have begun—they are all pained, injured, that I should defend [D. H.] Lawrence. They look sadly at me. I look forward with impatience to the day when I can defend your writing, as you defended Buñuel.

"I am glad I didn't blush before Fred. That day was the high peak of my love, Henry. I wanted to shout: 'Today I love Henry.' Perhaps you wish I had pretended casualness, I don't know. Write to me. I need your letters, as a human assertion of reality. One man I know wants to frighten me. When I talk about you he says, 'He cannot appreciate you.' He is wrong."

To Henry: "This is strange, Henry. Before, as soon as I came home from all kinds of places, I would sit down and write in my journal. Now I want to write to you, talk with you. Our 'engagements' are so unnatural—the spaces in between, when I have, like tonight, a desperate need of seeing you. I hinted to Hugo we might go out with you tomorrow night, but he wouldn't hear of it.

"I love when you say: 'All that happens is good.' I say, 'All that happens is wonderful.' For me it is all symphonic, and I am so aroused by living—God, Henry, in you alone I have found the same swelling enthusiasm, the same quick rising of the blood, the fullness. Before, I almost used to think there was something wrong. Everybody else seemed to have the brakes on. And when I feel your excitement about life flaring, next to mine, it makes me dizzy. What will we do, Henry, the night Hugo goes to Lyon? Today I would have liked to have been sewing curtains in your place while you talked to me.

"Do you think we are happy together because we feel

we are 'getting somewhere,' whereas you had the feeling with June that you were being led into more and more obscurity, mystery, entanglements?"

I meet Henry in the gray station, with an instantaneous rising of my blood, and recognize the same feelings in him. He tells me he could hardly walk to the station because he was crippled with his desire of me. I refuse to go to his apartment because Fred is there and I suggest the Hotel Anjou, where Eduardo took me. I see the suspicion in his eyes, and I enjoy it. We go to the hotel. He wants me to talk to the concierge. I ask her for room number three. She says it is thirty francs. I say, "You will give it to us for twenty-five." And I take the key off the board. I start up the stairs. Henry stops me midway to kiss me. We are in the room. He says with that warm laughter of his, "Anaïs, you are a devil." I don't say anything. He is so eager I do not have time to undress.

And here I stumble, because of inexperience, dazed by the intensity and savagery of those hours. I only remember Henry's voraciousness, his energy, his discovery of my buttocks, which he finds beautiful—and oh, the flowing of the honey, the paroxysms of joy, hours and hours of coition. Equality! The depths I craved, the darkness, the finality, the absolution. The core of my being is touched by a body which overpowers mine, inundates mine, which twists its flamed tongue inside of me with such power. He cries, "Tell me, tell me what you feel." And I cannot. There is blood in my eyes, in my head. Words are drowned. I want to scream savagely, wordlessly—inarticulate cries, without sense, from the most primitive basis of my self, gushing from my womb like the honey.

Tearful joy, which leaves me wordless, conquered, silenced.

God, I have known such a day, such hours of female submission, such a gift of myself there can be nothing left to give.

But I lie. I embellish. My words are not deep enough, not savage enough. They disguise, they conceal. I will not rest until I have told of my descent into a sensuality which was as dark, as magnificent, as wild, as my moments of mystic creation have been dazzling, ecstatic, exalted.

Before we met that day, he had written to me: "All I can say is that I am mad about you. I tried to write a letter and couldn't. I am waiting impatiently to see you. Tuesday is so far off. And not just Tuesday—I am wondering when you will come to stay overnight, when I can have you for a long spell. It torments me to see you just a few hours and then surrender you. When I see you, all that I wanted to say vanishes. The time is so precious and words are extraneous. But you make me so happy, because I *can* talk to you. I love your brightness, your preparations for flight, your legs like a vise, the warmth between your legs. Yes, Anaïs, I want to demask you. I am too gallant with you. I want to look at you long and ardently, pick up your dress, fondle you, examine you. Do you know I have scarcely looked at you? There is still too much sacredness clinging to you. I don't know how to tell you what I feel. I live in a perpetual expectancy. You come and the time slips away in a dream. It is only when you go that I realize completely your presence. And then it is too late. You numb me. I try to picture your life at Louveciennes but I can't. Your book? That too seems unreal. Only when you come and I look at you does the picture become clearer. But you go away so quickly, I don't know what to think. Yes, I see the Pouchkine legend clearly. I see you in my mind as sitting on that throne, jewels around your neck, sandals, big rings, painted fingernails, strange Spanish voice, living some kind of a lie which is not a lie exactly but a fairy tale. This is a little drunken, Anaïs. I am saying to myself: 'Here is the first woman with whom I can be absolutely sincere.' I remember your saying: 'You could fool me, I wouldn't know it.' When I walk along the boulevards and think of that, I can't fool you—and yet I would like to. I mean that I can never be absolutely loyal—it's not in me. I love women, or life, too much—which it is, I don't know. But laugh, Anaïs . . . I love to hear you laugh. You are the only woman who has had a sense of gayety, a wise tolerance—no, more, you seem to urge me to betray you. I love you for that. And what makes you do that—love? Oh, it is beautiful to love, and to be free at the same time.

"I don't know what I expect of you, but it is something in the way of a miracle. I am going to demand everything of you—even the impossible, because you encourage it. You are really strong. I like even your deceit, your treachery. It seems aristocratic to me. (Does aristocratic sound wrong in my mouth?)

"Yes, Anaïs, I was thinking how I could betray you, but I can't. I want you. I want to undress you, vulgarize you a bit—ah, I don't know what I am saying. I am a little drunk because you are not here. I would like to be able to clap my hands and voilà, Anaïs! I want to own you, use you, I want to fuck you, I want to teach you things. No, I don't appreciate you—God forbid! Perhaps I even want to humiliate you a little—why, why? Why don't I get down on my knees and just worship you? I can't, I love you laughingly. Do you like that? And dear Anaïs, I am so many things. You see only the good things now—or at least you lead me to believe so. I want you for a whole day at least. I want to go places with you—possess you. You don't know how insatiable I am. Or how dastardly. And how selfish!

"I have been on my good behavior with you. But I warn you, I am no angel. I think principally that I am a little drunk. I love you. I go to bed now—it is too painful to stay awake. I am insatiable. I will ask you to do the impossible. What it is, I don't know. You will tell me probably. You are faster than I am. I love your cunt, Anaïs—it drives me crazy. And the way you say my name! God, it's unreal. Listen, I am very drunk. I am hurt to be here alone. I need you. Can I say everything to you? I can, can't I? Come quickly then and screw me. Shoot with me. Wrap your legs around me. Warm me."

I felt as if I were reading his most unconscious feelings. I felt all life embracing me, in those words. I felt the supreme challenge to my worship of life, and I wanted to yield, to give myself to all life, which is Henry. What new sensations he arouses in me, what new torments, new fear and new courage!

No letter from him after our day. He felt a tremendous relief, satisfaction, fatigue, just as I did.

And then?

Yesterday he came to Louveciennes. A new Henry, or, rather, the Henry sensed behind the one generally known, the Henry beyond what he has written down, beyond all literal knowledge, my Henry, the man I love tremendously now, too much, dangerously.

He looked so serious. He had received a letter from June, in pencil, irregular, mad, like a child's, moving, simple, cries of her love for him. "Such a letter blots out everything." I felt the moment had come for me to release my June, to give him my June, "because," I said, "it will make you love her more. It's a beautiful June. Other days I felt you might laugh at my portrait, jeer at its naïveté. Today I know you won't."

I read him all I had written in my journal about June. What is happening? He is deeply moved, torn apart. He believes. "It is in that way I should have written about June. The other is incomplete, superficial. You have got her, Anaïs." But wait. He has left softness, tenderness out of his work, he has written down only the hate, the violence. I have only inserted what he has left out. But he has not left it out because he doesn't feel it, or know it, or understand (as June thinks), only because it is more difficult to express. So far his writing has only issued from violence, it has been whipped out of him, the blows have made him wail and curse. And now he sits and I confide in him completely, in the sentient, profound Henry. He is won.

He says, "Such a love is wonderful, Anaïs. I do not hate or despise that. I see what you give each other. I see it so well. Read, read—this is a revelation to me."

I read, and I tremble as I read, up to our kiss. He understands too well.

Suddenly he says, "Anaïs, I have just realized that what I give you is something coarse and plain, compared to that. I realize that when June returns . . ."

I stop him. "You don't know what you have given me! It is not coarse and plain! Today, for example . . ." I am choking with feelings that are too entangled. I want to tell him how much he has given me. We are oppressed by the same fear. I say, "You see a beautiful June now."

"No, I hate her!"

"You hate her?"

"Yes, I hate her," Henry says, "because I see by your notes that we are her dupes, that you are duped, that there is one pernicious, destructive direction to her lies. Insidiously, they are meant to deform me in your eyes, and you in my eyes. If June returns, she will poison us against each other. I fear that."

"There is something between us, Henry, a tie which is not quite possible for June to comprehend or to seize."

"The mind," he murmured.

"For that she will hate us, yes, and she will combat with her own tools."

"And her tools are lies," he said.

We were both so acutely aware of her power over us, of the new ties which bound us together.

I said, "If I had the means to help bring June back, would you want me to do it?"

Henry winced and suddenly lurched towards me. "Ah, don't ask me such a question, Anaïs, don't ask me."

One day we were talking about his writing. "Perhaps you couldn't write here at Louveciennes," I said. "It's too peaceful, nothing driving you."

"It would just be a different writing," he said. He was thinking of Proust, whose handling of Albertine haunts him.

How far we are from his drunken letter. Yesterday he was disarming; he was so whole. How he absorbed! June rarely confided in him. Will he turn around and deny all his feelings? I teased him. "Perhaps all I have written is untrue, untrue of June, untrue of me. Perhaps it's hypocrisy." "No! No!" He knew. Real passions, real loves, real impulses.

"For the first time I see some beauty in it all," says Henry.

I am afraid of not having been truthful enough. I am amazed at Henry's emotion.

"Am I not the Idiot?" I ask.

"No, you *see*, you just see more," says Henry. "What you see is there, all right. Yes." He reflects as he talks. He often repeats a phrase, to give himself time to reflect. What goes on behind that compact forehead fascinates me.

The extravagance of Dostoevsky's language has released both of us. He was a portentous author for Henry. Now, when we live with the same fervor, the same temperature, the same extravagance, I am in bliss. This is the life, the talk, these are the emotions which belong to me. I breathe freely now. I am at home. I am myself.

After being with Henry, I go to meet Eduardo. "I want you, Anaïs! Give me another chance! You belong to me. How I suffered this afternoon, knowing you were with Henry. I never knew jealousy before; and now it is so strong it is killing me." His face is terrifyingly white. He always smiles, as I do. Now he cannot. I am not yet accustomed to the sight of misery given by me; or, rather, given to Eduardo. It upsets me. Yet, deep down, I am cold. I sit there, seeing Eduardo's face distorted with pain, and I really feel nothing but pity. "Will you come with me?"

"No." I employ all the excuses that will not hurt him. I tell him everything except that I love Henry.

Finally, I win. I let him take me in a taxi to the station

to meet Hugo. I let him kiss me. I promise to come and see him Monday. I am weak. But I don't want to hurt his life, maim him, deprive him of his newborn self-confidence. Enough of my old love for him survives for that. I warned him that I could destroy him, although I hated to destroy, and that I had found a man I couldn't destroy, that he was the right man for me. I tried to make him hate me. But he said, "I want you, Anaïs." And the horoscope says: we are complements.

The important thing is the response to life. June and Henry respond extravagantly, as I do. Hugo is dimmer, more listless. Today he came out of the dimness to a realization of *The Possessed*. I made him write down his thoughts, they were so wonderful. His best moments are very profound.

He represents truth. He is Shatov, capable of love and faith. Then what am I? That Friday, when I lay in three men's arms, what was I?

To Eduardo: "Listen, *cousin chéri*, I'm writing you in the train, going home. I am trembling with pain over this morning. The day seemed so heavy to me I couldn't breathe. . . . You have been beautiful with activity, life, emotion, strength. It is a tragedy for me that you should be at your highest moment when I love you best, only not sensually, not sensually. We are destined never to meet with equal feelings. Just now it is Henry who owns my body. *Cousin chéri*, I tried today for the last time to direct life, according to an ideal. My ideal was to wait for you all my life, and I waited too long, and now I live by instinct, and the flow carries me to Henry. Forgive me. It isn't that you haven't the strength to hold me. Would you say that you didn't love me before because I was less lovable? No. It would be as untrue to say you lacked the strength as to say I have changed. Life is not rational; it is just mad and full of pain. Today I have not seen Henry nor will I see him tomorrow. I give these two days to the memory of our hours. Be a fatalist, yes, as I am today but have no mean or bitter thoughts such as the idea that I played with you for my vanity's sake. Oh, Eduardo, *querido*, I accept pain which comes not from such motives but from real sources—real pain, at the treachery of life, which hurts us both in different ways. Do not seek the *because*—in love there is no because, no reason, no explanation, no solutions."

I came home and threw myself on the couch; I found it hard to breathe. In answer to Eduardo's plea I met him early this morning. He had spent two days feeling jealous of Henry, realizing that he, the narcissist, was at last possessed by another. "How good it is to come out of one's self! I have thought of you continuously for two days, have slept badly, have dreamed that I struck you hard, oh, so hard and that your head fell off and I carried it about in my arms. Anaïs, I am going to have you all day. You promised me. All day." All I want is to dart out of the café. I tell him so. His pleadings, softness, intensity vaguely stir my old love and my pity, the Richmond Hill love, with its vague expectancies, the old habit of thinking: of course I want Eduardo.

I fear he might shut himself up again in narcissism because he cannot bear pain. "To think I have come to worship your very bones, Anaïs!" I am faintly, faintly stirred, yet I want most of all to run away from him. I don't know why, I obey him, follow him.

I feel hurt while reading *Albertine disparue*, because it is marked by Henry, and Albertine is June. I can follow each amplification of his jealousies, his doubts, his tenderness, his regrets, his horror, his passion, and I am invaded by a burning jealousy of June. For the moment this love, which had been so balanced between Henry and June that I could not feel any jealousy, this love is stronger for Henry, and I feel tortured and afraid.

Yet I dreamed of June last night. June had suddenly returned. We shut ourselves up in a room. Hugo, Henry, and other people were waiting for us to dress and have dinner together. I wanted June. I begged her to undress. Piece by piece I discovered her body, with cries of admiration, but in the nightmare I saw the defects of it, strange deformations. Still, she seemed altogether desirable. I begged her to let me see between her legs. She opened them and raised them, and there I saw flesh thickly covered with hard black hair, like a man's, but then the very tip of her flesh was snow-white. What horrified me was that she was moving frenziedly, and that the lips were opening and closing quickly like the mouth of the goldfish in the pool when he eats. I just watched her, fascinated and repulsed, and then I threw myself on her and said, "Let me put my tongue there," and she let me but she did not seem satisfied while I flicked at her. She seemed cold and restless. Suddenly she sat up, threw me down, and leaned over me, and as she lay over me I felt a penis touching me. I questioned her and she answered triumphantly, "Yes, I have a little one; aren't you glad?" "But how do you conceal it from Henry?" I asked. She smiled, treacherously. All through the dream there was a sense of great disorder, of movements which accomplished nothing, of everything being late, of everybody waiting, restless and defeated.

And yet I am jealous of all the suffering Henry experiences with her. I feel that I am sinking away from all wisdom and all understanding, that my instincts are howling like jungle animals. When I remember the afternoons with Henry in the Hotel Anjou, I suffer. Two afternoons which are branded on my body and on my mind.

When I came home from Eduardo yesterday I took refuge in Hugo's arms. I was loaded down with feelings of anxiety for Eduardo and yearning for Henry, and at the same time, lying in Hugo's arms and merely kissing his mouth and neck, I found a feeling so sweet and so profound that it seemed to conquer all the darkness and baseness of life. I felt as if I were a leper and that his strength was so great he could heal me instantly by a kiss. I loved him last night with a sincerity that surpasses all the climaxes my fever makes me crave. Proust writes that happiness is something from which fever is absent. Last night I knew happiness and I recognized it, and I can truly say that only Hugo has ever given it to me, and it runs undefeated by the leapings of my fevered body and mind.

Now, when I am living the richest period of my life, again my health fails me. All the doctors say the same thing: no illness, nothing wrong but general weakness, low stamina. The heart barely beats, I am cold, I am easily tired out. Today I was tired out for Henry. How precious the moment in the Clichy kitchen, with Fred, too. They were eating breakfast at two o'clock. Books piled up, the ones they want me to read and the one I brought them. Then in Henry's room, alone. He closes the door, and our talk melts into caresses, into deft, acute core-reaching fucking.

The talk is about Proust, and it brings this confession from Henry. "To be entirely honest with myself I like to be away from June. It is then I enjoy her best. When she is here I am morbid, oppressed, desperate. With you—well, you are *light.* I am satiated with experiences and pain. Perhaps I torment you. I don't know. Do I?"

I can't answer that very well, though it is clear to me that he is darkness to me. And why? Because of the instincts he has aroused in me? The word "satiation" terrified me. It seemed like the first drop of poison poured into me. Against his satiation, I match my fearful freshness, the newness in me, which gives intensity to what for him may be of less value. That first drop of poison, poured so accidentally, was like a foretelling of death. I don't know through what crevice our love will suddenly seep out and spend itself.

Henry, today I am sad for the moments I am missing, those moments when you talk with Fred until dawn, when you are eloquent or brilliant or violent or exultant. And I was sad that you missed a wonderful moment in me. Last night I was sitting by the fire and talking as I rarely talk, dazzling Hugo, feeling immensely and astonishingly rich, pouring out stories and ideas which would have amused you. It was about lies, the different kinds of lies, the special lies I tell for specific reasons, to improve on living. One time when Eduardo was being overanalytical I poured out the story of my imaginary Russian lover. He was in rapture. And by it I conveyed to him the necessity of folly, the richness in emotion which he lacks, because he is emotionally impuissant. When I am sorely in trouble, perplexed, lost, I invent the acquaintance of a wise old man with whom I converse. I tell everybody about him, how he looks, what he said, his effect on me (someone to lean on for a moment), and by the end of the day I feel strengthened by my experience with the wise old man, and as satisfied as if it were all true. I have also invented friends when the ones I had were not satisfying. And how I enjoy my experiences! How they fill me, add to me. Embroidery.

Today I meet Fred, and as we walk towards Trinité together the sun comes out of a rain cloud and blinds us. And I begin quoting from his writing about a sunny morning in the market, which touches him. He has told me I am good for Henry, that I give him things June couldn't give him. And yet he admits that Henry is entirely in June's power when she is there. June is stronger. I am growing to love Henry more than June.

Fred marvels at how Henry can love two women at the same time. "He is a big big man," he says. "There's so much room in him, so much love. If I loved you, I couldn't love another woman." And I was thinking: I am like Henry. I can love Hugo and Henry and June.

Henry, I understand your clasping June and me. One doesn't exclude the other. But June may not feel this, and certainly you didn't understand June clasping you and Jean together. No, you demanded a choice.

We are going to taste all we can give each other. Before June comes we are going to lie together as often as possible. Our happiness is in danger, yes, but we are going to devour it quickly, thoroughly. For every day of it I am thankful.

---

Letter to June: "This morning I awakened with a profound and desperate desire for you. I have strange dreams. Now you are small and soft and pliable in my arms, now you are powerful and domineering and the leader. At once mothlike and indomitable. June, what are you? I know you wrote Henry a love letter, and I suffered. I have found at least one joy and that is to be able to talk openly about you to Henry. I did it because I knew he would love you more. I gave him *my* June, the portrait of you I wrote down during the days we were together. . . . Now I can say to Henry, 'I love June,' and he does not combat our feelings, he does not abhor them. He is moved. And you, June? What does it mean that you have not written me? . . . Am I a dream to you, am I not real and warm for you? What new loves, new ecstasies, new impulses move you now? I know you don't like to write. I don't ask for long letters, only a few words, what you feel. Have you ever wished yourself back here in my house, in my room, and do you have regrets that we were so overwhelmed? Do you ever wish to live those hours over again and differently, with more confidence. June, I hesitate to write everything, as if I felt again that you would run downstairs to escape me, as you did that day, or almost.

"I'm sending you my book on Lawrence and the cape. I love you, June, and you know how acutely, how desperately. You know that no one can say or do anything to shake my love. I have taken you into myself, whole. You need have no fear of being unmasked, only loved."

To Fred: "If you want to be good to me, don't talk any more against June. Today I realized that your defense of me only engraves June more deeply into that groove of my being. Do you know how I learned this? Yesterday I listened to you, you remember, with a kind of gratitude. I didn't say very much for June. And then this morning I wrote June a love letter, moved by a selfless instinct of protection, as if I were punishing myself for having listened to praise of myself that lessened June's value. And Henry, I know, feels the same way and acts the same way. But I understand all you said and feel and are, and I like you for it, immensely."

Eduardo says to Dr. Allendy, his psychoanalyst, "I don't know if Anaïs loved me or not, whether she fooled me or fooled herself about her feelings."

"She loved you," said Allendy. "I can see that by her preoccupation with you."

"But you don't know her," said Eduardo. "You don't know the extent of her sympathy for others, her power of self-sacrifice."

To me Eduardo says, "What did happen, Anaïs? What intuition did you have at that moment when you asked me to let you go? What did you realize?"

"Just as I wrote you—an awareness of the importance of your conquering me, to give you the self-confidence you lacked, a stirring of the old love, which we mistook . . ." Oh, I am slippery.

So he rationalizes, in self-protection. "Then you, too, have a feeling of incest." The frailty of his confidence (If I conquer Anaïs, I have conquered everything) is so pitiable. I acted for his needs. I didn't obey my instincts, my imperative sureness that I want only Henry. But when I think I have done good and been utterly fair, it seems I have done evil, in a subtle, insidious way. I have suggested to Eduardo a doubt about his passion, which has been fostered by psychoanalysis, artificially stimulated by it. The scientific tampering with emotions. For the first time I am against analysis. Perhaps it did help Eduardo to realize his passion, but it does not add to his strength, basically. I feel it is a short-lived thing, something painfully squeezed out, a thin essence pressed out of herbs.

I see similarities between Henry and me in human relationships. I see our capacities for enduring pain when we love, our easily duped natures, our desire to believe in June, our quick rising to defend her from the hatred of others. He talks of beating June, but he would never dare. It is only a wish fulfillment, to dominate what he is dominated by. It is said in *Bubu de Montparnasse* that a woman submits to the man who beats her because he is like a strong government who can also protect her. But Henry's beating would be futile because he is not a protector of woman. He has let himself be protected. June has worked for him like a man, and so she can say, "I have loved him like a child." Yes, and it diminishes her passion. He has let her feel her own strength. And nothing of this can be changed, because it is engraved in both of them. All his life Henry will assert his manhood by destruction and hatred in his work; each time June appears he will bow his head. Now only hatred moves him. "Life is foul, foul," he cries. And with these words he kisses me and awakens me, I who have been sleeping one hundred years, with hallucinations hanging like curtains of spider webs over my bed. But the man who leans over my bed is soft. And he writes nothing about these moments. He doesn't even try to pull the spider webs down. How am I to be convinced the world is foul? "I am no angel. You have only seen me at my best, but wait. . . ."

I was dreaming of reading all this to Henry, everything

I have written about him. And then I laughed because I could hear Henry saying, "How strange; why is there so much gratefulness in you?" I didn't know why until I read what Fred wrote about Henry: "Poor Henry, I feel sorry for you. You have no gratitude because you have no love. To be grateful one must first know how to love."

Fred's words added to my own about Henry's hatred hurt me. Do I or do I not believe in them? Do they explain the profound amazement I felt, while reading his novel, at the savagery of his attacks on Beatrice, his first wife? At the same time I thought it was I who was wrong, that people must fight and must hate each other, and that hatred is good. But I took love for granted; love can include hatred.

I have constant slips of the tongue and say "John" instead of "Henry" to Hugo. There is no resemblance whatsoever between them, and I cannot understand the association in my mind.

"Listen," I say to Henry, "don't leave me out of your book out of delicacy. Include me. Then we'll see what happens. I expect much."

"But meanwhile," says Henry, "it is Fred who has written three wonderful pages about you. He raves about you, he worships you. I am jealous of those three pages. I wish I had written them."

"You will," I say confidently.

"For example, your hands. I had never noticed them. Fred gives them so much importance. Let me look at them. Are they really as beautiful as that? Yes, indeed." I laugh. "You appreciate other things, perhaps."

"What?"

"Warmth, for instance." I'm smiling, but there are so

many fine lacerations that Henry's words open. "When Fred hears me talk about June, he says I do not love you."

Yet he won't let me go. He calls out to me in his letters. His arms, his caresses, and his fucking are voracious. He says, with me, that no amount of thinking (Proust's words, or Fred's, or mine) will stop us from living. And what is living? The moment when he rings at Natasha's door (she is away and I have her place) and immediately desires me. The moment when he tells me he has had no thoughts of whores. I am so idiotically fair and loyal to June in every word I utter about her. How can I deceive myself about the extent of Henry's love when I understand and share his feelings about June?

He sleeps in my arms, we are welded, his penis still in me. It is a moment of real peace, a moment of security. I open my eyes, but I do not think. One of my hands is on his gray hair. The other hand is spread around his leg. "Oh, Anaïs," he had said, "you are so hot, so hot that I can't wait. I must shoot into you quickly, quickly."

Is how one is loved always so important? Is it so imperative that one should be loved absolutely or greatly? Would Fred say of me that I can love because I love others more than I love myself? Or is it Hugo who loves when he goes three times to the station to meet me because I have missed three trains? Or is it Fred, with his nebulous, poetic, delicate comprehension? Or do I love most when I say to Henry, "The destroyers do not always destroy. June has not destroyed you, ultimately. The core of you is a writer. And the writer is living."

"Henry, tell Fred we can go and get the curtains tomorrow."

"I'll come, too," said Henry, suddenly jealous.

"But you know Fred wants to see me, to talk with me." Henry's jealousy pleased me. "Tell him to meet me at the same place as last time."

"About four o'clock."

"No, at three." I was thinking we didn't have enough time together the last day we met. Henry's face is impenetrable. I never know by any sign on it what he feels. There are transitions, yes, when he is flushed and excited, or serious and chastened, or observant and introspective. The blue eyes are analytical, like a scientist's, or moist with feeling. When they are moist I am moved down to my toes because I remember a story about his childhood. His parents (his father was a tailor) used to take him with them on their Sunday outings, visiting, dragging the child along all day and late at night. They sat in the houses of their friends to play cards and smoke. The smoke would grow thick and hurt Henry's eyes. They would put him on the bed in the room next to the parlor, with wet towels over his inflamed eyes.

And now his eyes get tired with proofreading at the newspaper, and I would like to free him of it, and I can't.

Last night I couldn't sleep. I imagined being in Natasha's apartment again with Henry. I wanted to relive the moment when he came into me as we were standing. He taught me to encircle him with my legs. Such practices are so unfamiliar that they bewilder me. Afterwards, the joy bursts upon my senses, because it has unleashed a new kind of desire.

"Anaïs, I feel you, your hotness right down to my toes." In him, too, it is like lightning. He is always amazed by my moisture and my warmth.

Often, though, the passivity of the woman's role weighs on me, suffocates me. Rather than wait for his pleasure, I would like to take it, to run wild. Is it that which pushes me into lesbianism? It terrifies me. Do women act thus? Does June go to Henry when she wants him? Does she mount him? Does she wait for him? He guides my inexperienced hands. It is like a forest fire, to be with him. New places of my body are aroused and burnt. He is incendiary. I leave him in an unquenchable fever.

I have just been standing before the open window of my bedroom and I have breathed in deeply, all the sunshine, the snowdrops, the crocuses, the primroses, the crooning of the pigeons, the trills of the birds, the entire procession of soft winds and cool smells, of frail colors and petal-textured skies, the knotted gray-brown of old trees, the vertical shoots of young branches, the wet brown earth, the torn roots. It is all so savory that my mouth opens, and it is Henry's tongue which I taste, and I smell his breath as he sleeps, wrapped in my arms.

I expect to meet Fred, but it is Henry who comes to the rendezvous. Fred is working. My eyes open wide on Henry, the man who slept in my arms yesterday, and I have chill thoughts. I see his stained hat and the hole in his coat. Another day this would have moved me, but today I realize it is willed poverty, calculated, intentional, out of disdain for the bourgeois who holds a purse carefully. He talks marvelously about Samuel Putman and Eugene Jolas, and his work, and my work and Fred's. But then the Pernod affects him and he tells me of sitting in a café with Fred last night after work, and of whores talking to him, and of Fred's looking at him severely, because he had been with me that afternoon and shouldn't have been talking to those women; and they were ugly. "But Fred is wrong," I say, to

Henry's surprise. "The whores complement me. I understand the relief a man must feel to go to a woman without demands on his emotions or feelings." And Henry adds, "You don't have to write them letters!" As I laugh he realizes that I understand completely. I even understand his preference for Renoiresque bodies. *Voilà.* Yet I keep this picture of an outraged Fred worshiping me. And Henry says, "That's the nearest I came to being unfaithful to you."

I don't know that I so much want Henry's faithfulness, because I am beginning to realize that the very word "love" tires me today. Love or no love. Fred's saying Henry doesn't love me. I understand the need for relief from complications, and I desire it for myself, only women cannot achieve such a state. Women are romantic.

Suppose I don't want Henry's love. Suppose I say to him, "Listen, we are two adults. I'm sick of fantasies and emotions. Don't mention the word 'love.' Let's talk as much as we want and fuck only when we want it. Leave love out of it." They are all so serious. Just this moment I feel old, cynical. I'm tired of demands, too. For an hour today I feel unsentimental. In a moment I could destroy the entire legend, from beginning to end, destroy everything, except the fundamentals: my passion for June and my worship of Hugo.

Perhaps my intellect is playing another prank. Is that what it is to feel a sense of reality? Where are yesterday's feelings and this morning's, and what about my intuition that Henry instead of Fred would meet me? And what has it all got to do with the fact that Henry was drunk, and that I, not realizing it, read to him about his power to "break" me. He didn't understand, of course, while swimming in the sulphur-colored Pernod.

The burlesque of that hurt me. I asked him, "What is Fred like when he is drunk?"

"Merry, yes, but always a bit contemptuous with the whores. They feel it."

"Whereas you get friendly?"

"Yes, I talk to them like a cart driver."

Well, I had no joy from all this. It makes me cold and blank inside. Once, I joked and said that someday I would send him a telegram saying: "Never meet again because you don't love me." Coming home, I thought, tomorrow we will not meet. Or if we meet, we will never lie together again. Tomorrow I'll tell Henry not to bother about love. But the rest?

Hugo says tonight that my face is blazing. I can't restrain a smile. We ought to have a banquet. Henry has killed my seriousness. It couldn't survive his changing moods, from beggar to god, from satyr to poet, from madman to realist.

When he thrusts at me, I am saved from sobbing or hitting back because of my damned understanding. Whatever I understand, like Henry and the whores, I can't very well fight about. What I understand, I also simultaneously accept.

Henry is such a world in himself that it would not surprise me if he should want to steal, to kill, or to rape. So far I've understood everything.

Yesterday at the rendezvous I was seeing for the first time a malevolent Henry. He had come more to hurt Fred than to see me. He reveled when he said, "Fred is working. How it must gripe him." I didn't want to choose the curtains without Fred but Henry insisted on choosing them. I don't know whether I imagined it or not but it seemed to me he was exulting in insensibility. "I found as much pleasure doing evil . . ." said Stavrogin. To me, an unknown pleasure.

I had planned to send Henry a telegram while I was with Fred saying, "I love you." Instead, I wanted to go see Fred and blot out the hurt. Henry's pleasure was startling to me. He said, "I used to like borrowing from a certain man and then I would spend half the sum he gave me to send him a telegram." When stories like this rise out of drunken mists, I see in him a gleam of deviltry, a secret enjoyment of cruelty. June buying perfume for Jean while Henry starved, or taking pleasure in concealing a bottle of old Madeira in her trunk while Henry and his friends, penniless, wished desperately for something to drink. What startles me is not the act but the pleasure which accompanies it. Henry was pushed to torment Fred. June carries it all much further than he does, blatantly, such as when she wrestled with Jean at Henry's parents' house. This love of cruelty binds them together insolubly. They would both take pleasure in humiliating me, in destroying me.

I feel my past like an unbearable weight on me, like a curse, the source of every movement I make, every word I utter. At certain moments the past surmounts me, and Henry recedes into unreality. A terrible reserve, an unnatural purity envelops me, and I close out the world completely. Today I am the *jeune fille* of Richmond Hill, writing on an ivory white desk about nothing at all.

I have no fear of God, and yet fear keeps me awake at night, fear of the devil. And if I believe in the devil, I must believe in God. And if evil is abhorrent to me, I must be a saint.

Henry, save me from beatification, from the horrors of static perfection. Precipitate me into the inferno.

Seeing Eduardo yesterday crystallized my mental chill. I listen to his explanation of my feelings. It sounds very plausible. I have suddenly turned cold towards Henry because I witnessed his cruelty to Fred. Cruelty has been the great conflict of my life. I witnessed cruelty in my childhood—Father's cruelty towards Mother and his sadistic punishment of my brothers and me—and the sympathy I felt for my mother reached hysteria when she and my father quarreled, acts which paralyzed me later. I grew up with such an incapacity for cruelty it amounts to a weakness.

Seeing a small aspect of it in Henry brought a realization of his other cruelties. And more than that, Fred aroused all the reserve in me, filling me with recollections of my childhood, which is what Eduardo describes as retrogression, falling back again into a childish state, which could keep me from progressing any further into maturer living.

I had wanted to confide in someone, I even wanted to let myself be guided. Eduardo said the moment had come for me to be psychoanalyzed. He had always wanted this. He could help me by talking things over, but only Dr. Allendy could be a guide, a *father* (Eduardo loves to tempt me with a father figure). Why did I insist, instead, on making Eduardo my psychoanalyst? That was only postponing the real task. "Perhaps I like to look up to you," I said.

"In place of the other relationship, which you don't want?"

Somehow the talk seemed eminently effective to me. I was already singing. Hugo was off at a bank function. Eduardo went on analyzing. He was looking extraordinarily handsome. All during dinner I was affected by his forehead and his eyes, his profile, his mouth, his sly expression—the introvert gloating over his secrets. This great handsomeness I took into myself later when he desired me, but I took it as one breathes air, or swallows a snowflake, or yields to the sun. My laughter released him from seriousness. I told him about the allure of his face and his green eyes. I wanted him and took him, a casual lover. But a bad psychoanalyst, I teased, because he made love to his patient.

As I ran upstairs to comb my hair, I knew that the next day I would rush to see Henry. All he does to combat my phantoms is to push me against the wall of his room and kiss me, to tell me in a whisper what he wants of my body today, what gestures, what attitudes. I obey, and I enjoy him to frenzy. We rush along over phantasmagoric obstacles. Now I know why I have loved him. Even Fred, before he left us, seemed less tragic, and I confided to Henry that I didn't want a perfect love from him, that I knew he was tired of all that, as I was, that I felt a surge of wisdom and humor, and that nothing could stop our relationship until we just didn't want to make love any more. For the first time, I think I understand what pleasure is. And I am glad I laughed so much last night, and sang this morning, and moved irresistibly towards Henry. (Eduardo was still here when I left, carrying the package containing Henry's curtains.)

Just before this, my brother Joaquin and Eduardo were talking about Henry, in my presence. (Joaquin has read my journal.) They think that Henry is a destructive force who has elected me, the most creative of forces, to test his power on, that I have succumbed to the magic of tons of literature (it is true that I love literature), that I will be saved—I forget how, but somehow in spite of myself.

And as I lay there, already happy because I had decided I would have my Henry today, I smiled.

On the first page of a beautiful purple-covered diary book Eduardo gave me, with an inscription, I have already written Henry's name. No Dr. Allendy for me. No paralyzing analysis. Just living.

*APRIL*

When Henry hears Hugo's beautiful, vibrant, loyal, heart-stirring voice over the telephone, he is angry at the amorality of women, of all women, of women like myself. He himself practices all the disloyalties, all the treacheries, but the faithlessness of a woman hurts him. And I am terribly distressed when he is in such a mood, because I have a feeling of being faithful to the bond between Hugo and me. Nothing that I live outside of the circle of our love alters or diminishes it. On the contrary, I love him better because I love him without hypocrisy. But the paradox torments me deeply. That I am not more perfect, or more like Hugo, is to be despised, yes, but it is only the other side of my being.

Henry would understand my abandoning him out of consideration for Hugo, but to do so would be hypocritical of me. One thing is certain, though: If one day I were forced to choose between Hugo and Henry, I would choose Hugo without hesitation. The liberty which I have given myself in Hugo's name, like a gift from him, only increases the richness and potency of my love for him. Amorality, or a more complicated morality, aims at the ultimate loyalty and overlooks the immediate and literal one. I share with Henry an anger, not at the imperfections of women, but at the foulness of living itself, which perhaps this volume proclaims more loudly than all Henry's curses.

Henry threatened yesterday to make me absolutely drunk, which became effective only when I read Fred's powdered and crystallized letters to Céline. Our talk breaks and splashes like a kaleidoscope. When Henry goes to the kitchen, Fred and I talk as if we had thrown a bridge from fortress to fortress and there is nothing we can hold back. Words, like a procession, rush across a bridge which is usually drawn up and has even grown rusted from the love of solitude. Then there is Henry, constantly in communication with the world, as if sitting forever at the head of a gigantic banquet.

In the small kitchen, without moving, we three almost touch each other. Henry moved to put a hand on my shoulder and to kiss me, and Fred would not look at the kiss. I sat bowed under the two kinds of love. There was Henry's warmth, his voice, his hands, his mouth. And there were Fred's feelings for me, touching a more delicate region, so that while Henry kissed me I wanted to extend my hand to Fred and hold both loves.

Henry was bursting with universal generosity: "I give you Anaïs, Fred. You see how I am. I want everybody to love Anaïs. She's wonderful."

"She's too wonderful," said Fred. "You don't deserve her."

"You are a wasp," cried Henry, the hurt giant.

"Besides," said Fred, "you haven't given me Anaïs. I have my own Anaïs, a different one from yours. I've taken her without asking either of you. Stay all night, Anaïs. We need you."

"Yes, yes," cried Henry.

I sit like an idol, and it is Fred who criticizes the giant because the giant does not worship me.

"Curse it, Anaïs," Henry says, "I don't worship you, but I love you. I feel I can give you as much as Eduardo, for example. I could not hurt you. When I see you sitting there, so fragile, I know I won't hurt you."

"I don't want worship," says the idol. "You give me—well, what you give me is better than worship."

Fred's hand trembles when he offers me a glass of wine. The wine stirs the center of my body, and it is throbbing. Henry goes out for a moment. Fred and I are silent. It is Fred who has said, "No, I don't like big banquets. I love a dinner like this, for two or three." Now we are heavily silent, and I feel bowed down. Henry returns and asks Fred to leave us. He has scarcely pulled the door after him when Henry and I are tasting each other's flesh. We fall together into our savage world. He bites me. He makes my bones crack. He makes me lie with legs wide open and digs into me. Our cravings grow wild. Our bodies are convulsed.

"Oh, Anaïs," he says, "I don't know how you learned it, but you can fuck, you can fuck. I've never said it before, as strongly, but listen now, I love you madly. You've got me, you've got me. I'm crazy about you."

And then something I say arouses a sudden doubt in him. "It isn't only the fucking, is it? You *do* love me?"

The first lie. Mouths touching, breaths mingling; I, with his wet, hot penis in me, say I love him.

But as I say it I know it is not true. His body has a way of arousing mine, of answering mine. When I think of him I want to open my legs. Now he is asleep in my arms, heavily asleep. I hear an accordion. It is Sunday night, in

Clichy. I think of *Bubu de Montparnasse*, of hotel rooms, of the way Henry pushes up my leg, of his loving my buttocks. I am not myself at this moment, the vagabond. The accordion swells my heart, the white blood of Henry has filled me. He lies asleep in my arms and I do not love him.

I think I told Fred I didn't love Henry when we sat there silently. I told him I loved his own visionariness, his hallucinations. Henry carries the power to fuck, to flow, to curse, to enlarge and vitalize, to destroy and create suffering. It is the demon in him I admire, the indestructible idealist, the masochist who has found a way of inflicting pain on himself, because he suffers from his treacheries, his crudenesses. It touches me when he is humble before something like my house. "I know I am a boor and that I do not know how to behave in such a house, and so I pretend to despise it, but I love it. I love the beauty and fineness of it. It is so warm that when I come into it I feel taken up in the arms of a Ceres, I'm ensorcelled."

And then Hugo drives me home in the car, and he says, "Last night I was awake, and I thought of how there is a love which is bigger and more wonderful than fucking." Because he had been ill for a few days and we had not made love, but slept in each other's arms.

I felt as if I would burst from my fragile shell. I felt my breasts heavy and full. But I was not sad. I thought, Darling, I am so rich tonight, but it is for you, too. It is not all for myself. I'm lying to you every day now, but see, I give you the joys I am given. The more I take into myself, the greater my love for you. The more I deny myself, the poorer I would be for you, my darling. There is no tragedy, if you can follow me in that equation. There are equations which are more obvious. Such a one would be: I love you and therefore I renounce the world and life for you. You would have a prostrate nun before you, poisoned by demands you could not answer and which would kill you. But see me tonight. We are driving home together. I have known pleasure. But I do not shut you out. Come into my dilated body and taste it. I carry life. And you know it. You cannot see me naked without desiring me. My flesh seems to you innocent and entirely your possession. You could kiss me where Henry bit me and find pleasure. Our love is inalterable. Only knowledge would hurt you. Perhaps I am a demon, to be able to pass from Henry's arms into yours, but literal faithfulness is for me empty of meaning. I cannot live by it. What is a tragedy is that we should live so close together without your being able to perceive this knowledge, that such secrets should be possible, that you should only know what I wish to tell you, that there should be no trace on my body of what I live through. But lying, too, is living, lying of the kind I do.

Fred's presence restrains me, as though my very own eyes were watching the extension of myself into spheres I should renounce. With Fred I could live out something delicate and intricate. But I do not want to live with myself. I am flying from myself. Still, I am not deforming my true nature but manifesting the sensuality which exists in me. Henry answers a strength in me that had not been answered before. His sexual vitality is in accord with mine. When I took up dancing it was a Henry I craved. It is a Henry I sought, erroneously, in John.

My thoughts, like elastic, are stretched to their tensest meaning. With Henry one does not talk to the depths of things. He is no Proust, lingering and stretching. He is in movement. He lives by gusts. It is the gusts I enjoy in Henry. I may sit for a whole day after a gust and sail my river boat slowly down the feelings that he has dispersed with prodigality.

Eduardo says I have never really entirely given myself, but that seems impossible when I see how I submit to the nobility and perfection of Hugo, to the sensualism of Henry, to the beauty of Eduardo himself. The other night at the concert I stood transfixed before him. He has learned not to smile, which is what I must learn. The color of his skin alone attracts me. He has the golden pallor of the Spanish but with a Northern glow, too, a rosiness under the tan. And the color of his eyes, that changeful green, unbearably cool. It is the mouth and nostrils which promise. But again I have the sensation of Eduardo and me walking through the world and knocking our heads together. Our heads alone meet and knock. I would have nothing else. I like his mind, which is like a sanctuary, very rich with his continuous plumbing and analysis. He seems without will because he obeys his unconscious, and, like Lawrence, cannot always tell why.

Henry has noticed what neither a Hugo or an Eduardo would notice. I was lying in bed and he said, "You always seem to be taking poses, in an almost Oriental way."

He demands strong words from me when he fucks, and I cannot give them. I cannot tell him what I feel. He teaches me new gestures, prolongations, variations.

Eduardo asked me the other day if I would like to try June's way: plunge into an absolute denial of scruples, to lie (to one's self, principally), to deform one's nature so as to allow no impediment, like my incapacity for cruelty. Yesterday, in the very paroxysm of sensual joy, I could not bite Henry as he wanted me to.

Eduardo is afraid of my journal. He is afraid of an indictment, and that I should not have understood. He confessed this fear to his psychoanalyst.

I have a sense of all that I leave out—the lacunae, especially the dreams, the hallucinations. Also, the lies are left out, a desperate necessity to embellish. So I do not write them down. The journal is therefore a lie. What is left out of the journal is also left out of my mind. At the moment of writing I rush for the beauty. I disperse the rest, out of the journal, out of my body. I would like to come back, like a detective, and collect what I have washed off. For example, the terrible, divine credulity of Hugo. I think of what he could have noticed. The time I came back from Henry's room and washed myself, he could have seen the few drops of water that fell to the floor; stains on my underclothes; rouge rubbed off on my handkerchiefs. He could have questioned my saying to him, "Why don't you try and come twice?" (as Henry does), my excessive fatigue, the rings under my eyes.

I keep my diary very secret, but how often I have written in it while sitting at his feet by the fire, and he has not tried to read over my shoulder. When Eduardo made Hugo lie down, close his eyes, and respond to words—"love," "cat," "snow," "jealousy"—his reactions were amazingly slow and vague. Jealousy alone brought an immediate response. He seems to refuse to register, to realize. That is good. It is his self-protection. It is the basis of the odd liberty I have in spite of his powerful jealousy. He does not want to see. This arouses such a pity in me that at times it maddens me. I would like him to punish me, beat me, imprison me. It would relieve me.

I go to meet Dr. Allendy to talk about Eduardo. I see a handsome, healthy man, with clear, intelligent, seer's eyes. My mind is alert, expecting him to say something dogmatic, formulistic. I want him to say it, because if he does, this will be another man I cannot lean on, and I will have to go on conquering myself alone.

We talked first about Eduardo, how he had gained in strength. Allendy was glad I had noticed a keen difference. But now we came to a difficult point. "Did you know," asked Allendy, "that you have been the most important woman in his life? Eduardo has been obsessed with you. You are his image. He has seen you as mother, sister, and unattainable woman. To conquer you means conquering himself, his neuroses."

"Yes, I know. I want him to be cured. I do not want to deprive him of his newborn confidence by telling him that I don't love him sensually."

"How do you love him?"

"I have always been attached to him ideally. I am now, but not sensually. There is another man, a more animal man, who really holds me strongly."

I tell him a little about Henry. He is surprised that I should divide my loves thus. He asks me what my true feelings were about my experience with Eduardo.

"I was entirely passive," I say. "I felt no pleasure. And I am afraid that he might realize this and blame himself for it. It will be worse than ever, worse than if I say now, 'Listen, I love Henry and so I can't love you.' Because if it goes on it becomes like a competition, as if I had allowed rivalry and comparison and *then* abandoned him. It seems more dangerous to me. But then," I ask laughing, "do men know when they give a woman pleasure or not?"

Dr. Allendy laughs, too. "Eighty percent of them never know," he says. "Some men are sensitive, but many more are vain and they want to believe they do, and many others do not really know." (I remembered Henry's question in the hotel: "Do I satisfy you?")

Then I say, "Rather than continue the sexual comedy, would it not be better to tell him *I* am ill, neurotic, that there is something wrong with me?"

"And, of course, you may be," says Allendy. "There is something strange in the way you divide up your loves. It is as if you lacked confidence."

He touches a sensitive spot now. A few minutes ago he had made a mistake, when I talked about the separation between animal and ideal love. He had jumped to the banal conclusion that at the age of puberty I may have witnessed some brutal aspect of love and been disgusted and turned to the ethereal. But now he approaches a truth: lack of confidence. My father did not want a girl. He said I was ugly. When I wrote or drew something, he did not believe it was my work. I never remember a caress or a compliment from him, except when I nearly died at the age of nine. There were always scenes, beatings, his hard blue eyes on me. I remember the unnatural joy I felt when Father wrote me a note here in Paris which began: "Ma jolie." I got no love from him. I suffered with my mother. I remember our arrival in Arcachon, where he was vacationing, after my illness. His face showed he did not want us. What he meant for Mother I also took for myself. Yet

I felt hysterical sorrow when he abandoned us. And all through my schooldays in New York I craved for him. I was always fearful of his hardness and coldness. Yet I repudiated him in Paris. It was I who was severe and unsentimental.

"And so," said Allendy, "you withdrew into yourself and became independent. Instead of trustingly giving yourself entirely to one love, you seek many loves. You even seek cruelty from older men, as if you could not enjoy love without pain. And you are not sure . . ."

"Only of my husband's love."

"But you need more than one."

"Always his, and an older man's."

I was amazed that a child's confidence, once shaken and destroyed, should have such repercussions on a whole life. Father's insufficient love and abandonment remain indelible. Why was it not effaced by all the loves I inspired since then?

Eduardo wanted Dr. Allendy and me to talk for the sake of what I would write down. And I am willing, but on my own terms. That is, I go to him infrequently, which gives me time to absorb the material and work inspirationally and which also makes me less dependent. Yet yesterday when he said, "You seem very well equilibrated, and I don't believe you need me," I suddenly felt a great distress at being left alone again. My work stabilizes me, I utilize my sufferings, but I would like to confide to a human being what I confide to my journal. There is always something barred from my relationships. With Eduardo I cannot talk about Henry. I can only talk about my illness. With Henry I cannot talk about analysis. He is not an analyst, he is an epic writer, an unconscious Dostoevsky. With Fred I can be surrealistic but not the woman who wrote a study of Lawrence.

Allendy said, "You acted beautifully towards Eduardo in all this, as few women would act, for, in general, a woman considers man as an enemy, and she is glad when she can humiliate him or demolish him."

Joaquin says that when he read my journal he became aware that there was more in Henry's gift to me than just a sensual experience; that he did answer to some needs which Hugo could not satisfy. He still thinks that I lose myself in Henry, give myself to experiences which are not really true to my nature.

Allendy, too, begins to imply that I normally should not love a Henry, and that the cause of my loving him must be removed. Here I turn fiercely against science and feel a great loyalty to my instincts.

Psychoanalysis may force me to be more truthful. Already I realize certain feelings I have, like the fear of being hurt. When Henry calls up, I am suspended to every inflection of his voice. If he is busy at the newspaper office, if there is somebody there, or he sounds casual, I am immediately distressed.

Today Henry awoke and said to himself, "To hell with angelical or literary women!" Then he tells me he has written me two letters since Sunday, which are waiting for me at Natasha's, and I am so elated. I despise my own oversensitiveness, which requires so much reassurance, but which also makes me so aware of other people's sensitivity. Hugo's great love should have given me confidence, and my continued craving to be loved and understood is certainly abnormal.

Perhaps I reassert my confidence by trying to conquer older men. Or am I courting pain? What do I feel when I see Henry's rather cold blue eyes on me? (My father had icy blue eyes.) I want them to melt with desire for me.

There is now a great tension between Fred and me; we cannot bear each other's eyes. He wrote something about me so exact, so piercing that I felt invaded in the most secret precincts of my being. His writing about Henry also terrified me, as if he had come too close to my own fears and doubts. He writes occultly. I could barely talk after reading those pages. And he was reading my journal. He said, "You should not let me read this, Anaïs." I asked why. He seemed stunned. He bowed his head, his mouth trembled. He is like a ghost of me. Why was he stunned? Did I reveal the similitude, the recognition? He is a part of me. He could understand my entire life. I would put all my journals in his hands. I do not fear him. He is so tender with me.

Henry talks beautifully to me, in a cool, sagelike mood. He says, "I love you," while I lie in his arms, and I say, "I do not believe you." He realizes I am in a devilish mood. He insists: "Do you love *me*?" And I answer vaguely. When we are sensually bound together I cannot believe that we are close only physically. When I awake from the deliriousness and we talk quietly, I am surprised that he should talk about our love so seriously.

"Sunday night after you left I slept a while, then I went out for a walk, and I felt so happy, Anaïs, happier than I have ever felt before. I realized a terrible truth: that I don't want June to come back. I need you terribly—absolutely. At certain moments I even feel that if June should come back and disappoint me and I should not care any more for her, I would be almost glad. Sunday night I wanted to send her a cablegram telling her I did not want her any more."

But my wisdom prevented me from believing. He, too, knows, because he adds, "I'm weak in June's hands, Anaïs. If, when she comes back, I act exactly as she wants me to act, you must not feel that I disappoint you or fail you." This surprises me, because it seems to me that when I first rushed into my passion, with characteristic intensity, and sensed the instability, the tragedy in the situation, I pulled back and diminished the importance of our relationship. I exhausted my capacity for tragedy with John Erskine. I suffered then to the limit. I don't know if I can ever suffer as much again, and I believe Henry's feelings are similar. I want to enjoy the present hour deeply, thoughtlessly. Henry bending over me, desirous, Henry's tongue between my legs, Henry's vigorous, torrential possessiveness.

"You are the only woman I can be faithful to. I want to protect you."

When I see June's photograph in Henry's room, I hate June, because at this moment I love Henry. I hate June, and yet I know that I also am in her power, and that when she comes back . . .

"What I feel with you that I don't feel with June is that beyond love, we are friends. June and I are not friends."

One cannot escape from one's own nature, although Henry said yesterday, "There are flaws in your goodness." Flaws. What a relief. Fissures. I may escape through them. Some perversity drives me outside of the role I am forced to play. Always imagining another role. Never static. When Henry wants to read my journal, I tremble. I know he suspects that I betray him constantly. I would like to, and I cannot. Since he has come to me I have practiced instinctively the faithfulness of the whores: I do not take any pleasure except with him. My greatest fear is Hugo's desiring me the same day, and it happens frequently. Last night he was ardent, ecstatic—and I, obedient and deceptive. Simulating enjoyment. He thought it an exceptional night. His pleasure was tremendous.

When I seem to be overflowing and calling for all the sensual pleasures obtainable, do I mean it? If I felt attracted to some woman in the street or a man I danced with, would I really be able to satisfy my desire? Is there a desire? The next time such a feeling overtakes me, I will not resist it. I must know.

Tonight I surrender to a craving for Henry. I want him, and I want June. It is June who will kill me, who will take Henry away from me, who will hate me. I want to be in Henry's arms. I want June to find me there: it will be the only time she will suffer. After that it is Henry who will suffer, at her hands. I want to write her and beg her to come back, because I love her, because I want to give up Henry to her as the greatest gift I can make her.

Hugo undresses me every night as if it were the first time and I a new woman for him. My feelings are in a chaos I cannot clarify, cannot order. My dreams tell me nothing except that I have a terror of being driven again to the point of suicide.

One does not get healed just by living and loving, or I would be healed. Hugo heals me at times. We walked out in the fields today, under cherry trees, sat down on the grass, in the sun, talking like two very young lovers. Henry heals me, takes me up in his vital arms, his giant's arms. And so some days I believe myself well.

Hugo has gone away on a trip, and he kissed me so desperately and sorrowfully. I am surrounded by signs of him, small things which sing his habits, his defects, his divine goodness: a letter he has forgotten to mail, his worn-out underwear (because he will never buy anything for himself), his notes on work to be done, a golf ball—which reminds me that he said yesterday, "Not even golf is pleasure for me, because I prefer to be with you. It is all part of my damned work"—a toothbrush, an open jar of brilliantine, a half-smoked cigarette, his suit, his shoes. I have hardly kissed him good-bye, and the green gate is barely closed after him when I say to Emilia, "Clean my rose dress and wash my lace underwear. I may go and visit a friend for a few days."

I did not forget yesterday to be so good to Eduardo that he must have grown at least two feet. And the same evening I wanted to dissolve into Hugo's body, to be imprisoned in his arms, in his goodness. At such a moment passion and fever seem unimportant. I cannot bear to see Hugo jealous, but he is sure of my love. He says, "I have never loved you as much, I have never been as happy with you. You are my whole life." And I know that I love him as much as I can love him, that he is the only one who possesses me eternally. Yet for three days I have visualized life with Henry in Clichy. I say to Hugo, "Send me a telegram every day, please." And I may not be home to read them.

---

I have run away. My pajamas, comb, powder, perfume are in Henry's room. I find a Henry so utterly profound that I am dazed.

We are walking to the Place Clichy, in rhythm. He makes me aware of the street, of people, of reality. I walk like a somnambulist, but he is smelling the street, he is observing, his eyes are wide open. He shows me the whore with a wooden stump who stands near the Gaumont Palace. He does not know what it is to live in a world where the only distinct personage is one's self, as Eduardo and I know. We sit in several cafés and talk about life and death, in Lawrence's sense.

Henry says, "If Lawrence had lived . . ." Yes, I know the end of the sentence. I would have loved him. He would have loved me. Henry can visualize the changing aspect of my writing room. John's photographs. John's books. Lawrence's photograph and Lawrence's books. Henry's watercolors and Henry's manuscripts. For a moment Henry and I sit and reflect sardonically on the spectacle of our lives.

Eduardo said there is no pattern to Henry's writing or living. Exactly. If there were, he would be an analyst. If he were an analyst, he would not be a living, chaotic force.

When I tell Henry about John Erskine, he is amazed at my sacrilegiousness. John, the man Hugo revered. I say quietly, "It may seem sacrilegious, and yet, look how natural: I loved in John what bound Hugo to him."

We were sitting in the kitchen in Clichy at 2:00 A.M. with Fred, eating and drinking, and smoking heavily. Henry had to get up and wash his eyes with cold water, the irritated eyes of the little German boy. I could not bear this and I said, "Henry, let's drink to the end of your work for the newspaper. You will never do it again. I say so."

This seemed to hurt Fred. He dropped into a black mood. We said good night. I went to Henry's room.

We were enjoying our being together, undressing, talking, placing our clothes on the chair. Henry was admiring my red silk Japanese pajamas, which looked so strange in the plain room, on the rough blanket.

The next day we discovered that Fred had not slept there. "Don't take him too seriously," said Henry. We had breakfast together at five in the afternoon. And then I sewed the gray curtains and Henry hammered on the curtain rods. Later Henry made a hearty dinner; we drank Anjou, and were very gay. Early in the morning I went back to Louveciennes.

When I returned to Clichy, Fred was home and very sad. We had our dinner, but silently, and I was miserable. Fred threw off his mood to please me and exclaimed, "Let's do something; let's go to Louveciennes."

We are off.

I feel the magic of my own house lulling me. We all sit by the fire. This is the moment when the house diffuses a charm, and the fire melts one's nerves. I can sit complete, as though I were part of a mural. Their admiration and love is sweet to me. I lose my sense of secrecy. I open the iron boxes and show them my early journals. Fred grasps the first volume and begins to cry and laugh over it. I have given Henry the red journal, all about himself, a thing I have never done with anyone. I read over his shoulder.

Henry and I are waiting for the train on a high platform. The rain has washed the trees. The earth pours out essences like a woman a man has ploughed and seeded. Our bodies draw close.

At the moment I do not think of how June and I stood

pressed against each other in the same way. I think of it now because yesterday, for the first time, he hurt me, although I was prepared for his sarcasm and ridicule. I knew about his love of finding defects, because of all he had written about June. We were reading my red journal. He came to an entry where Fred had said that I was beautiful. "You see," said Henry. "Fred thinks you are beautiful. I don't. I think you have great charm, yes." I was sitting close to him. I looked at him with bewilderment and then swiftly put my head on the pillow and cried. When he put his hand on my face and felt the tears, he was amazed. "Oh, Anaïs, I never thought that could mean anything to you. I hate myself for having said it so cruelly. But you remember, I also told you I didn't think June was beautiful. The most powerful women have not been the most beautiful. But to think I could make you cry, that I could do that, when it is one thing I never wanted to do to *you*."

He now sat in front of me, and I lay sunk in the pillows, hair rumpled and eyes swimming in tears. At that moment I remembered what the painters thought of me, and I told him. And suddenly I *kicked* him. I pawed him, like a cat, he said. And when that was over, which amused him, we felt strangely closer, until I said teasingly, in the train—because he was telling me that he had thought me beautiful the first day he had seen me, but had begun to think not because Fred insisted on it so much; and because of June, too—I said, "You've got bad taste!"

But all the wonderful things he had said to me about my journal paled now. My confidence wavered. It did not heal me to think what a relative thing beauty is and that each man has his own individual response to it. It is unnatural to be so hurt. Yet I took this hurt into myself and said, "I'm going to bear it. I'm going to live it down, I'm not going to care." And for a few hours I waved my courage about, until we were undressing that night and Henry said, "I want to watch you undress. I've never done that." I sat on his bed, and I was overcome by a feeling of timidity. I did something to distract his attention from my undressing, and I slipped into the bed. I wanted to cry. Only two moments before, he said, "I have the feeling that I am a very ugly man. I never want to look at myself in the mirror." And I found something evasive and lovely to say. I told him what I liked about him. I didn't say to him, "I have needed Eduardo's beauty these days as never before."

At three-thirty the next day I was in Allendy's salon, in terrible need of him.

I went to Henry and found him at work. He received me with a joyous kiss. We worked together. I sat at my table next to his, looking over fragments to be inserted in my book. I was filled with the strength of his writing. When he got hungry, I offered to cook the dinner. "Let me play at being the wife of a genius." And I went to the kitchen in my stately rose dress.

Henry's very voice lifts me. I think of his saying, "When I write about you, I will have to write of you as an angel. I cannot put you on a bed."

"But I don't behave like an angel. You know I don't."

"I know, yes, I know. You've tired me out these past days. You're a sexual angel, but you're an angel just the same. Your sensuality doesn't convince me."

"I'll punish you for that," I said. "From now on I'll behave like an angel."

Two hours later Fred has gone to work and Henry is

kissing me in the kitchen. I want to play at resisting him, but even a kiss on my neck melts me. I say no, but he puts his hands between my legs. He charges me like a bull.

When we lie quiet, I love him still, his hands, his wrists, his neck, his mouth, the warmth of his body, and the sudden leaping of his mind. Afterwards we sit eating and talking about June and Dostoevsky while the cock crows. That Henry and I can sit and talk about our love of June, about her grandiose moments, is to me the greatest of victories.

The long, tranquil hours with Henry are the most potent. He falls into a thoughtful quietness as he sits over his work, chuckling sometimes. He has in him something of a gnome, a satyr, and a German scholar. There are hard bumps on his forehead, which look as if they were about to burst. His body suddenly appears fragile, bowed.

As he sits there, I feel that I can see his mind as I see his body, and it is labyrinthine, fertile, sentient. I am loaded with adoration for everything that his head contains and for the impulses which blow in gusts.

He is lying in bed, body arched against my back, his arm around my breast. And in the circumference of my solitude I know I have found a moment of absolute love. His greatness fills the wounds and closes them, silences the desires. He is asleep. How I love him! I feel like a river that has overflowed.

"Anaïs, when I came home last night I thought you were here, because I smelled your perfume. I missed you. I realized I didn't tell you when you were here how wonderful it was to have you here. I never say those things. Look, here is a drawer full of your clothes—stockings. I want you to leave your perfume all through the place."

I think he loves me with tenderness, with sentimentality. It is June who inspires the passions. And I am there to cull his thoughts, his musings, his recollections, his confidences. I stand by Henry the writer, and I am given his other love.

Now alone in Louveciennes, I still feel the imprint of his body asleep against mine. I wish today were the last day. I always want the high moment to be the last. June can come back and blow at us like the simoom. Henry will be tormented by her, and I will be hypnotized.

There will remain, here in my journal, the things Henry has said. I receive them like gifts of jewels, incense, and perfumes. Henry's words fall, and I catch them with such care that I forget to talk. I am the slave fanning him with peacock feathers. He talks about God, Dostoevsky, and the finesse of Fred's writing. He draws a distinction between that finesse and his own dramatic, sensational, potent writing. He can say with humility, "Fred has a finesse which I lack, erudition, the quality of an Anatole France."

And I say, "But don't you see, he lacks the passion, just as France lacked it. It is what you have!"

At the thought of this, as we walk along a boulevard, I want to kiss the man whose passion rushes like lava through a chill intellectual world. I want to give up my life, my home, my security, my writing, to live with him, to work for him, to be a prostitute for him, anything, even to be fatally hurt by him.

Late in the night he tells me about a book I have not read, Arthur Machen's *Hill of Dreams*. And I am listening with my soul. He says softly, "I'm talking almost paternally to you."

At that moment I know I am half woman, half child.

That a portion of me conceals a child who loves to be amazed, to be taught, to be directed. When I listen, I am a child, and Henry becomes paternal. The haunting image of an erudite, literary father reasserts itself, and the woman becomes small again. I remember other phrases, like "I would not hurt you—not you," his unusual delicacy with me, his protectiveness. I feel myself betrayed. Overwhelmed with the wonder of Henry's work, I have become a child. I can imagine another man saying to me, "I cannot make love to you. You are not a woman. You are a child."

I awake from dreams of utter sensuality. And then in anger I want to dominate, to work like a man, support Henry, get his book published. I want more than ever to fuck and to be fucked, to assert the sensual woman. Henry says one day, "Listen, I believe you could have ten lovers and handle them all. You're insatiable." And another day, "Your sensuality doesn't convince me."

He has seen the child!

Hateful, infuriating. I run away from Clichy and think I carry my secret away with me. I have the hope that Henry has not grasped it too well. I fear the uncanny analysis of his eyes. I slip out of his bed and run away while he sleeps. I rush home and fall asleep, deeply, for many hours. I must choke the child. Tomorrow I can meet Henry, face him, be woman.

This would have remained a vague, meaningless incident. Now, because of psychoanalysis, it is heavy with significance. Analysis makes me feel as if I were masturbating instead of fucking. Being with Henry is to live, to flow, to suffer, even. I do not like to be with Allendy and to press dry fingers on the secrets of my body.

When I talk just a little about the fear of cruelty to

Eduardo, he says what I say, "But one uses one's weaknesses. One can make something of them." And I have done that. Yet I can see no good in my childish admiration of older men, my adoration of John and Henry. I can see nothing in it but interference with the progress of maturity, the abdication of my own personality. As Henry says, "It is beautiful to see you sleep. You lie like a doll, where one has put you. Even in sleep you do not sprawl and take too much room."

Allendy's questions crackle at me. "What did you feel about our first talk?"

"I felt that I needed you, that I didn't want to be left alone to think my life over."

"You loved your father devotedly, abnormally, and you hated the sexual reason which caused him to abandon you. This may have created in you a certain obscure feeling against sex. This feeling asserts itself in your unconscious in that scene with John. You willed him to a kind of castration."

"Then why was I so unhappy, in such despair when it happened, and why did I love him for two years?"

"Perhaps you loved him more because of what happened."

"But I have despised him since then for his lack of impulsive passion."

"The ambivalent need of dominating man, of being conquered by him and of being superior to him. You really loved him because he did not dominate you, because you were superior to him in passion."

"No, because now that I have found a man who has conquered me I am tremendously happy."

Allendy asks questions about Henry. He finally notes

that I dominate him socially. He notes also that I have chosen to put myself in the situation of the rival of a woman I know will conquer, therefore seeking pain for myself. That I have loved men weaker than I and have suffered from this. At the same time I have an extreme fear of pain, and it makes me divide my loves so that each one serves as a refuge against another. Ambivalence. I want to love a stronger man and cannot do so.

He says that I have a sense of inferiority due to my physical frailness as a child. It seemed to me that men only loved healthy, fat women. Eduardo talked to me about fat Cuban girls. Hugo's first attraction was for a fat girl. Everybody used to comment on my slenderness, and my mother quoted the Spanish proverb: "Bones are for the dogs." When I went to Havana, I doubted being able to please because I was thin. This theme continues right down to the moment when Henry hurt me by his admiration of Natasha's body because it seemed rich to him.

Allendy: "Do you know that sometimes the sense of sexual inferiority is due to a realization of one's frigidity?"

It is true I was quite indifferent to sex until I was eighteen or nineteen, and even then, tremendously romantic but not really sexually awake. But afterwards! "And if I were frigid, would I be so preoccupied by sex?"

Allendy: "All the more so."

Silence. I am thinking that with all the tremendous joys Henry has given me I have not yet felt a real orgasm. My response does not seem to lead to a true climax but is disseminated in a spasm that is less centered, more diffuse. I have felt an orgasm occasionally with Hugo, and when I have masturbated, but perhaps that is because Hugo likes me to close my legs and Henry makes me open them so much. But this, I would not tell Allendy.

From my dreams he culls the consistent desire to be punished, humiliated, or abandoned. I dream of a cruel Hugo, of a fearful Eduardo, of an impotent John.

"This comes from a sense of guilt for having loved your father too much. Afterwards I am sure you loved your mother much more."

"It is true. I loved her tremendously."

"And now you seek punishment. And you enjoy the suffering, which reminds you of the suffering you endured with your father. In one of your dreams, when the man forces himself into you, you hate him."

I feel oppressed, as if his questions were thrusts. I am in a terrible need of him. Yet analysis does not help. The pain of living is nothing compared to the pain of this minute analysis.

Allendy asks me to relax and tell him what goes on in my mind. But what goes on in my mind is the analysis of my life.

Allendy: "You are trying to identify yourself with me, to do my work. Have you not wished to surpass men in their own work? To humiliate them by your success?"

"Indeed not. I constantly help men in their work, make sacrifices for them." I encourage, admire, applaud them. No, Allendy is very wrong.

He says, "Perhaps you are one of those women who are friends not enemies of man."

"More than that. My original dream was to be married to a genius and serve him, not to be one. When I wrote my book on Lawrence, I wanted Eduardo to collaborate with me. Even now I know he could have written a better one, only it is I who have the energy, the impulse."

Allendy: "You know about the Diana complex, the woman who envies man his sexual power."

"I have felt that, yes, sexually. I would have liked to have been able to possess June and other beautiful women."

There are ideas which Allendy abandons, as though he were sensing my susceptibility. Every time he touches upon my lack of confidence I suffer. I suffer when he touches on my sexual potency, my health, or my feeling of solitude, because there is no one man in whom I could confide entirely.

I lie back and I feel an inrush of pain, despair. Allendy has hurt me. I cry. I cry also with shame, with self-pity. I feel weak. I don't want him to see me cry and I turn away. Then I stand up and face him. His eyes are very soft. I want him to think me a superior woman. I want him to admire me. I like it when he says, "You have suffered a great deal."

When I leave him, I am in a dream, relaxed, warm, as if I had traversed fantastic regions. Eduardo says I am like a hen sitting on her eggs.

Allendy: "Why, exactly, were you upset last time?"

"I felt that some of the things you said were true."

I would like simply to talk to him about the days I have spent with Henry. After Henry, analysis is distasteful to me. I begin with docility but I feel a growing resistence. I admit to Allendy that I do not hate him but that I enjoyed, in a female way, his having succeeded in making me cry. "You proved stronger than I. I like that."

However, as the hour progresses I begin to feel that he is arousing difficulties which I could easily live down, that he reawakens my fears and doubts. For that, I hate him. As he reads my dreams he notes that they are written with a more than masculine directness. Now I find him probing the masculine elements in me. Do I love Henry because I identify myself with him and his love and possession of

June? No, this is false. I think of the night Henry taught me to lie over him and how I disliked it. I was happier when I lay under him, passively. I think of my uncertainty with women, not being sure of the role I want to play. In a dream it is June who has a penis. At the same time, I admit to Allendy, I have imagined that a freer life would be possible to me as a lesbian because I would choose a woman, protect her, work for her, love her for her beauty while she could love me as one loves a man, for his talent, his achievements, his character. (I was remembering Stephen in *The Well of Loneliness*, who was not beautiful, who was even scarred in the war, and who was loved by Mary.) This would be a relief from the torment of lack of confidence in my womanly powers. It would eliminate all concern with my beauty, health, or sexual potency. It would make me confident because everything would depend on my talent, inventiveness, artistry, in which I believe.

At the same time I realized that Henry loved me for these last things, too, and I was becoming accustomed to it. Henry, also, gives a smaller importance to my physical charms. I could be healed by the sheer courage of continuing to live. I could heal myself. I don't really need you, Allendy!

Whenever he asks me to close my eyes and relax and talk, I go on with my own analysis. I say to myself, "He is telling me little that I do not know." But this is not true, because he has made clear to me the idea of guilt. I understood suddenly why both Henry and I wrote love letters to June when we were falling in love with each other. He has also made clear the idea of punishment. I take Hugo to the rue Blondel and incite him to infidelity to punish myself for my own infidelities. I glorify June to punish myself for having betrayed her.

I elude Allendy's further questions. He fumbles. He

can find nothing definite. He suggests many hypotheses. He also probes to discover my feelings about him, and I tell him about my interest in his books. I have a mischievous awareness that he expects me to become interested in him, and I don't like playing the game while knowing it is a game. Yet my interest is sincere. I also tell him I don't mind any more whether he admires me or not. And that is a victory over myself.

It humiliates me to confess my doubts to him. So today I hated him. When I stood before him, ready to leave, I thought, "At this moment I have less confidence in myself than ever. It is intolerable."

With what joy I gave myself to Henry the following day.

The house is asleep. The dogs are quiet. I feel the weight of solitude. I wish I were in Henry's apartment, if only to dry the dishes he washes. I see his vest, unbuttoned, because the discarded suit given to him is too small for him. I see the very frayed lapel under which I love to slip my hand, the tie I finger while he talks to me. I see the blond hair on his neck. I see the expression he has when he takes the garbage can away, surreptitious, half ashamed. Ashamed, too, of his orderliness, which forces him to wash the dishes, to tidy the kitchen. He says, "This is what June objected to—said it was unromantic." I remember, from Henry's notes, the royal disorder she affected. I don't know what to say. They are both in me: the woman who acts as Henry does and the woman who dreams of acting like June. Some vague tenderness draws me to Henry, so seriously washing the dishes. I cannot taunt him. I help him. But my imagination is out of the kitchen. I only love the kitchen because

Henry is there. I have even wished that Hugo would stay away much longer so that I could live in Clichy. It is the first time I have ever wished such a thing.

"It is this way," says Henry. "I have overdrawn the cruelty and evil of June because I was interested in evil. That is just the trouble; there are no really evil persons in the world. June is not really evil. Fred is right. She tries desperately to be. It was one of the first things she told me the night I met her. She wanted me to think her a *femme fatale*. I'm inspired by evil. It preoccupies me, as it did Dostoevsky."

The sacrifices June made for Henry. Were they sacrifices, or were they things she did to heighten her personality? It is I who question this. She makes no obscure sacrifices. Flamboyant ones, yes. Dramatic ones. I have made obscure sacrifices, whether small or big. But I prefer June's prostitution, gold digging, comedies. In between, Henry can starve. She will serve him unreliably and fantastically or not at all. She urged Henry to leave his job. She wanted to work for him. (Secretly I have envisaged prostitution, and to say it is for Henry is only to find a justification.) So June has found a magnificent justification. She has made heroic sacrifices for Henry. And all of it has contributed to the personality of June.

I say to Henry, "Why are you so savage about her defects? And why do you write less about the magnificence?"

"That is what June says. She repeats, 'And you forget this, and you forget that. You only remember the wrongs.' The truth is, Anaïs, that I take goodness for granted. I expect everybody to be good. It is evil which fascinates me."

I remember a feeble effort at living out one of my own fantasies. I came back to Henry one afternoon after he had teased me, full of the devil. I told him that I was going out with a woman the next evening. In Gare St. Lazare I had seen a whore I wanted so much to talk to, and I imagined myself going out with her. Now, bursting into Henry's apartment, as June might have done, I could have brought about a curious event, which Henry would have liked to have heard about later. But instantly I became aware that he had been writing, he was in a serious mood, I had disturbed him. He had been hoping I would sit down with him and help him organize his book. My mood evaporated. I even felt contrite.

June would have interrupted the writing, precipitated Henry into more experiences, delayed the digestion of them, shone with the brilliancy of a Fate in motion, and Henry would have cursed her and then said, "June is an interesting character."

So I went home to Louveciennes and slept. And the next day when Henry asks me, "What did you do last night?" I wish I had something to tell him. I assume a strange look. He thinks he will read about it later in the journal.

I wonder how it feels to have read the whole of my red journal. Henry did not say very much while he was reading, but he shook his head occasionally or laughed. He did say that my journal was terribly frank, and that the descriptions of sensual feelings were unbelievably strong. I didn't mince my words. I had drawn him well, flatteringly but truly. What I said about June was all true. He expected something like my affair with Eduardo. He was sexually stirred by my dream of June and by other pages. "Of course," he said, "you are a narcissist. That is the raison d'être of the journal. Journal writing is a disease. But it's all right. It's very interesting. I don't know of any journal more interesting. I don't know of any woman writing so frankly."

I protested, because I thought a narcissist was one who only loved himself, and it seemed to me . . .

It was narcissism anyway, said Henry. But I feel that he admired the journal. He did tease me about Fred, saying he feared I would give myself to him as I did to Eduardo, out of sympathy, and he was jealous. He kissed me as he said this.

Hugo comes back, and he seems like a young son to me. I feel old, battered but tender and joyful. I am resting on the flesh bed of an enormous fatigue. Everything I carry away from Henry is enormous.

If I fall asleep, it is because I am overloaded. I sleep because one hour with Henry contains five years of my life, and one phrase, one caress answers the expectations of a hundred nights. When I hear him laugh, I say, "I have heard Rabelais." And I swallow his laughter like bread and wine.

Instead of cursing he is sprouting, covering all the spaces he missed in his sensational strides with June. He is at rest from torment, venomousness, drama, madness. And he says in a tone I have never heard from him before, as if to engrave it, "I love you."

I fall asleep in his arms, and we forget to finish the second fusion of ourselves. He falls asleep with his fingers dipped in the honey. To sleep this way I must have found the end of pain.

I walk the streets with a steady tread. There are only two women in the world: June and I.

Anaïs: "Today I frankly hate you. I am against you."

Allendy: "But why?"

"I feel that you have taken away from me the little confidence I had. I feel humiliated because I have confessed to you, and I so rarely confess."

"Are you afraid to be loved less?"

"Yes. Quite definitely. I keep a kind of shell around me. I want to be loved."

I tell him about my acting like a child with Henry, through my admiration. How I had feared this would desensualize Henry.

Allendy: "On the contrary, a man loves to feel this sense of importance you give him."

"I immediately imagined he would love me less."

Allendy was amazed at the extent of my lack of confidence. "To an analyst, of course, it is very clear, even in your appearance."

"In my appearance?"

"Yes. I saw immediately that you have seductive manners and bearing. Only people who are unsure act seductively."

We laughed at this.

I told him I had imagined seeing my father at my dance recital in Paris, when it was proved he was in St. Jean de Luz at the time. It had given me a shock.

"You wanted him to be there. You wanted to dazzle him. At the same time you were frightened. But because you have wanted to seduce your father since you were a child and did not succeed, you have also developed a strong sense of guilt. You want to dazzle physically, but when you succeed, something makes you stop. You tell me you haven't danced since."

"No. I have even had a very strong feeling against it. It was also due to bad health."

"I have no doubt that if you should succeed in your writing you would also give that up to punish yourself."

Other women who are talented but ugly are self-satisfied, confident, magnificent, and I who am talented and attractive, so Allendy tells me, weep because I do not look like June and inspire passion.

I try to explain this to him. I have put myself in the worst position of all by loving Henry and sharing him with a June who is my greatest rival. I am exposing myself to a final death blow since I am sure that Henry will chose June (as I would choose her if I were a man). I also know that if June comes back, she would not choose me in preference to Henry. So I can only lose both ways. And I am risking this. Everything pushes me into it. (Allendy tells me it is masochism.) I again seek pain. If I should give up Henry now, of my own free will, it would only be to suffer less.

I feel two impulses: one masochistic and resigned, the other seeking escape. I yearn to find a man who will save me from Henry and this situation. Allendy listens and broods on this.

One evening in Henry's kitchen—he and I alone—we talk ourselves empty. He takes up the subject of my red journal, tells me what faults I have to beware of, and then says, "Do you know what baffles me? When you write about Hugo, you write wonderful things, but at the same time they are unconvincing. You do not tell anything that would cause your admiration or love. It sounds strained."

I immediately become distressed, as if it were Allendy questioning me.

"It isn't for me to be asking questions, Anaïs," Henry continues, "but listen, I am not being personal now. I myself like Hugo. I think he is fine. But I am just trying to understand your life. I imagine that you married him when your character was not yet formed, or for the sake of your mother and brother."

"No, no, not for that. I loved him. For my mother and brother I should have married in Havana, in society, richly, and I couldn't do that."

"That day Hugo and I went out for a walk, I tried to grasp him. The truth is, if I had seen only him in Louveciennes, I would have come once, said here's a nice man, and forgotten all about it."

"Hugo is inarticulate," I said. "It takes time to know him." And all the while my old, secret, immense dissatisfaction wells up like a poison, and I keep saying foolish things about the bank subduing him, and how different he is on vacations.

Henry curses. "But it's so obvious that you are superior to him." Always that hateful phrase—from John, too. "Only in intelligence," I say.

"In everything," says Henry. "And listen, Anaïs, answer me. You are not just making a sacrifice. You're not really happy, are you? You want to run away from Hugo at times?"

I cannot answer. I bow my head and cry. Henry comes and stands over me.

"My life is a mess," I say. "You're trying to make me

admit something I will not even admit to myself, as you could see by the journal. You sensed how much I *want* to love Hugo and in just what way I do. I'm all broken up with visions of what it might have been here, with you, for instance. How satisfied I have been, Henry."

"And now, only with me," says Henry, "you would blossom so quickly that you would soon exhaust all I can give and pass on to another. There are no limits to what your life could be. I have seen how you can swim in a passion, in a large life. Listen, if anybody else did the things you have done, I would call them foolish, but somehow or other you make them seem so terribly right. This journal, for instance, is so rich, so terribly rich. You say my life is rich but it is only full of events, incidents, experiences, people. What is really rich are these pages on so little material."

"But think what I would make of more material," I say. "Think of what you said about my novel, that the theme [faithfulness] was an anachronism. That stung me. It was like a criticism of my own life. Yet I cannot commit a crime, and to hurt Hugo would be a crime. Besides, he loves me as nobody has ever loved me."

"You haven't given anybody else a real chance."

I am remembering this while Hugo is gardening. And to be with him now seems as if I were living in the state of being I was in at twenty. Is it his fault, this youthfulness of our life together? My God, can I ask about Hugo what Henry asks about June? He has filled her. Have I filled Hugo? People have said there is nothing in him but me. His great capacity for losing himself, for love. That touches me. Even last night he talked about his inability to mix with other people, saying that I was the only one he was close to, happy with. This morning in the garden he was in bliss. He wanted me there, near him. He has given me love. And what else?

I love the past in him. But all the rest has seeped away.

After what I revealed to Henry about my life, I was in despair. It was as if I were a criminal, had been in jail, and were at last free and willing to work honestly and hard. But as soon as people discover your past they will not give you work and expect you to act like a criminal again.

I am finished with myself, with my sacrifices and my pity, with what chains me. I am going to make a new beginning. I want passion and pleasure and noise and drunkenness and all evil. But my past reveals itself inexorably, like a tattoo mark. I must build a new shell, wear new costumes.

While I wait for Hugo in the car I write on a cigarette box (on the back of the Sultanes there is a good bit of rosy space).

Hugo has found out that: I have not seen the gardener about the garden, the mason about the cracked pool, have not done my accounts, have missed my fitting for an evening dress, have broken all routine.

One evening Natasha calls up. I am supposed to have spent the nights in her studio. And she asks me, "What have you been doing these last ten days?" I cannot answer her or Hugo will hear me. "Why does Natasha call you up?" he asks.

Later, in bed. Hugo is reading. As I write, almost under his eyes, he cannot suppose that what I am writing is so treacherous. I am thinking the worst about him I have ever thought.

---

Today while we worked in the garden I felt as if I were in Richmond Hill again, wrapped up in books and in trances, with Hugo passing by, hoping for a glimpse of me. *Mon Dieu*, for a moment today, I was in love with him, with the soul and the virgin body of those earlier days. A part of me has grown immeasurably, while I have clung to my young love, to a memory. And now the woman lying naked in the vast bed watches her young love bending over her and does not want him.

Since that talk with Henry, when I admitted more than I had ever admitted to myself, my life has altered and become deformed. The restlessness which was vague and nameless has become intolerably clear. Here is where it stabs me, at the center of the most perfect, the most steadfast structure, marriage. When this shakes, then my whole life crumbles. My love for Hugo has become fraternal. I look almost with horror on this change, which is not sudden, but slow in appearing on the surface. I had closed my eyes to all the signs. Above all, I dreaded admitting that I didn't want Hugo's passion. I had counted on the ease with which I would distribute my body. But it is not true. It was never true. When I rushed towards Henry, it was all Henry. I am frightened because I have realized the full extent of my imprisonment. Hugo has sequestered me, fostered my love of solitude. I regret now all those years when he gave me nothing but his love and I turned into myself for the rest. Starved, dangerous years.

I should break up my whole life, and I cannot do it. My life is not as important as Hugo's, and Henry doesn't need me because he has June. But whatever in me has grown outside and beyond Hugo will go on.

*MAY*

I never have seen as clearly as tonight that my journal writing is a vice, a disease. I came home at seven-thirty worn out by a magnificent night with Henry and three hours with Eduardo. I didn't have the strength to go to Henry again. I had dinner, smoked dreamily. I glided into my bedroom, felt a sense of being enclosed, of falling into myself. I got my journal from its last hiding place under my dressing table and threw it on the bed. And I had the feeling that this is the way an opium smoker prepared his pipe. The journal, like a fragment of myself, shares my duplicities. Where has my tremendous fatigue gone? Occasionally I stop writing and feel a profound lethargy. And then some demoniac feeling urges me on.

I confide in Allendy. I talk profusely about my childhood, quote from my early journals obvious phrases about Father—so intelligible now, my passion for him. Also my sense of guilt; I felt I did not deserve anything.

We discuss finances and I tell him the cost of the visits prevents me from seeing him more often. He not only reduces his fee by half but offers to let me pay in part by working for him. I am flattered.

We talk about physical facts. I am underweight. A few pounds more would give me security. Will Allendy add medicine to the psychic treatment? I confess the fear I have that my breasts are small perhaps because I have masculine elements in me and half of my body may therefore be adolescent.

Allendy: "Are they absolutely undeveloped?"

"No." As we flounder in talk I say, "You are a doctor; I'll simply show them to you." And I do. Then he laughs at my fears. "Perfectly feminine," he says, "small but well outlined—lovely figure. A few pounds more, yes," but how disproportionate my self-criticisms.

He has observed the unnaturalness of my personality. As if enveloped in a mist, veiled. No news to me, except that I did not know it could be so plainly read. For example, my two voices, which have become quite apparent lately: one, according to Fred, is like that of a child before its First Communion, timid, soundless. The other is assured, deeper. This one appears when I have a great deal of confidence.

Allendy thinks that I have created a completely artificial personality, like a shield. I conceal myself. I have constructed a manner that is seductive, affable, gay, and within this I am hidden.

I had asked him to help me physically. Was this a sincere action, showing him my breasts? Did I want to test my charm on him? Wasn't I pleased that he should be complimentary? That he should show more interest in me?

Is it Allendy or Henry who is curing me?

Henry's new love has me in a state of bliss such as I have never known. He wanted to hold off. He didn't want to put himself in my power. He didn't want to add himself to "the list" of my lovers. He didn't want to get serious. And now! He wants to be my husband, to have me all the time; he writes love letters to the child I was at eleven, who has touched him profoundly. He wants to protect me and give me things.

"I never thought such a frail little thing could have so

much power. Did I ever say you were not beautiful? How could I say it! You're beautiful, you're beautiful!" When he kisses me now I do not hold back.

I can now bite him when we lie in bed. "We devour each other, like two savages," he said.

I lose my fear of showing myself naked. He loves *me*. We laugh at my gaining weight. He has made me change my hair because he did not like the severe Spanish style. I have thrown it back and high over my ears. I feel windblown. I look younger. I do not try to be the *femme fatale*. It is useless. I feel loved for myself, for my inner self, for every word I write, for my timidities, my sorrows, my struggles, my defects, my frailness. I love Henry in the same way. I cannot even hate his rushing towards other women. Despite his love for me, he is interested in meeting Natasha and Mona Paiva, the dancer. He has a diabolical curiosity about people. I have never known a man with so many sides, with such a range.

To have a summer day like today and a night with Henry—I ask nothing more.

Henry shows me the first pages of his next book. He has absorbed my novel and written a fantastic parody of it, incited partly by his jealousy and anger, because the other morning when I left him, Fred called me into his room and wanted to kiss me. I did not let him, but Henry heard the silence and imagined the scene and my faithlessness. The pages elated me—their perfection and finesse and sharpness, and the fantastic tone. There is poetry in them, too, and a secret tenderness. He has made a special nook in himself for me.

He expected me to have written ten pages at least about

that night we spent talking until dawn. But something has happened to the woman with a notebook. I have come home and sunk into my enjoyment of him as into a warm summer day. The journal is secondary. Everything is secondary to Henry. If he did not have June, I would give everything to live with him. Each different aspect of him holds me: Henry correcting my novel with amazing care, with interest, with sarcasm, with admiration, with complete understanding; Henry, without self-confidence, so extraordinarily modest; Henry, the demon pumping me, making diabolical notes; Henry concealing his feelings from Fred and displaying to me a tremendous tenderness. Last night in bed, half asleep, he was still murmuring, "You're so wonderful, there is no man good enough for you."

He has made me more honest with myself. And then he says, "You give me so much, so much and I give you nothing."

He, too, lacks confidence. He is uneasy in certain social situations if they are the least bit chic. He is not sure of my love. He believes that I am extremely sensual and therefore I could easily leave him for another man and still another. At this I laugh. Yes, of course I would love to be fucked five times a day, but I would have to be in love. That is certainly a drawback, an inconvenience. And I can only love one man at a time. "I want you to stop with me," Henry says. "I love your not being promiscuous. I was terribly worried when you were interested in Montparnasse." And then he begins to kiss me. "You've got me, Anaïs." He has playful, almost childish caresses for me sometimes. We rub noses, or he chews my eyelashes, or runs his thumb over the outlines of my face. And I then see a sort of gnomelike Henry, a little Henry, so tender.

Fred is sure Henry is hurting me fearfully. But Henry cannot hurt me any more. Even his faithlessness could not hurt me. Besides, I require less tenderness. Henry is toughening me. When I find out he does not like my perfume because it is too delicate, at first I am a bit offended. Fred loves Mitsouko, but Henry likes acrid, powerful perfumes. He always demands assertion, potency.

It is like his asking me to change my hair style because he likes wildness in hair. When he uttered the word "wildness" I responded to it, as though it were something I had been wanting. Wild hair. His stocky, firm hands go through my hair. My hair is in his mouth when we sleep. And when I clasp my hands behind my head, raising my hair, in a Grecian way, he exclaims, "That is the way I love it."

I feel at home in Clichy. Hugo is not necessary to me. I only bring to him my weariness from sleepless nights, a joyful weariness. Early in the morning when I slip out of Henry's apartment, the Clichy workmen are awake. I carry away my red journal, but that is only a habit, for I carry away no secrets; Henry has read my journals (this one, not yet). I also carry away a few pages of Fred's book, delicate as a watercolor, or a few pages from Henry's book, which are like a volcano. The old pattern of my life is shattered. It hangs around me in shreds. Great things are going to happen from all this. I feel the fermentation. The train which takes me home to Louveciennes shakes phrases in my mind like dice in a dice box.

My journal writing breaks down, because it was an intimacy with myself. Now it is interrupted constantly by Henry's voice, his hand on my knee.

Louveciennes is like a casket, petal-lined, carved, golden,

with walls of newborn leaves, blossoms, neatly raked alleys, names of flowers on sticks, old trees, hoary ivy, mistletoe. I will fill it with Henry. I walk up the hill remembering him grave, withdrawn, watching dancers. I ring the bell thinking of one of his humorous corrections of my book. In my bedroom I take off my stained underwear. I remember phrases of his that I will savor in the night. The taste of his penis is still in my mouth. My ear is burning from his bites. I want to fill the world with Henry, with his diabolical notes, plagiarisms, distortions, caricatures, nonsense, lies, profundities. The journal, too, will be filled with Henry.

Yet I told him that he had killed the journal. He had been teasing me about it, and I had just discovered vegetative enjoyment. I was lying in bed after dinner, rose dress crumpled and stained. The journal was a disease. I was cured. For three days I had not written. I had not even written about our mad night of talking, when we heard the birds, looked out of the kitchen window and saw the dawn. I had missed so many dawns. I didn't care about anything except lying there with Henry. No more journal writing. Then his teasing vanished. Oh, no, that would be a pity, he said. The journal must not die. He would miss it.

It did not die. I can find no other way of loving my Henry than filling pages with him when he is not here to be caressed and bitten. When I left him this morning, early, he was asleep. I wanted so much to kiss him. I felt despair as I quietly packed my black valise. Hugo will be home in four hours.

Henry said that in my novel it was curious to note the difference between the me who talks to Hugo and the one who talks to John. With Hugo, I behave youthfully, naïvely, almost religiously. With John, I show maturity and dexterity. It is the same even now. To Hugo I give idealistic explanations of my actions, because that is what he craves. Quite the opposite of what I give Henry. Henry says that after reading my book he can never again be sure of me. His worldliness helps him to catch every unconscious revelation, every innuendo. I feel that the book would hurt Hugo, whereas Henry feels I have, in the end, glorified him. And it is true. Henry even helped me to discard a few passages which weakened Hugo's character. But I will never again write about Hugo, because what I write for him and about him is hypocritical and youthful. I write about him as one writes about God, with traditional faith. His qualities are precious to me but not the most inspiring. All that is over now. And in dropping the constant effort to exalt my love of Hugo, I also drop the last vestiges of my immaturity.

I remember the afternoon Henry came to Louveciennes after reading my childhood diary, expecting to find a girl of eleven. He was still moved by its pages. But my deviltry laughed away the child, and very soon I had him stirred up, saying mad things and fucking me. I wanted to triumph over the child. I refused to become sentimental, to retrogress. It was like a duel. The woman in me is strong. And Henry said he was drunk with looking at me. I told him I didn't want him for a husband (why, I don't know). I laughed at his passionateness. And the minute he was gone I wanted to have him back, to love him with ferocity. I had been more moved by his German seriousness and sentimentality than I had wanted to show. Heinrich! How I love his jealous questions, his cynical suspicions, his curiosity. The streets of Paris belong to him, the cafés and the whores. Modern writing belongs to him; he does it better than any. Every potency, from the whip of the wind to a revolution, belongs to him.

I love his defects, too. One of them is fault finding, a demoniac habit of contradiction. But does it matter, since we understand each other so well that he cannot imagine us quarreling seriously over anything? When I think of him talking about June, I see a very hurt man. This man in my arms is not very harmful to me, because he needs me. He even says, "It's strange, Anaïs, but with you I feel relaxed. Most women make a man feel strained and tense. And I feel at my best because of that." I give him a feeling of absolute intimacy, as if I were his wife.

Hugo is lying in bed beside me, and I am still writing about Henry. The idea of Henry sitting alone in the kitchen at Clichy is unbearable to me. And yet Hugo has grown these days. We laugh together about it. Now that we are both free of fears, we are living easily. He has been traveling with a man from the bank, a plain, simple, joyous man. And they have drunk together, exchanged obscene stories, and danced in cabarets. Hugo has at last been taken up by men. He has loved it. And I say: "Go away, travel a great deal. We both need that. We can't have it together. We can't give it to each other."

I think of Fred observing Henry's sacrileges against good taste: lighting a match on the sole of his shoe, putting salt on the pâté de foie gras, drinking the wrong wines, eating sauerkraut. And I love it all.

Yesterday Henry received a cable from June: "I miss you. I must join you soon." And Henry is angry. "I don't want June to come and torture me and hurt you, Anaïs. I love you. I don't want to lose you. As soon as you left the other day I began to miss you. 'Miss' is not the word; to crave for you. I want to be married to you. You're precious, rare. I see all of you now. I see the face of the child, the dancer, the sensual woman. You've made me happy. Terribly happy."

We come together with despair and frenzy. I am in such ecstasy I'm weeping. I want to be soldered to him.

"It is not me," he says. "It's something you've created out of your own wonderful self." I force him to admit it is he himself I love, a Henry I know well. But I know June's power over both of us. I say to him, "June has power over me, but it is you I love. There is a difference. Do you see it?"

"That is the way I love you," he answers. "And you have power, too, of another kind."

"What I'm afraid of is that June will separate us not only physically but completely."

"Don't give in to June," says Henry. "Keep your wonderful mind. Be strong."

"I could say the same to you," I answer. "Yet I know all of your mind will be of no use to you."

"It will be different this time."

The menace. We have talked. We are quiet. Fred has come into the room. We are plotting so I can spend a few days with Henry before I go away on vacation. Fred leaves us. Henry kisses me again. God, what kisses. I can't sleep when I think of them. We lie close together. Henry says I am wrapped around him like a cat. I kiss his throat. When his throat shows in the open shirt I can't talk, desire moves me so. I whisper hoarsely in his ear, "I love you," three times in such a tone that he is frightened. "I love you so much I even want to give you women!"

Today I can't work because yesterday's feelings lie ready to pounce on me out of the softness of the garden.

They are in the air, in the smells, in the sun, on myself, like the clothes I wear. It is too much to love this way. I need him near me every moment—more than near, inside of me.

I hate June, and yet there is her beauty. June and I melted together, as it should be. Henry must have both. I want both, too. And June? June wants everything; because her beauty demands it.

June, take everything from me but not Henry. Leave me Henry. He is not necessary to you. You do not love him as I do today. You can love many men. I will love only a few. For me, Henry is rare.

I am giving Henry the courage to dominate and dazzle June. He is filling himself with the strength my love gives him. Every day I say I cannot love him more, and every day I find more love in me for him.

Heinrich, another beautiful day with you is finished, always too early. And I am not empty of love yet. I loved you as you sat yesterday with the light on your gray-blond hair, the warm blood showing through your Nordic skin. Your mouth open, so sensual. Your shirt open. In your stocky hands you held your father's letter. I think of your childhood in the streets, your serious adolescence—but always sensual—many books. You know how tailors sit like Arabs over their work. You learned to cut out a pair of pants when you were five years old. You wrote your first book during a two weeks' vacation. You played jazz on the piano for the grownups to dance to. You were sometimes sent to get your father, who was drinking in a bar. You could slip under the swinging doors, you were so small. You tugged at his coat. You drank beer.

You abhor kissing a woman's hand. You laugh at it.

You look so fine in all your cast-off suits, shabby clothes. I know your body now. I know what deviltries you are capable of. You are something to me that I never read in your writings or heard about from June or your friends. Everybody thinks of the noise and the power of you. But I have heard and felt the softness. There are words in other tongues I must use when I talk about you. In my own, I think of: *ardiente, salvaje, hombre.*

I want to be there wherever you are. Lying next to you even if you are asleep. Henry, kiss my eyelashes, put your fingers on my eyelids. Bite my ear. Push back my hair. I have learned to unbutton you so swiftly. All, in my mouth, sucking. Your fingers. The hotness. The frenzy. Our cries of satisfaction. One for each impact of your body against mine. Each blow a sting of joy. Driving in a spiral. The core touched. The womb sucks, back and forth, open, closed. Lips flicking, snake tongues flicking. Ah, the rupture—a blood cell burst with joy. Dissolution.

The three of us are on the couch, looking at a map of Europe. Henry asks me, "Are you still gaining weight?"

"Yes, continuously."

"Oh, Anaïs, don't gain weight," says Fred. "I like you as you are."

Henry smiles. "But Henry likes Renoiresque bodies," I say.

"It's true," says Henry.

"But I love slenderness. I love virginal breasts."

"I should really love you, Fred. It was a mistake."

Henry does not smile. I know his jealous expressions now, but Fred and I continue to banter. "Fred, after I spend a few days with Henry, I'll spend two days with you, in a hotel, so I can take Henry there. He loves to be taken to hotels where I have been before. Two days."

"We'll have breakfast in bed. Mitsouko perfume. A chic hotel. Yes?"

Later Henry says, "It's all right to be joking, but Anaïs, don't torment me. I'm jealous, terribly jealous." I want to laugh because I have already forgotten about the Renoir bodies, the virginal breasts.

When Henry telephones, I feel his voice in my veins. I want him to talk into me. I eat Henry, I breathe Henry, Henry is in the sun. My cape is his arm around my waist.

Café de la Place, Clichy. Midnight. I asked Henry to write something in the diary. He wrote: "I imagine that I am now a very celebrated personage and I am being given one of my own books to autograph. So I write with a stiff hand, a little pompously. *Bonjour, Papa!* No, I can't write in your journal now, Anaïs. Someday you will lend it to me, with a few blank pages towards the end—and I will write an index—a diabolical index. Heinrich. Place Clichy. There's nothing sacred about this book except you."

To encourage him I had said, "There is nothing sacred about this book, and you can even write sideways or upside down in it."

He was wearing a beret and looked thirty years old.

Last night when Hugo had to go to a bank function and I realized I could go to Henry, on a soft summer night, I wanted to shout. In the taxi, alone, I sang and rocked my joy, murmuring, "Henry, Henry." And I kept my legs closed tight, against the invasion of his blood. When I arrived, Henry saw my mood. It flowed from my body and my face.

Warm white blood. Henry screwing. There is no other word.

His kisses are wet like rain. I have swallowed his sperm. He has kissed the sperm off my lips. I have smelled my own honey on his mouth.

I go to Allendy in a state of tremendous elation. I tell him first about the article I am doing for him, which I found discouragingly difficult. He tells me of a simpler way of doing it. Then I tell him of a dream I had in which I had asked him to come to Joaquin's piano concert because I needed him there. In the dream he was standing up in the aisle and towering over other people. My reading of his books has raised him very much in my estimation. I asked him if he would really come to the concert. I know he is tremendously busy, yet he accepted.

I told him about my "watery" dreams and the dream of a King's ball. He said the wetness symbolized fecundation, and the love of the King was the conquest of my father through other men. For the moment, he thought, I was on a peak and scarcely needed him. I told him I could not believe psychoanalysis worked so swiftly. I praised its effects extravagantly. His manner towards me affected me joyously, too. I observed again the beauty of his Celtic eyes. Then he made a masterful analysis of my marriage, from bits gleaned here and there.

"But," says Allendy, "now comes the test of absolute maturity: passion. You have molded Hugo like a mother, and he is your child. He cannot arouse your passion. He knows you so intimately that perhaps his passion, too, will turn to another. You have gone through phases together, but now you will drift apart. You yourself have experienced passion with someone else. Tenderness, understanding, and passion are not usually linked together. But then, tenderness and understanding are so rare."

"But they are immature," I said. "Passion is so powerful."

Allendy smiled, sadly, I thought. Then I said, "This analysis, it seems to me, might apply to Eduardo's feelings, too."

"No. Eduardo really loves you, and you love him, I believe."

Allendy was wrong. When I left him, still buoyant and courageous, I talked with Eduardo. "Listen, darling," I said. "I think we really love each other, fraternally. We can't do without each other, because there is so much understanding between us. If we had married, it would have been a marriage like that of Hugo and me. You would have worked, developed, been happy. We are so delicate and careful with each other. We also want passion. But I can never look at you as I look at other men. You cannot have a passion for me as you would for a woman whose soul you don't know. Believe me, I'm right. Don't be hurt. I feel close to you. You need me. We need each other. We'll find passion elsewhere."

Eduardo realizes I am partly right. We sit very close in the café. We walk together very close. We are half sad, half joyous. It is warm. He smells my perfume. I look at his beautiful face. We desire each other. But it's a mirage. It's only because we are so young, and it is summer, and we are walking body against body.

Hugo is coming to take me home, and so Eduardo and I kiss, and that is all.

At Joaquin's concert Eduardo sits next to me, so beautiful. My lover Henry is sitting where I cannot see him. When we all rise for the intermission, Allendy stands in the aisle. Our eyes meet. There is sadness in them, a seriousness, which moves me. As I walk about with feline movements I know I am seducing Allendy and Eduardo and Henry and others. There is a fiery, handsome Italian violinist. There is my father, who changes his seat to place himself in front of me. There is a Spanish painter.

One layer of physical confidence, one layer of timid seductiveness, one layer of childish despair, because Mother made such a scene when she saw Father arriving at the concert. And poor Joaquin was upset and nervous, but he played superbly.

Henry was intimidated by the crowd. I pressed his hand very hard. He seemed strange and distant. I faced my father with a statuelike poise. I felt the child in me still frightened. Allendy towered over the crowd. I wanted to walk up to him, as in the dream, and stand by his side. Would he give me strength? No. He himself has sometimes weakened. Everybody has his timidities, his self-doubts. I carry layers of feelings, sensations. The heavy lamé on my naked body. The caress of the velvet cape. The weight of the full sleeves. The hypnotic glow of the lights. I am aware of my trailing walk, of hands shaking mine.

Eduardo is drugged. With my words, my perfume (Narcisse Noir). When he met Henry, he drew himself up, proud, beautiful. In the car his leg seeks mine. Joaquin covers me with his cape. As I enter the Café du Rond Point everybody looks at me. I see I have fooled them. I have concealed the smaller me.

Hugo is paternal, protective. He pays for the champagne. I am longing for Henry, who could scatter all the layers stifling me, break open the oyster hypnotized with her fear of the world.

I said to Henry, "You have known much passion, but you have never known closeness, intimacy with a woman, understanding." "That's so true," he said. "Woman for me was an enemy, a destroyer, one who would take things from me, not one whom I could live with closely, be happy with."

I begin to see the preciousness of what Henry and I feel for each other, of what it is he gives me that he has not given June. I begin to understand Allendy's thoughtful smile when I depreciate tender love, friendship.

What he does not know is that I must complete the unfulfilled portions of my life, that I must have what I have missed so far, to complete myself and my own story.

But I cannot enjoy sexuality for its own sake, independent of my feelings. I am inherently faithful to the man who possesses me. Now it is a whole faithfulness to Henry. I tried to enjoy Hugo today, to please him, and I couldn't. I had to pretend.

If there were no June in the world today, I could know the end of my restlessness. I awoke one morning crying. Henry had said to me, "I really take no pleasure in your body. It isn't your body I love." And the sorrowfulness of that moment comes back. Yet, the last time we were together he had said wild things about the beauty of my legs and of my knowing so well how to fuck. Poor woman!

Both Hugo and Henry like to watch my face when they make love to me. But now, for Hugo, my face is a mask.

Allendy told Hugo at the concert that I was a very interesting subject, that I responded so sensitively and quickly.

That I was almost cured. But that evening I again had the sensation of wanting to dazzle Allendy, while concealing some secret part of my real self. There must always be something secret. From Henry I conceal the fact that I rarely get ultimate sexual satisfaction because he likes my legs wide open, and I need to close them. I don't want to diminish his pleasure. Besides, I get a kind of disseminated pleasure which, even if it is less keen, lasts longer than an orgasm.

Henry wrote me a letter after the concert. I put it under my pillow last night: "Anaïs, I was dazzled by your beauty! I lost my head, I felt wretched. I have been blind, blind, I said to myself. You stood there like a Princess. You were the Infanta! You looked thoroughly disappointed in me. What was the matter? Did I look stupid? I probably was. I wanted to get down on my knees and kiss the hem of your dress. So many Anaïses you have shown me—and now this one!—as if to prove your Protean versatility. Do you know what Fraenkel said to me? 'I never expected to see a woman as beautiful as that. How can a woman of such femininity, such beauty, write a book [on D. H. Lawrence]?' Oh, that pleased me no end! The little tuft of hair coming up over the crown, the lustrous eyes, the gorgeous shoulder line, and those sleeves I adore, regal, Florentine, diabolistic! I saw nothing below the bosom. I was too excited to stand off and survey you. How much I wanted to whisk you away forever. Eloping with the Infanta—ye gods. Feverishly I sought out the Father. I think I spotted him. His hair was the clue. Strange hair, strange face, strange family. Presentiment of genius. Ah, yes, Anaïs, I am taking everything quietly—because you belong in another world. I see nothing in myself to recommend your interest. Your *love*? That seems fantastic to me now. It is some divine prank, some cruel jest you are playing on me . . . *I want you.*"

I said to Allendy, "Don't analyze me today. Let's talk about you. I am enthusiastic over your books. Let's talk about death."

Allendy assents. Then we discuss Joaquin's concert. He said my father looked like a young man. Henry made him think of a famous German painter—too soft, perhaps double sided? an unconscious homosexual? Now I am surprised.

My article was good, says Allendy, but why do I not want to be analyzed? As soon as I begin to depend on him I want to win his confidence, analyze *him*, find a weakness in him, conquer him a little because I have been conquered.

He is right. "Yet," I protest, "it seems to me it is a sign of sympathy." He says yes, because that is the way I treat all those I love. Although I want to be conquered, I do all I can to conquer, and when I have conquered, my tenderness is aroused and my passion dies. And Henry? It is too soon to tell.

Allendy says that although I appeared to be seeking domination and cruelty and brutality in Henry (I found them in his writing), my real instinct told me there was a softness in the man. And that although I appear to be surprised that Henry should be so gentle, so scrupulous with me, I am now really glad. I have conquered again.

I have been cruel to Hugo. Yesterday I didn't want him to come home. I felt a terrible hostility. And it showed. Henry and his friend Fraenkel were there in the evening. I stopped Hugo when he was reading out loud, something too long, monotonously, and I changed the subject once so brusquely that Fraenkel noticed it. But Fraenkel liked Hugo, thought highly of him. Once Hugo moved his chair, after having put some books and manuscripts on the floor. Later he sat on it, and Henry's manuscript was right under a leg of the chair. That made me restless. I finally got up and tenderly picked it up.

There was a humorous moment when Fraenkel was talking about Henry's sound way of sleeping and how long he slept. I looked mischievously at Henry and said, "Is that so? Really?"

My Henry listened like a big bear to little, sinuous Fraenkel explaining complex abstract ideas. Fraenkel has a passion for ideas. Fraenkel, as Henry says, *is* an idea. A year ago those ideas would have filled me with joy. But Henry has done something to me, Henry the man. I can only compare what I feel to Lady Chatterley's feelings about Mellors. I cannot even think about Henry's work or Henry himself without a stirring in my womb. Today we had time only for kisses, and they alone melted me.

Hugo tells me his instinct assures him there is nothing between Henry and me. Last night when I slipped Henry's letter under my pillow, I wondered if the paper would crackle and Hugo would hear it, if he would read the letter while I lay asleep. I am taking great risks, with exhilaration. I want to make big sacrifices for my love. My husband, Louveciennes, my beautiful life—for Henry.

Allendy says, "Give yourself wholly to one person. Depend. Lean. Have confidence. Have no fear of pain."

I think I have, with Henry. And yet I still feel alone and divided.

He left me at the Gare St. Lazare last night. I began to write in the train, to balance the seven-leagued-boot leaping of my life with the ant activity of the pen. The ant words rushed back and forth carrying crumbs: such heavy crumbs. Bigger than the ants. "Have you enough heliotrope ink?" Henry asked. I should not be using ink but perfume. I should be writing with Narcisse Noir, with Mitsouko, with jasmine, with honeysuckle. I could write beautiful words that would exhale the potent smell of woman's honey and man's white blood.

Louveciennes! Stop. Hugo is waiting for me. Retrogression. The past: The train to Long Beach. Hugo in a golf suit. His legs stretched out near mine arouse me. I have brought iodine because he gets sudden toothaches. I wear an organdy dress, stiff and fresh, and a picture hat with cherries dangling on the right, in a dip of the large soft wing. The Sunday crowd is flushed, sunburnt, tattered, ugly. I return loaded with my first true kiss.

In the train again—this time to meet Henry. When I ride this way, with my pen and my journal, I feel extraordinarily secure. I see the hole in my glove and a mend in my stocking. All because Henry must eat. And I am happy that I can give Henry security, food. At certain moments, when I look into his unreadable blue eyes, I have a sensation of such torrential happiness that I feel emptied.

Eduardo and I were going to spend the whole afternoon together. We began with an abundant lunch in the Rotisserie de la Reine Pédaque, a place which makes one hungry. Malicious, psychoanalytical conversation. Fresh strawberries. Eduardo warming, melting, desirous. So I say, "Let's go to the movies. I know one we should see."

He is obstinate. But there is no more pity or weakness in me. I am just as obstinate. Eduardo with the Hotel Anjou in mind. I with Henry's blood in my veins. All during the lunch I thought how much I would like to bring Henry to the place. Give him food out of those enormous, fairy-tale banquet dishes. Eduardo is very angry, in a chill way. He says, "I'll take you to the Gare St. Lazare. You can make the two-twenty-five."

But I have a rendezvous with Henry at six. We walk a bit together and then we separate, both angry, with barely any words. I see him walking aimlessly and desolately. I cross the street and walk into the Printemps. I go to the counter with necklaces and bracelets and earrings, which dazzle me always. I stand like a fascinated savage. Glitter. Amethyst. Turquoise. Shell pink. Irish green. I would like to be naked and cover myself with cold crystal jewelry. Jewelry and perfume. I see two very broad flat steel bracelets. Handcuffs. I am the slave of bracelets. They are soon clasped on my wrists. I pay. I buy rouge, powder, nail lacquer. I do not think of Eduardo. I go to the coiffeur, where I can sit still and frozen. I write with a wrist encircled in steel.

Later, Henry asks questions. I refuse to answer. I resort to women's tricks. I keep the secret of my faithfulness. We press each other's arms as we walk through the streets of Paris. A dangerous hour. I have already experienced today the strange pleasure of hurting Eduardo. Now I want to stay with Henry and hurt Hugo. I can't bear to be going home alone, while Henry goes to Clichy. I am tormented by the desire we couldn't satisfy. It is he who is now afraid of my madness.

Today Allendy drives his questions relentlessly. I cannot escape. When I try to change the subject, he answers me but returns to the subject I am eluding. He is confused by what I tell him about Eduardo, about wanting to be cruel to Hugo the same day, and about the bracelets. Henry is obviously the favored one just now. But since Allendy proceeds from the assumption that I love Eduardo, he is certain to get lost, although he does see quite clearly the struggle between my wanting to conquer and my wanting to be conquered. I sought domination in Henry, and he does dominate me sexually, but I was deceived by his writing and his enormous experience.

Allendy did not understand the bracelets. I bought two of them, he says, in contradiction to my feeling of satisfaction at hurting Eduardo and Hugo. As soon as I achieve cruelty, I want to prostrate myself. One bracelet for Hugo and one for Eduardo.

This, I do not believe. I chose the two bracelets with a feeling of absolute subjection to Henry and liberation from the tenderness which binds me to Hugo and Eduardo. When I showed them to Henry, I stretched out both my wrists as one does in being handcuffed.

Allendy is probing the moment at the concert when I imagined him sad and troubled. What exactly did I imagine? Did he have financial worries, concern over his work, emotional troubles?

"Emotional," I said quickly.

"What did you think of my wife?"

"I observed that she was not beautiful, and it gave me pleasure. I also asked your maid if it was your wife who decorated your house, because I liked the decoration. I think

I was making comparisons between us. I am sorry I said that about your wife not being beautiful."

"That is not very wicked, if that is all you thought."

"But I also felt that I was beautiful the night of the concert."

"You certainly were *en beauté*. Is that all?"

"Yes."

"You are repeating the experience of your childhood. Identifying my wife, who is forty years old, with your mother and wondering if you can win your father (or me) from her. My wife represents your mother and that is why you dislike her. You must have been, as a child, very jealous of your mother."

He talks a great deal about a woman's need to be subjugated, the joy I do not know yet, he believes, of letting go entirely. Physically first, because Henry has aroused me so deeply.

I begin to find flaws in his formulas, to be irritated at his quick filing away of my dreams and ideas. When he is silent, I analyze my own actions and feelings. Of course, he could say that I am trying to find him defective, to make an equal of him, because he obtained my confidence about his wife. At the moment I feel he is distinctly stronger than I, and I want to balance this by doing some independent analysis about the bracelets. I am therefore half submissive, half rebellious.

Allendy accentuates the ambivalence of my desires. He senses that he is also approaching the sexual key to my neuroses, and I realize he is, too, like a deft detective.

To test Hugo I have mentioned once or twice the idea of an "evening off"—once a week, perhaps, when we might each go out separately. It is understood that he finds no pleasure in going out with Henry because of an obscure jealousy.

Finally we agreed that I could go to the movies with Henry and Fred while he went out with Eduardo. At the last moment Eduardo could not go. I offered to postpone my engagement. Hugo would not hear of it. He said he would go out anyway, and that it was a good thing for both of us. He said this in a normal tone of voice. I don't know for sure whether he was secretly hurt by my request for independence. He maintained that he was not. Whether he is hurt or not, it is necessary. I feel that gradually he will make good use of his own liberty.

"Do you think liberty simply means that we are growing apart?" he asked anxiously. This, I denied. Certainly I have grown away from him sexually, and if there is any jealousy in me now, it is not due to physical passion for him but to sheer possessiveness. And since I do not give him my body in the complete sense, he has a full right to his liberty and more. It would only be fair if he should find elsewhere the same joys I have found with Henry. If what Allendy says is true, both of us must find passion outside of our love. Naturally, this costs me an effort. I could keep Hugo for myself. The idea of liberty had not occurred to him. It is I who have suggested it. Natasha would call me a fool.

What can I do with my happiness? How can I keep it, conceal it, bury it where I may never lose it? I want to kneel as it falls over me like rain, gather it up with lace and silk, and press it over myself again.

Henry and I lie fully dressed under the coarse blanket

of his bed. He talks about his own profound joy. "I can't let you go tonight, Anaïs, I want you the whole night. I feel that you belong to me." But later, as we sit close together in a café, he reveals his lack of confidence, his doubts. The red journal made him sad. He read about his sensual power over me. "Is that all, is that all?" he wants to know. Is he only that for me? Then it will soon be over, a passing infatuation. Sexual desire. He wants my love. He needs the security of my love. I tell him I have loved him since I spent those few days with him in Clichy. "At the beginning, yes, it was perhaps purely sensual. Not now."

It seems to me I cannot love him more than I do. I love him as much as I desire him, and my desire is immense. Every hour I spend in his arms could be the last. I give myself to it with frenzy. At any moment, before I see him again, June could return.

How does June love Henry?—how much, how well? I ask myself in torment.

When people are surprised to find him soft and timid, I am amused. I, too, bowed to the brutality of his writing, but my Henry is vulnerable, sensitive. How humbly he seeks to make Hugo like him, how pleased he is when Hugo is kind to him.

Last night Hugo went to a movie, enjoyed the novelty of the experience, danced in a cabaret with a Martinique girl, felt nostalgia for me when he heard the music, as if we were very far away from each other, and came home eager to possess me.

After the soft, easy way Henry slips into my body, Hugo is terrible to bear. At such moments I feel I may go mad and reveal everything.

Henry has a picture of Mona Paiva, the dancer, tacked

over his washstand, along with two photos of June, one of me, and some of his watercolors. I give him a tin box for his letters and manuscripts, and inside the lid he pastes the program of Joaquin's concert. On his door he tacks notes on Spain.

I cut out the top of my box of powder—*N'aimez que Moi, Caron, Rue de la Paix.* He carries this in his vest pocket. He also carries one of my wine-colored handkerchiefs.

Last night he said, "I am so rich because I have you. I feel that there will always be a lot doing between us, that there will always be changes and novelties."

He almost said, "We'll be connected and interested in each other beyond the connection of the moment." And at this thought, my heart tightened, and I felt the need to touch his suit, his arm, to know he was there and, temporarily, all mine.

I float along, basking in memories of Henry—how his face looks at certain moments, the mischief of his mouth, the exact sound of his voice, at times husky, the firm square hold of his hand, how he looked in Hugo's discarded green coat, his laughter at the movies. He cannot make a movement which does not reverberate in my body. He is no taller than I am. Our mouths are on the same level. He rubs his hands when he is excited, repeats words, shakes his head like a bear. He has a serious, chaste look on his face when he works. In a crowd, I guess at his presence before I see him.

I realized today, with great amusement, the extent to which Henry has shaken down my old gravity, with his literary pranks, his crazy manifestos, his contradictions, his changes of mood, his grotesque humor. I can see myself as a ridiculous person, because of my constant efforts to understand others. We heard that Richard Osborn had gone mad. "Hurrah!" said Henry. "Let's go and see him. Let's have a drink first. This is rare, superb; it doesn't happen every day. I hope he is really insane." I was at first a bit disconcerted, but very quickly I caught the flavor of the humor, and I asked for more. Henry has taught me to play. I had played before, in my own way, with sandal-footed humor, but his is a lusty humor, which I have enjoyed to the point of hysteria—like the morning the dawn caught us still talking. Henry and I fell on his bed, exhausted, but he was still talking deliriously about the strainer that was thrown by mistake in the water closet, about black lace underwear and coral, etc., out of which he later created that inimitable parody of my novel.

The other night we talked about the trick of literature in eliminating the unessential, so that we are given a concentrated dose of life. I said almost indignantly, "It's a deception and the cause of much disappointment. One reads books and expects life to be just as full of interest and intensity. And, of course, it isn't so. There are many dull moments in between, and they, too, are natural. You, in your writing, have played the same trick. I expected all our talks to be feverish, portentous. I expected you always drunk, and always delirious. Then when we lived together for a few days, we fell into a profound, quiet, natural rhythm."

"Are you disappointed?"

"It is very different from what I expected, yes, less sensational, but I'm satisfied."

I have lost that tranquil Seine-like rhythm of my adolescence. And yet when Henry and I sit together in the

Café de la Place Clichy, we enjoy the profound feverless currents of our love.

It is June who gives fever. But it is only a superficial fever. The true, indelible fever lies in Henry's writing. As I read his latest book I am almost petrified with admiration. I try to think about it, to tell him how it affects me, and I can't. It is too enormous, too potent.

Everything is so sweet between Hugo and me. Great tenderness and much deception on my part about my true feelings. I was touched by his behavior the other night and tried to repay it by giving him much pleasure. The way I think of Henry terrifies me: it is so obsessional. I must try and spread out my thoughts.

When Henry and I talk about June, I do not think of her now except as a "character" I admire. As a woman, she threatens my one great possession, and I cannot love her any more. If June would die—I often think of it—if only she would die. Or if she would cease loving Henry, but that, she will not. Henry's love is the refuge she returns to, always.

Whenever I have gone to Henry's apartment and he has been writing a letter to June, or rewriting a passage about her in his book, or marking what fits her in Proust or Gide (he finds her everywhere), I have an intolerable fear: He is hers again. He has realized he loves no one but her. And each time, with surprise, I see him drop his book or letter and turn wholly to me, with love, desire. The last test, June's cable, gave me profound reassurance. But each time we talk about her I feel the same terrible anxiety. This cannot last. I will not fight events. The minute June returns, I relinquish Henry. Yet it is not so simple. I cannot relinquish living so closely to Henry as I do in these pages, for the sake of eluding pain.

Allendy was a superman today. I will never be able to describe our talk. There was so much intuition, so much emotion throughout. To the very last phrase he was so human, so true.

I had come in a mood of confidence, of recklessness, thinking: I do not want Allendy to admire me unless he can do so when he knows me exactly as I am. My first effort at complete sincerity.

I tell him first of all that I was ashamed of what I had said last time about his wife. He laughed and said he had forgotten all about it and asks, "Is there anything else which worries you?"

"Nothing in particular, but I would like to ask you if my strong sensual obsession is a reaction against too much introspection? I have been reading Samuel Putnam, who writes that 'the quickest way out of introspection is a worship of the body, which leads to sexual intensity.' "

I cannot remember his exact answer, but I sense his connection of the word "obsession" with a frantic search for satisfaction. Why the effort? Why dissatisfaction?

Here, I feel an imperative need to tell him my biggest secret: In the sexual act I do not always experience an orgasm.

He had guessed this from the very first day. My talk on sex had been crude, bold, defiant. It did not harmonize with my personality. It was artificial. It betrayed an uncertainty.

"But do you know what an orgasm is?"

"Oh, very well, from the times I did experience it, and particularly from masturbation."

"When did you masturbate?"

"Once, in the summer, in St. Jean de Luz. I was dissatisfied and had a strong sexual urge." I am ashamed to admit that when I was alone for two days I masturbated four and five times a day, and also often in Switzerland, during our vacation, and in Nice.

"Why only once? Every woman does it and very often."

"I believe it is wrong, morally and physically. I was terribly depressed and ashamed afterwards."

"That's nonsense. Masturbation is not physically harmful. It is only the feeling of guilt we have about it that oppresses."

"I used to fear it would diminish my mental power, my health, and that I would disintegrate morally."

Here, I add other details, which he listens to silently, trying to coordinate them. I tell him things I have never entirely admitted to myself, and which I have not written in my journal, things I wanted to forget.

Allendy is piecing the fragments together and talks about my partial frigidity. He discovers that I also consider this an inferiority and believe it is due to my frail physique. He laughs. He attributes it to a psychic cause, a strong sense of guilt. Sixty out of a hundred women feel as I do and never admit it and, most important of all, Allendy says, if I only knew what little difference this makes to men and how unaware they are of it. He always transforms what I term an inferiority into a natural thing, or one whose curse can be easily removed. I immediately feel a great relief and lose my terror and secretiveness.

I tell him about June, of my desiring to be a *femme fatale*, of my cruelty towards Hugo and Eduardo, and my surprise that they should love me as much or more afterwards. We also discuss my frank, bold sex talk, how I reverse my true, innate modesty and exhibit a forced obscenity. (Henry says he doesn't like my telling obscene stories, because it doesn't suit me.)

"But I am full of dissonances," I say, feeling that strange anguish Allendy creates—half relief, because of his exactness, half sorrow for no specific reason, the feeling of having been discovered.

"Yes, and until you can act perfectly naturally, according to your own nature, you will never be happy. The *femme fatale* arouses men's passions, exasperates them, torments them, and they want to possess her, even to kill her, but they do not love her profoundly. You have already discovered that you are loved profoundly. Now you have also discovered that cruelty to both Eduardo and Hugo has aroused them, and they want you even more. This makes you want to play a game which is not really natural to you."

"I have always despised such games. I have never been able to conceal from a man that I loved him."

"But you tell me profound loves do not satisfy you. You crave to give and to receive stronger sensations. I understand, but that is only a phase. You can play the game now and then, to heighten passion, but profound loves are the loves which suit your true self, and they alone will satisfy you. The more you act like yourself the nearer you come to a fulfillment of your real needs. You are still terribly afraid to be hurt; your imaginary sadism shows that. So afraid to be hurt that you want to take the lead and hurt first. I do not despair of reconciling you to your own image."

These are his words, crudely restated and only half remembered. I was so overcome by the sensation of his loosening innumerable tensions, of liberating me. His voice was so gentle and compassionate. Before he had finished I was sobbing. My gratitude was immense. I wanted to tell him I admired him and finally did. He was silent while I sobbed, and then he asked me his gentle question: "I didn't say anything to hurt you?"

I would like to cover the last pages with yesterday's joys. Showers of kisses from Henry. The thrusts of his flesh into mine, as I arched my body to better weld it to his. If a choice were to be made today between June and me, he tells me, he would surrender June. He could imagine us married and enjoying life, together. "No," I say, half teasing, half serious. "June is the only one. I am making you bigger and stronger for June." A half truth; there is no choice. "You're too modest, Anaïs. You do not realize yet what you have given me. June is a woman who can be effaced by other women. What June gives I can forget with other women. But you stand apart. I could have a thousand women after you and they could not efface you."

I listen to him. He is elated, and so he exaggerates, but it is so lovely. Yes, I know, for a moment, June's rareness and mine. The balance leans towards me for the moment. I look at my own image in Henry's eyes, and what do I see? The young girl of the diaries, telling stories to her brothers, sobbing much without reason, writing poetry—the woman one can talk to.

## *JUNE*

Last night Henry and I went to the movies. When the story became tragic, harrowing, he took my hand, and we locked fingers tightly. With every pressure I shared his response to the story. We kissed in the taxi, on the way to meet Hugo. And I could not tear myself away. I lost my head. I went with him to Clichy. He penetrated me so completely that when I returned to Louveciennes and fell asleep in Hugo's arms, I still felt it was Henry. All night it was Henry at my side. I curled my body around him in my dreams. In the morning I found myself tightly entangled with Hugo, and it took me a long time to realize it was not Henry. Hugo believes I was so loving last night, but it was Henry I loved, Henry I kissed.

Since Allendy has fully won my confidence I came ready to talk very frankly about frigidity. I confess this: that when I found pleasure in sexual intercourse with Henry I was afraid of having a baby and thought that I should not have an orgasm too frequently. But a few months ago a Russian doctor told me it could not happen easily; in fact, if I wanted a child I would have to subject myself to an operation. The fear of having a baby, then, was eliminated. Allendy said the very fact that I did not try to reassure myself on this score for seven years of my married life proved I did not really give it any importance, that I used it merely as an excuse for not letting go in coition. When this fear vanished, I was able to examine more closely the true nature of my feelings. I expressed a restlessness at what I termed the enforced passivity of women. Still, perhaps two times out of three, I kept myself passive, waiting for all the activity in the man, as if I did not want to be responsible for what I was enjoying. "That is to abate your sense of guilt," Allendy said. "You refuse to be active and feel less guilty if it is the other who is active."

After the previous talk with Allendy I had felt a slight change. I was more active with Henry. He noticed it and said, "I love the way you fuck me now." And I felt a keen pleasure.

What astonishes me most about June are Henry's stories of her aggressivity, her taking him, seeking him at her own will. When I occasionally try aggressivity, it gives me a feeling of distress, shame. I sense now an occasional psychic paralysis in me somewhat similar to Eduardo's, except that it is more serious for a man.

Allendy pressed me to admit that since the last analysis I had complete confidence in him and that I had become very fond of him. All is well, then, as this is necessary for the success of the analysis. At the end of the session he could use the word "frigidity" without offending me. I was even laughing.

One of the things he observed was that I was dressing more simply. I have felt much less the need of original costuming. I could almost wear ordinary tailored clothes now. Costume, for me, has been an external expression of my secret lack of confidence. Uncertain of my beauty, Allendy said, I designed striking clothes which would distinguish me from other women.

"But," I said, laughing, "if I become happy and banal, the art of costuming, which owes its existence purely to a sense of inferiority, will be mortally affected." The pathological basis of creation! What will become of the creator if I become normal? Or will I merely gain in strength, so as to live out my instincts more fully? I will probably develop different and more interesting illnesses. Allendy said that what was important was to become equal to life.

My happiness hangs in suspense, and what happens now is determined by June's next move. Meanwhile I wait. I am overcome with a superstitious fear of starting another journal. This one is so full of Henry. If I should have to write on the first page of the new one, "June is here," I will know that I have lost my Henry. I will be left with only a small purple-bound book of joy, that is all, so quickly written, so quickly lived.

Love reduces the complexity of living. It amazes me that when Henry walks towards the café table where I wait for him, or opens the gate to our house, the sight of him is sufficient to exult me. No letter from anyone, even in praise of my book, can stir me as much as a note from him.

When he is drunk, he becomes sentimental in such a human, simple way. He begins to visualize our life together, I as his wife: "You will never seem as beautiful as when I see you roll up your sleeves and work for me. We could be so happy. You would fall behind in your writing!"

Oh, the German husband. At this, I laugh. So, I fall behind in my writing and I become the wife of a genius. I had wanted this, among other things, but no housework. I would never marry him. Oh, no. I know that he is delighted with the liberty I give him but that he is extremely jealous and would not let me act as freely.

Yet when I see him so childishly happy with my love, I hesitate at playing the game of worrying him, deceiving him, tormenting him. I do not even want to arouse his jealousy too painfully.

It is Fred's role, unconsciously, to poison my happiness. He points to the inadequacies of Henry's love. I do not deserve a half love, he says. I deserve extraordinary things. Hell, Henry's half love is worth more to me than the whole loves of a thousand men.

I imagined for a moment a world without Henry. And I swore that the day I lose Henry I will kill my vulnerability, my capacity for true love, my feelings by the most frenzied debauch. After Henry I want no more love. Just fucking, on the one hand, and solitude and work on the other. No more pain.

After not seeing Henry for five days, due to a thousand obligations, I couldn't bear it. I asked him to meet me for an hour between two engagements. We talked for a moment and then we went to the nearest hotel room. What a profound need of him. Only when I am in his arms does everything seem right. After an hour with him I could go on with my day, doing things I do not want to do, seeing people who do not interest me.

A hotel room, for me, has an implication of voluptuousness, furtive, short lived. Perhaps my not seeing Henry has heightened my hunger. I masturbate often, luxuriously, without remorse or after distaste. For the first time I know what it is to eat. I have gained four pounds. I get frantically hungry, and the food I eat gives me a lingering pleasure. I never ate before in this deep carnal way. I have only three desires now, to eat, to sleep, and to fuck. The cabarets excite me. I want to hear raucous music, to see faces, to brush against bodies, to drink fiery Benedictine. Beautiful women and handsome men arouse fierce desires in me. I want to dance. I want drugs. I want to know perverse people, to be intimate with them. I never look at naïve faces. I want to bite into life, and to be torn by it. Henry does not give me all this. I have aroused his love. Curse his love. He can fuck me as no one else can, but I want more than that. I'm going to hell, to hell, to hell. Wild, wild, wild.

Today I carried my mood to Henry, or what I could hold of it, for it seemed to me that it overflowed like lava, and I was sad when I saw him so quiet, serious, tender, not crazy enough. No, not as crazy as his writing. It is June who burns Henry with words. In his arms I forgot my fever for an hour. If only we could be alone for a few days. He wants me to go to Spain with him. There, will he throw off his gentleness and be crazy?

Is it always to be the same? One does not meet the match to one's state of being, one's phase, one's mood, never. We are all sitting on seesaws. What Henry is tired of, I am hungry for, with a brand-new, fresh, vigorous hunger. What he wants of me, I am not in the mood to give. What opposition in our own rhythms. Henry, my love, I don't want to hear any more about angels, souls, love, no more profundities.

An hour with Henry. He says, "Anaïs, you overwhelm me. You arouse the strangest sensations. When I left you last time, I adored you." We sit on the edge of his bed. I put my head on his shoulder. He kisses my hair.

Soon we are lying side by side. He has penetrated me, but his penis suddenly ceases to move and becomes soft.

I say, smiling, "You didn't want to fuck today."

He says, "It isn't that. It's because I have been thinking a great deal these days about growing old and how one day . . ."

"You're crazy, Henry. Old, at forty! And you, who never think at such moments. Why, you'll be fucking when you are a hundred."

"This is so humiliating," says Henry, hurt, bewildered.

I can only think for the moment of his humiliation, his fears. "It is natural," I say. "It happens to women, too, only in women it doesn't show! They can conceal it. Hasn't it ever happened to you before?"

"Only when I didn't want my first mistress, Pauline. But I want you desperately. I have a terrible fear of losing you. Yesterday I was worrying like a woman. How long will she love me? Will she get tired of me?"

I kiss him.

"Now you kiss me as if I were a child, you see."

I observe that he is ashamed of himself. I say and do everything to make everything natural. He imagines he will be impotent from now on. As I comfort him I conceal the beginning of my own fears and my own despair. "Perhaps," I say, "you feel that you must always fuck me when I come to see you so that I will not be disappointed." This strikes him as the truest explanation. He accepts it. I myself am against our unnatural meetings. We cannot meet when we want each other. That is bad. I want him more when he is not there. I beg him not to take it seriously. I convince him. He promises to go out that night, to the same play where I must go with some bank people.

But in the taxi my own disproportionate fears return. Henry loves me, but not fuckingly, not fuckingly.

That same night he came to the play and sat up in the balcony. I felt his presence. I looked up at him, so tenderly. But the heaviness of my mood stifled me. For me everything was finished. Things die when my confidence dies. And yet . . .

Henry went home and wrote me a love letter. The next day I telephoned and said, "Come to Louveciennes if you are not in the mood to work." He came immediately. He was gentle, and he took me. We both needed that, but it did not warm me, resuscitate me. It seemed to me that he, too, was fucking just to reassure himself. What a leaden weight on me, on my body. We had only one hour together. I walked with him to the station. As I walked back I reread his letter. It seemed insincere to me. Literature. Facts tell me one thing, my instincts another. But are my instincts just my old neurotic fears?

Strange, I forgot my appointment with Allendy today and I didn't telephone him. I need him terribly, and yet I want to fight alone, grapple with life. Henry writes a letter, comes to me, appears to love me, talks to me. Empty. I am like an instrument which has stopped registering. I don't want to see him tomorrow. I asked him again the other day, "Shall I send money to June so that she can come, instead of giving it to you so you can go to Spain?" He said no.

I begin to think a great deal about June. My image of a dangerous, sensual, dynamic Henry is gone. I do all I can to recapture it. I see him humble, timorous, without self-confidence. When I said playfully the other day: "You'll never have me again," he answered, "You're punishing me." What I realize is that his insecurity is equal to mine, my poor Henry. He wants as much to prove to me how beautifully he can make love, prove his potency, as I want to know that I arouse potency.

Yet I showed courage. When that scene, so unbearably like the one with John, happened, I showed no concern, no surprise. I stayed in his arms, quietly laughing and talking. I said, "Love spoils fucking." But this was more bravado than anything else. The way I suffered was a truer self-revelation.

Despite all this I risked my marriage and happiness to sleep with Henry's letter under my pillow, with my hand on it.

---

I am going to Henry without joy. I am afraid of that gentle Henry I am going to meet, too much like myself. I remember that from the first day I expected him to take the lead, in talk, in action, in all things.

I thought bitterly of June's magnificent willfulness, initiative, tyranny. I thought, it isn't strong women who make men weak, but weak men who make women overstrong. I stood before Henry with the submissiveness of a Latin woman, ready to be overwhelmed. He has let me overwhelm *him*. He has constantly feared to disappoint me. He has exaggerated my expectations. He has worried about how long and how much I would love him. He has let thinking interfere with our happiness.

Henry, you love your little whores because you are superior to them. You really have refused to meet a woman on your own level. You were surprised how much I could love without judging, adoring you as no whore ever adored. Well, then, are you no happier to be adored by me, and doesn't it make you infinitely superior? Do all men shrink before the more difficult love?

For Henry, everything is flowing as before. He did not observe my hesitation when he suggested we go to the Hotel Cronstadt. Our hour seemed just as rich as ever, and he was so adoring. Yet I had the feeling of making an effort to love him. Perhaps he has just frightened me. I expected him to be impotent again. I didn't have the same wild confidence. Tenderness, yes. The cursed tenderness. I recaptured my happiness, but it was a cold happiness. I felt detached. We got drunk, and then we were very happy. But I was thinking of June.

Driving home after much white wine: Fourth of July fireworks bursting from the tops of street lamps. I am swallowing the asphalt road with a jungle roar, swallowing the houses with closed eyes and geranium eyelashes, swallowing telegraph poles and *messages téléphoniques,* stray cats, trees, hills, bridges. . . .

I mailed my surrealistic piece to Henry, adding, "Things I forgot to tell you: That I love you, and that when I awake in the morning I use my intelligence to discover more ways of appreciating you. That when June comes back she will love you more because I have loved you. There are new leaves on the tip of your already overrich head."

I feel the need of telling him I love him because I do not believe it. Why has Henry become to me little Henry, almost a child? I understand June's leaving him and saying, "I love Henry like my own child." Henry, who, before, was a gigantic menace, a terrorizer. It cannot be!

Cabaret Rumba. Hugo and I are dancing together. He is so much taller than I that my face nestles under his chin, against his chest. An inordinately handsome Spaniard (a professional dancer) has been looking at me like a hypnotist. He smiles at me over the head of his partner. I answer his smile, I stare into his eyes. I drink in their message. I answer with the same mixture of sensual enjoyment and amusement. His smile is lightly sketched on his face. I experience such acute pleasure to be communicating with this man while nestled in Hugo's arms. I am planning, as I smile at him, to return to the place and to dance with him. I feel a tremendous curiosity. I have looked into this man, I have imagined him naked. He has looked into me, too, with narrow animal eyes. The emotion of duplicity releases an insidious poison. All the way home the poison spreads. I understand now how to play for a moment with those feelings I have held too sacred. Next week instead of going out with my quiet "husband," Henry, I'll go and see the Spaniard. And women—I want women. But the masculine lesbians in Le Fétiche cabaret did not please me at all.

I now also understand the carnation in Carmen's mouth. I was smelling mock orange. The white blossoms touched my lips. They were like the skin of a woman. My lips pressed them, opened and closed gently around them. Soft petaled kisses. I bit into the white blossoms. Morsel of perfumed flesh, silkiness of skin. Carmen's full mouth biting her carnation; and I, Carmen.

It is too bad Henry has been good to me, too bad he is a good man. He is becoming aware of a subtle change in me. Yes, he says, I may look immature at first sight, but when I am undressed and in bed, how womanly I am.

The other day Joaquin came downstairs unexpectedly, into the salon, to ask me a trivial question, and Henry and I had been kissing. It showed on Henry's face, and he was embarrassed. I did not feel troubled or ashamed. I was resentful of the intrusion, and I said to Henry, "Well, it serves him right for coming here when he shouldn't."

If Henry realizes that I am becoming shameless, strong, sure of my actions, refusing to be impressed by others, if he realizes the true course of my life now, will he change towards me? No. He has his needs, and he needs the woman in me who was soft, timid, good, incapable of hurting, of running wild. Instead of that, every day I grow nearer to June. I begin to want her, to know her better, to love her more. Now I realize that every interesting move in their life together was made by June. Without her he is a quiet watcher, not a participant. Henry and I combine beautifully for companionship but not for living. I expected those first days (or nights) in Clichy to be sensational. I was surprised when we fell into deep, quiet talks and did so little. I expected Dostoevskian scenes and found a gentle German who could not bear to let the dishes go unwashed. I found a husband, not a difficult and temperamental lover. Henry was, at first, even uneasy as to how to entertain me. June would have known. Yet I was happy and deeply satisfied then because I loved him. It is only these past days that I have felt my old restlessness.

I suggested to Henry that we go out, but I was disappointed when he refused to take me to exotic places. He was content with a movie and sitting in a café. Then he refused to introduce me to his rakish friends (to protect and keep me). When he did not take the lead, I began to suggest going here or there.

One night we had gone from Gare St. Lazare to a movie and then to a café. In the taxi on the way to meet Hugo, Henry began kissing me, and I clung to him. Our kisses grew frenzied, and I said, "Tell the taxi driver to drive us to the Bois." I was intoxicated by the moment. But Henry was frightened. He reminded me of the hour, of Hugo. With June, how different it would have been! I left him with sadness. There is really nothing crazy about Henry except his feverish writing.

I make an effort to live externally, going to the hairdresser, shopping, telling myself: "I must not sink, I must fight." I need Allendy, and I cannot see him until Wednesday.

I want to see Henry, too, but now I do not count on his strength. That first day in the Viking, he said, "I am a weak man," and I did not believe him. I do not love weak men. I feel tenderness, yes. But, my God, in a few days he has destroyed my passion. What has happened? The moment when he doubted his potency was only a spark. Was it because his sexual power was his unique power? Was it in this way only that he held me? Was it a change in me?

By evening I begin to feel it isn't very important that I am disappointed. I want to help him. I am happy his book is written and that I have given him a feeling of security and well-being. I love him in a different way, but I love him.

Henry is precious to me, as he is. I melt when I see his frayed suit. He fell asleep while I was dressing for a formal dinner. Then he came to my bedroom and watched me adding the last touches. He admired my Oriental green dress. He said I moved about like a princess. My bedroom window was open on the luxurious garden. It made him think of the setting of *Pelléas and Mélisande.* He lay on the couch. I sat next to him for a moment and cuddled him. I said, "You must get yourself a suit," wondering how I would get the money for it. I couldn't bear to see the frayed sleeves around his wrists.

We sit close together in the train. He says, "You know, Anaïs, I am so slow that I cannot realize I am going to lose you when we get to Paris. I will be walking alone in the streets, perhaps twenty minutes later, and suddenly I will feel keenly that I do not have you any longer and that I miss you."

And he had told me in a letter, "I look forward to those two days [Hugo is going to London], to spending them quietly with you, absorbing you, being your husband. I adore being your husband. I will always be your husband whether you want it or not."

At the dinner my happiness made me feel natural. In

my mind I was lying on the grass with Henry over me; I beamed at the poor ordinary people around the table. They all felt something—even the women, who wanted to know where I shopped for my clothes. Women always think that when they have my shoes, my dress, my hairdresser, my make-up, it will all work the same way. They do not conceive of the witchcraft that is needed. They do not know that I am not beautiful but that I only appear to be at certain moments.

"Spain," said my dinner partner, "is the most wonderful country in the world, where women are really women!"

I was thinking, I wish Henry could taste this fish. And the wine.

But Hugo felt something, too. Before the banquet we were to meet at the Gare St. Lazare. Henry was supposed to have come to Louveciennes to help me with my novel. When Henry and I arrived at the station together, Hugo was not happy. He began to talk quickly, severely about Osborn, "the child prodigy." Poor Hugo, and I could still smell the grass of the forest.

I walked with him so lightly. And where was Henry? Was he missing me already? Sensitive Henry, who has a fear of being disliked, despised, a fear that Hugo should "know everything" or that I will be ashamed of him before people. Not understanding why I love him. I make him forget humiliations and nightmares. His thin knees under the threadbare suit arouse my protective instincts. There is big Henry, whose writing is tempestuous, obscene, brutal, and who is passionate with women, and there is little Henry, who needs me. For little Henry I stint myself, save every cent I can. I cannot believe now that he ever terrified me, intimidated me. Henry, the man of experience, the adventurer. He is afraid of our dogs, of snakes in the garden, of people when they are not *le peuple.* There are moments when I see Lawrence in him, except that he is healthy and passionate.

I wanted to tell my dinner partner last night, "You know, Henry is so passionate."

I failed to go to my last appointment with Allendy. I was beginning to depend on him, to be grateful to him. Why did I stop for a week, he asks. To stand on my own feet again, to fight alone, to take myself back, to depend on nobody. Why? The fear of being hurt. Fear that he should become a necessity and that, when my cure was finished, our relationship would end and I would lose him. He reminds me that it is part of the cure to make me self-sufficient. But by not trusting him, I have shown that I am still ill. Slowly he will teach me to do without him.

"If you dropped me now, I would suffer as a doctor from not succeeding in my cure of you, and I would suffer personally because you are interesting. So you see, in a way, I need you as much as you need me. You could hurt me by dropping me. Try to understand that in all relationships there is dependency. Don't be afraid of dependency. It is the same with the question of domination. Don't try to tip the scales. The man must be the aggressor in the sexual act. Afterwards he can become like a child and depend on the woman and need her like a mother. You are not domineering intrinsically, but in self-defense—against pain, against the fear of abandonment, which perpetually recalls to you your father's abandonment of you—you try to conquer, to dominate. I see that you do not use your power for evil or cruelty, but just to satisfy yourself of its effectiveness.

You have conquered your husband, Eduardo, and now Henry. You do not want weak men, but until they have become weak in your hands you are not satisfied. Be careful of this: drop your defensive attitude, drop, above all, your fears. Let go."

Henry writes me a thoughtless letter about the little nineteen-year-old Paulette Fred has brought to Clichy to live with him. Henry is joyous because she is doing the housekeeping and urges Fred to marry her because she is adorable. This letter tore into my flesh. I visualized Henry playing with Paulette while Fred went to work. Oh, I know my Henry. I withdrew into myself like a snail, I didn't want to write in my journal, I refused to think, but I must cry out. If this is jealousy, I must never again inflict it on Hugo, on anyone. Paulette, in Clichy; Paulette, free to do everything for Henry, eating with him, spending the evenings with him while Fred is at work.

A summer evening. Henry and I are eating in a small restaurant wide open to the street. We are part of the street. The wine that runs down my throat runs down many other throats. The warmth of the day is like a man's hand on one's breast. It envelops both the street and the restaurant. The wine solders us all, Henry and me, the restaurant and the street and the world. Shouts and laughter from the students preparing for the Quatz Arts Ball. They are in barbaric costumes, red-skinned, feathered, overflowing from buses and carts. Henry is saying, "I want to do everything to you tonight. I want to lay you on this very table and fuck you before everybody. I'm nuts about you, Anaïs. I'm crazy about you. After dinner we're going to the Hotel Anjou. I'll teach you new things."

And then, inchoately, he feels a sudden need for confession: "That day I left you in Louveciennes, rather drunk—would you believe it, while I was having dinner, a girl came and sat next to me. She was just an ordinary prostitute. Right in the restaurant I put my hand under her skirt. I went to a hotel with her, thinking of you all the time, hating myself, remembering our afternoon. I had been so satisfied. So many thoughts I had, that when the moment came, I couldn't fuck the girl. She was so contemptuous. Thought me impotent. I gave her twenty francs, and I remember being glad it was not more because it was your money. Can you understand that, Anaïs?"

I try to keep my eyes steady, mechanically I say I understand, but I am bewildered, hurt beyond words. And now he feels the need to continue: "Only one more thing. I must tell you one more thing, and then it is all. One night Osborn had just got his pay, he took me to a cabaret. We began to dance and then took two girls home to Clichy. When we were sitting in the kitchen they asked us to talk business. They asked a big price. I wanted them to go, but Osborn paid them what they wanted and they stayed. One was an acrobatic dancer and showed us some of her tricks naked, with only slippers on. Then Fred came home at three o'clock, furious to find I had used his bed, took the sheets off and showed them to me, saying: 'Yes, yes, and then you say you love your Anaïs.' And I do, Anaïs. I even think you might have found a perverse pleasure in seeing me."

Now I bow my head and the tears come. But I go on saying I understand. Henry is drunk. He sees that I am hurt. And then I shake it off. I look at him. The earth is rocking. Shouts and laughter from the students in the street.

At the Hotel Anjou we lie like lesbians, sucking. Again, hours and hours of voluptuousness. The hotel sign, in red lights, shines into the room. The warmth heaves in. "Anaïs," Henry says, "you have the most beautiful ass." Hands, fingering, ejaculations. I learn from Henry how to play with a man's body, how to arouse him, how to express my own desire. We rest. A big bus of students is passing. I jump and run to the window. Henry is asleep. I would like to be at the ball, to taste everything.

Henry awakens. He is amused to find me naked at the window. We play again. Hugo may be at the ball, I think. When I gave him his liberty, I know he planned to go. Hugo is at the ball with a woman in his arms, and I am in a hotel room with Henry, with red light shining through the window, a summer night filled with the cries and laughter of the students. I have run naked to the window twice.

All this is a dream now. At the time it happened I had a feeling in my body as before a cloudburst. My body remembers the hotness and fever of Henry's caresses. A story. I must write it a hundred times. But now it brings me pain. In self-protection I will have to detach myself from Henry. I cannot bear this. I hold on while Henry flows carelessly from woman to woman.

Today for a moment I softened: It does not matter. Let him have his ordinary little women if it makes him happy. The relief of opening one's hand and letting go was immense. But soon after, I tightened again. A desire for revenge, a strange revenge. I give myself to Hugo with such feelings against Henry that I experience a great physical pleasure. My first infidelity to Henry.

What subtle forces act on the sensual being. A small hurt, a moment of hatred, and I can enjoy Hugo completely, frenziedly, as much as I have enjoyed Henry himself. I cannot bear jealousy. I must kill it by balance. For every one of Henry's whores I will avenge myself but in a more terrible way. He has often said that of the two of us, I, in a sense, commit by far the more profane acts.

Behind my own drunkenness there is always a certain consciousness, enough to make me refuse to answer Henry's questions and doubts about me. I do not try to make him jealous, but neither do I admit my stupid fidelity. It is in this way women are pushed into war with men. There is no possibility of absolute confidence. To confide is to put yourself in someone else's hands and to suffer. Oh, tomorrow, how I will punish him!

Already I am glad that when Hugo came back from London I let him kiss me for a long while and carry me in his arms, to the back of the garden, among the mock orange bushes.

While he was away, I met with Henry, carrying my pajamas and comb and toothbrush, but poised for flight. I let him talk. "This Paulette and Fred," he says, "they are cute together. I don't know how it will end. She is younger than she said. We were afraid at first her parents would make trouble for Fred. He asks me to take care of her in the evening. I have taken her to the movies, but the truth is, she bores me. She is so young. We have nothing to say to each other. She is jealous of you. She read what Fred wrote about you. 'We're all expecting the goddess today.' "

I laugh and tell him what I have been thinking. I can see in his face how uninterested he is in Paulette, although he admits it is the first time he is indifferent. "Why, Paulette is nothing," he says. "I wrote that letter enthusiastically because I enjoyed their enthusiasm, participated in it."

This became a subject of teasing. It was an ordeal for

me to go to Clichy to meet Paulette. I was afraid of her and I had wanted to bring her a gift, because she was a foreign presence, a new person in our Clichy life, living there in the way I would like to be living.

She was nothing but a child, thin and graceless, but temporarily attractive because she had just been made woman by Fred, and because she was in love. Henry and I enjoyed their childish cooing for a while and then got tired of them, and for the remaining days I spent in Clichy we fled from them.

One night when I arrived, Henry had a stomach ache. I had to take care of him as I do of Hugo—hot towels, massage. He was lying on the bed, showing a beautiful white stomach. He slept a while and awoke cured. We read together. We had an amazing fusion. I slept in his arms. In the morning he awoke me with caresses, mumbling something about my expression.

Henry's other face, with which he may someday repudiate all this, is for the moment impossible for me to visualize.

Just before this, I had one visit with Allendy, in which I clearly showed a retrogression. I returned to him a rubber *préventif* he advised me to wear. Interpretation: I wanted to show him I was in a mood of repentence for my "loose life." This, because Joaquin was taken ill with appendicitis, giving me a feeling of guilt.

Then I confessed that certain practices in sexual games do not really appeal to me, like penis sucking, which I do to please Henry. In connection with this, I remembered that a few days preceding my liaison with Henry I couldn't swallow food. I had a feeling of nausea. Since food and sexuality have a connection, Allendy believes I showed an unconscious resistance to sexuality. Also, the resistance returns more strongly when some incident reawakens my sense of guilt.

I realized that my life was stopped again. I cried. But perhaps because of this talk with Allendy I was able to go on, to go to Henry, to conquer my jealousy of Paulette. I suppose it is an indication of my pride and independence to say that I find it difficult to give entire credit to psychoanalysis for my various victories, and I am apt to believe it is due to Henry's great humanness or my own efforts.

Eduardo pointed out to me how quickly I forget the true source of my new confidence and how this very confidence (given to me by Allendy) is what makes one believe in one's own powers. In short, I don't know enough about psychoanalysis yet to realize that I owe everything to Allendy.

I have not let myself dwell sentimentally on him. In fact, I am glad that I do not love him. Need him, yes, and admire him, but without sensuality. I have a feeling that I am waiting for him to become upset by me. I enjoy it when he admits I intimidated him the first day we met or when he talks about my sensual charm. Here, the awareness that transference is an artificially stimulated emotion inspires me with more mistrust than ever. If I doubt genuine manifestations of love, how much more do I doubt this mentally aroused attachment.

Allendy talks about finding my true rhythm. He developed this from an acutely visual dream I had. As far as he could see, from studying me, I was fundamentally an exotic Cuban woman, with charm, simplicity, and purity.

All the rest was literary, intellectual. There was nothing wrong with acting roles except that one must not take them seriously. But I become sincere and go all the way. And I then become uneasy and unhappy. Allendy also believes my interest in perversions to be a pose.

Long after he said this, I remembered that the place where I have been most soundly happy is Switzerland, where I lived washed of all external roles. Do I think myself interesting in a picture hat, soft dress, little make-up, as I am in Switzerland? No. But I think myself interesting in a Russian hat! Lack of faith in my fundamental values.

At this point I began to balk a little. If psychoanalysis is going to annihilate all nobility in personal motives and in art by the discovery of neurotic roots, what does it substitute in place of them? What would I be without my decoration, costume, personality? Would I be a more vigorous artist?

Allendy says I must live with greater sincerity and naturalness. I must not overstep the bounds of my nature, create dissonances, deviations, roles (as June has done), because it means misery.

I am waiting in Allendy's salon. I hear a woman's voice in his office. I feel jealous. I am annoyed because I hear them laughing. He is late, too, for the first time. And I am bringing him an affectionate dream—the first time I have allowed myself to think of him physically, amorously. Perhaps I should not tell him the dream. It is giving him too much, while he . . .

My bad feelings vanish when he appears. I tell him the dream. This, he realizes, is an improvement. A few months ago I would have withdrawn. He is glad of the warmth now appearing in our relationship. But he shows me how the dream betrays that my happiness comes more from his neglect of other people to give me all his attention than from the attention itself. "We come to the sensitive point again. Your unsureness, the need to be loved exclusively. There is in all your dreams a great possessiveness, too. To cling in love is bad, and it only comes from lack of confidence. Therefore when someone understands you and loves you, you are inordinately grateful."

Allendy always restores sincerity. He finds that I suppress my jealousies and my anger, turn them upon myself. He says I must express them, get rid of them. I practice a false goodness. I am not really good. I force myself to be generous, forgiving. "For a time," says Allendy, "act as angrily as you want to."

Terrible results from this suggestion. I found coming to the surface a thousand causes for resentment against Henry, his too easy acceptance of my sacrifices, his unreasoned defense of anything that is attacked, his praise of ordinary, common women, his fear of intelligent women, his vituperations against June, the magnificent being.

I awoke with a feeling that Allendy was going to kiss me during our appointment. The day seemed set for it, too, a luxuriant, tropical day. I felt languid and very sad to be parting from him.

When I arrived and told him I would not be coming again, he put aside the analysis and we talked. I looked at his Moujik nose and wondered if a man like that would be sensual. I was conscious of taking my usual poses. But I felt very panicky. At the end of our talk he took my hands. I eluded him a little. I put on my hat and cape, but when

I was about to leave he leaned over and said, *"Embrassez moi."*

Two impressions stand out very clearly: that I wished he had taken a good hold of me and kissed me without asking, and that the kiss was too short and chaste. Afterwards, I wanted to go back for another. It seemed to me I had been timid, and he, too, and we could have kissed better. He was distinctly handsome that day, brilliant, dreamy, interesting, and so firm. Really a giant.

I was very happy after Allendy's kiss. At the same time I know that Henry's most casual kiss can shake the foundations of my body. I realized this keenly today when I saw him after five days' separation. What a convergence of bodies. It is like a furnace when we meet. Yet day by day I realize more completely that only my body is stirred. My best moments with Henry are in bed.

## *JULY*

But when Hugo left for London Monday, I rushed off to Henry. Two nights of ecstasy. I still bear the traces of his bites, and last night he was so frenzied he hurt me. Our love-making was broken by profound talks.

He is jealous. He took me to Montparnasse, and a handsome Hungarian sat next to me and made advances to me, boldly. Henry talked afterwards of wanting to keep me under lock and key, that I was made for intimacy. When he saw me in Montparnasse, he felt that I was too soft and delicate for the crowd; he wanted to protect me, to hide me.

He has been debating with himself whether or not to

give up June. With me he feels whole, and he knows I have loved him better. We lie awake in the night talking about this, but I know he cannot and must not think of giving up June, his passion. I, in his place, would not give her up. June and I do not efface each other; we complement one another. Henry needs both of us. June is the stimulant and I the refuge. With June he knows despair and with me harmony. All this I say while I hold him very firmly in my arms.

And then I have Hugo. I would not give him up for Henry. What I cannot say to Henry is that he is primarily a physical man and that this is why June is essential to him. Such a man inspires sensual love. I, too, love him sensually. And in the end, this tie cannot last. He is destined to lose me. What I give him would be tremendous to a man less sensual. But not to a Henry.

We lie awake in the night, talking, and although my arms clasp him firmly my wisdom already relinquishes him. He is begging me not to take risks during the summer; he is still kissing me, after the convulsions of our fucking, which was, as he said, as if the thermometer had broken.

I have conquered a man least conquerable. But I also know the limits of my power, and I know it takes June and me together to answer the demands of men. I accept this with a sad elation.

Henry has loved me; oh, I am his love. I have had all I could have of him, the most secret layers of his being, such words, such feelings, such looks, such caresses, each flaming for me uniquely. I have felt him lulled by my softness, exultant in my love, passionate, possessive, jealous. I have grown on him, not bodily, but like a vision. What does he remember most vividly of our moments together? The afternoon he lay on the couch in my bedroom while I finished dressing for a dinner, in my deep green Oriental dress, perfuming myself, and he, overtaken by a sense of living in a fairy tale, with a veil between himself and me, the princess! That is what he remembers while I lie warm in his arms. Illusions and dreams. The blood he pours into me with groans of joy, the biting into my flesh, my odor on his fingers, all vanish before the potency of the fairy tale.

"You are a child," he says, half-puzzled, while at the same time he says, "You certainly know how to fuck. Where did you learn, where?"

And yet when he compares me to Paulette, the real child, he observes the seductiveness of my gestures, the maturity of my expression, the mind which he loves. "I am at one with you, Anaïs. I need you. I don't want June to come back."

When one knows the brutality that existed between Henry and June, it is strange to see how attentive he is to the least sign from me of boredom or fatigue. He has developed new perceptions and a new softness. To tease him, when he talked about my lack of hard-boiledness, I said that I had expected to get that from him, I had hoped to clash with him, to face ridicule, brutality, to learn to fight and hit back and talk louder, but that he had completely failed to give me that experience. I had disarmed the Bubu who was going to make a hard-boiled woman out of me. I don't even get criticized. With me he quickly surrenders his impulsive judgments, like calling Paulette adorable. By patience and gentleness I gain equilibrium in a man who is all reactions, oscillations, contrariness. Sometimes when he marvels at the deftness of my fingers, whether I am carving fish or arranging his tie, I think of Lawrence, so irritable and so bitter and so nervous, and I think I am playing on somewhat the same instrument. I still feel his kisses on the palms of my hands, and I hate to bathe because I am impregnated with wonderful odors.

Hugo is coming home in a few hours, and so life goes on like this in contradictory patterns. How long, I wonder, will I crave the sensualist? Before falling asleep, he said to me, "Listen, I am not drunk, and I am not sentimental, and I tell you you are the most wonderful woman in the world."

When I say I love him sensually, I do not altogether mean that; I love him in many other ways—when he is laughing at the movies, or talking very quietly in the kitchen; I love his humility, his sensitiveness, the core of bitterness and fury in him.

He was going to write June a crushing letter, full of accusations. And at that moment I brought him a document which justifies all her actions. It was as if he had raised his hand to strike her and I had to stop him. I know now June is a drug addict. I have found descriptions in a book that verify what I have vaguely sensed.

Henry was overwhelmed. He can be so easily duped. June talked constantly about drugs, like the criminal who returns to the scene of the crime. She needed to mention the subject while violently denying ever taking drugs (two or three times, perhaps). Henry began to piece the fragments together. When I saw his despair, I grew frightened. "You must not be too sure of what I say. I am sometimes too quick to synthesize." But I felt I was right.

Here, he passed the only ethical judgment I have ever heard him pass on self-destruction, that taking drugs denoted a deficiency in one's nature. This is what made the relationship hopeless.

I felt such pity for him when he began to question how much June loved him, comparing her love with mine. I defended her, saying she loves him in her own way, which is inhuman and fantastic. But it is true that I would not leave him as she does. It is true, as he says, that her greatest love is self-love. But it is her self-love that has made her a great character.

Henry is sometimes amazed by my admiration of June. Last night he said, "At the beginning you very much wanted June to come back. Am I right in thinking you don't want it now?"

"Yes." And I have also admitted other things, after never answering his questions about lovers. Once, in his arms, he pressed me so feelingly, saying, "Tell me you haven't deceived me; it would hurt me terribly, tell me," that I told him I had not. I gave away my mystery, knowing I shouldn't, yet incapable of anything else.

To exasperate a man may be a pleasure; but to lie in Henry's arms and surrender to him so entirely seemed a greater pleasure to me—to feel his body relaxing and to see him falling asleep with his happiness. The day after, I can always recover my feminine shield, take up the unnecessary and hateful war. In broad daylight I can give him back a little anguish, jealousy, fear, because he wants them, Henry, the Eternal Husband. He loved his suffering with June, even though he also loves his relief from suffering with me.

We had an amusing talk about our beginnings. Henry had wanted to kiss me the day we were first alone, the day of our walk to the woods, talking about June.

"But confess it was a game for you, at the beginning," I said.

"Not in the very beginning. In Dijon, yes, I had cruel, cold ideas, of using you. But the day I came back to Paris and saw your eyes—oh, Anaïs, the look in your eyes in the restaurant when I came back. That got me. But your life, your seriousness, your background scared me. I would have been very slow if you hadn't . . ."

I laugh now, as I think of it—what I read him from the red journal, the dream about his writing. It was I who broke the shell, because I desperately wanted him to know me. And what a surprise I was to him, he tells me. I followed an impulse, daringly, boldly. Was it because I could see more quickly and knew that Henry and I . . . Or was it naïveté?

We confess the most humorous doubts about each other. I have imagined Henry saying to June, "No, I don't love Anaïs. I acted as you do, for the sake of what she could do for me." And he has imagined me talking contemptuously about him in a few months. We sit in the kitchen exchanging these diabolical outgrowths of overfertile minds, which a caress will dissipate in a moment. I am in my pajamas. Henry's hand slips around my shoulder, and we laugh, wondering what will prove to be the truth.

The contrast between Hugo's sensuality and Henry's torments me. Could Hugo be made more sensual? It lasts so short a time with him. He thinks himself a phenomenon because he took me six nights in succession, but with quick, stabbing movements. Even after a paroxysm Henry's tenderness is more penetrating, more lingering. His soft little kisses, like rain, stay in my body almost as long as his violent caresses.

"Are you ever dry?" he teases me. I confess that Hugo has to use Vaseline. Then I realize the full significance of this confession, and I am overwhelmed.

Last night in my sleep I touched Hugo's penis as I learned to touch Henry's. I caressed it and pressed it in my hand. In my half-sleep I thought it was Henry. When Hugo became excited and began to take me, I awakened fully and was deeply disappointed. My desire died.

I love Hugo passionlessly, but tenderness is a strong tie, too. I will never leave him while he wants me. I believe that this passion for Henry will be burned out.

It is for the men who are not primarily physical that I am the essential woman, men like Hugo, Eduardo, even Allendy. Henry can do without me. Yet it is extraordinary to see how I have changed him, how he has become whole, how he rarely attacks windmills and rails illogically now. It is I who cannot live altogether without Henry. I have changed, too. I feel restless, spirited, adventurous. To be absolutely truthful, I hope secretly to meet someone else, to go on living as I am living, sensually. I have erotic imaginings. I do not want solitude, introspection, work. I want pleasure.

These days I occupy myself with frivolities. I serve the goddess of beauty, hoping she may grant me gifts. I work for a dazzling skin, vibrant hair, good health. True, I have no new clothes, because of Henry, but that doesn't matter. I have dyed and altered and rearranged things. On Monday I'm going to risk an operation which will forever efface the humorous tilt of my nose.

After a night together, Henry and I couldn't separate. I had promised to go home Sunday and spend the evening with Eduardo. But Henry said he would come to Louveciennes with me, whatever happened. I shall never forget that day and night. The maids were out; we had the house to ourselves. Henry explored it and enjoyed it to the utmost. When he threw himself on our big soft bed, the voluptuousness of it affected him. I joined him, and he penetrated me swiftly, hungrily.

We talked, read together, danced, listened to guitar recordings. He read bits of the purple journal. If he felt the fairy-taleness of the place, I began to feel a kind of ensorcellement, too, in which Henry was an extraordinary being, a saint, a stupendous master of words, with a dazzling mind. I am astonished by his sensitiveness. He wept as he watched me listening to the records; and he refused to read on in the journal, upset by its too intimate revelations—Henry, who holds nothing sacred.

Eduardo came at four o'clock and we let him ring the bell. Henry was enjoying it, but not I. "You're too human," he said, adding, "Now I know how you will feel about me when you put me in the same situation." Henry and I lying in bed, and Eduardo ringing the bell, walking away, and trying again a half hour later.

At half past one Monday Henry left me, thinking I was leaving that night for a vacation. At two o'clock I was at the clinic. I was amazed at my going there, all alone, to take a great risk with my face. I lay on the operating table aware of every gesture of the surgeon. I was at once calm and frightened. I had told nobody about this. My sense of solitude was immense, and with it I felt a sureness which comes to me at all big moments. It carried me through. If the operation failed and my face were marred, I even planned to disappear completely, never see loved ones again. Then came the moment when I saw my nose in the mirror, blood-stained and straight—Greek! Afterwards, bandages, swelling, a painful night, dreams. Would my nostrils ever quiver again?

In the morning the nurse brings me writing paper stamped with the name of the clinic. This suggests an idea. I write to Eduardo, in a faltering hand, that I went to the country, took cocaine and was brought to the hospital because I would not awaken. I play with the idea, chuckling as I write. To make life more interesting. To imitate literature, which is a hoax.

What you imagine is something you want. How would it have been, that day and night in Louveciennes alone with June, if there had been cocaine?

I am home, haunted by the wonder of the hours with Henry and by a belated horror of the clinic. My nose is heavy but beautiful.

I put off seeing Allendy until I am presentable. He tells me he has seen Eduardo and that he is very unhappy. I also want Allendy to believe the cocaine story.

There is sunshine on the bed but no feeling of sacrilege because Henry has slept here. It seems natural to me. The house is in order. My trunk is packed and in the entrance. I have Austrian money in my bag and a ticket for Innsbruck.

Henry was in despair the day after our talk, which was supposed to settle everything. We decided we should not run away together. I told him sadly, "You will lose me soon because you don't love me enough." But we are not there yet.

As my passion spreads, so does my tenderness for Hugo. The more distance I create between our two bodies, the more exotic to me his perfection, his goodness, the more keen my gratitude, the more aware I am that he, among all of us, knows best how to love. While he is traveling and I sit alone I do not feel bound to him, I do not imagine myself at his side, I do not wish for him, yet he has given me the most precious of all gifts, and when I think of him I see a vastly generous, warm man who has kept me from misery, suicide, and madness.

Madness. It would be easy for me to again feel the mood I had aboard the ship to New York when I wanted to drown myself. When I write Eduardo my imaginary letter, I say, "I am glad to have escaped the inferno for twenty-four hours of dreams." I mean this. My attraction to drugs is based on an immense desire to annihilate awareness. When I left Henry the other day, I knew so deeply I was leaving him that I could easily have turned to the taxi driver and ordered him to drive me straight into the Seine.

What I invented for Eduardo will happen someday. How long I will be able to bear the awareness of living depends on my work. Work has been my only stabilizer. The journal is a product of my disease, perhaps an accentuation and exaggeration of it. I speak of relief when I write; perhaps, but it is also an engraving of pain, a tattooing of myself.

Henry thinks the journal becomes important only when I write truths, like the details of my deceptions.

It seems to me that I follow only the most accessible thread. Three or four threads may be agitated, like telegraph wires, at the same time, and if I were to tap them all I would reveal such a mixture of innocence and duplicity, generosity and calculation, fear and courage. I cannot tell the whole truth simply because I would have to write four journals at once. I often would have to retrace my steps, because of my vice for embellishment.

Hotel Achenseehof, Tirol. Last night in bed I stretched out my hand desolately and wished to touch that ever lively, sensual Henry. I was sorry when he confessed he had written me a passionate letter from Dijon and then destroyed it because my letter contained some allusion to his hypersexuality, which I had not meant as a reproach, but which he took as one.

Oh, to sleep until I am whole again, to awaken free and light. The idea of the many letters I must write distresses me. Even to Henry I have only sent a small note. Mountains, heavy clouds, mists, quilts, blankets, and me, lying still as a dormouse. Nose normal. I hide my journal in the stove, with the ashes.

For Henry, I awoke and wrote a letter. I awoke to remember my dream: June had arrived. She came to see me before seeing Henry, again looking sullen and indifferent, as in other dreams. I was asleep. She awoke me with a kiss but began immediately to tell me how disappointed she was in me and to criticize my appearance. When she said my nose was too thick, I explained to her about the operation. Then I immediately regretted it because I realized she would tell Henry. I told her that I realized quite well she was more beautiful than I. She asked me to masturbate her. I did so very skillfully and experienced the sensation as if I were doing it to myself. She was grateful for the pleasure and left thanking me. "Now I am going to see Henry," she said.

Letter to Henry: "Last night I wondered how I could show you, by what it would cost me most to do, that I love you; and I could only think of sending you money to spend on a woman. I thought of the Negress. I like her because at least I can feel my own softness melting into her. Please don't go to too cheap, too ordinary a woman. And then don't tell me about it, since I am sure you have already done it. Let me believe I have given it to you."

At the same time with what joy I receive Hugo here. And I have found great pleasure, even frenzy in his love-making. Somehow, in a place like this, I cannot miss Henry, because Henry doesn't belong with mountains, lakes, health, solitude, sleep. Hugo triumphs here, with his very beautiful legs in Tyrolean shorts. I rest here with him, and my life in Paris with Henry is like my night dreams.

Hugo and I take up our tenderness and teasing. A week away from me matures him. I believe we cannot mature together. Together we are soft, weak, young. Depending on each other too much. Together we live in an unreal world. And we live in the outside world, as Hugo says, only because we have this one, ours, to fall back on.

He was distressed by my perfect nose. "But I loved that funny little tilt. I don't like to see you change." Finally I convinced him of the aesthetic progress. I wonder what Henry will say.

In a way I dread receiving a letter from him. It will bring fever. I have fallen back on the security of Hugo's devotion. I rest on his big hairy chest. Occasionally I get a little bored and impatient, but I do not show it. We are happy together over little things. People take us, as always, for honeymooners.

What I wonder about now is whether I stay in Hugo's world because I lack courage to venture out completely, or is it that I have not yet loved anyone enough to want to give up my life with Hugo? If he were to die, I would not go to Henry; that is clear to me.

I feel great joy at receiving a long letter from Henry. I realize that he and June have made Dostoevsky alive and terrible to me. At some moments I melt with gratitude at the thought of what Henry has given me, in just being what he is; at others, I am in despair over the liberated instincts which make him such a bad friend. I remember that he showed more hurt vanity than love when the Hungarian tried to put his hands under my dress that night at the Select. "What did he think I was, a fool?" When drunk, he is capable of anything. Now he has his head shaved like a convict's, in self-abasement. His love of June is self-laceration. In the end, all I know is that he has fecundated me in more than one way and that I will have few lovers as interesting as Henry.

As we again begin our duel of letters—mad, merry, free letters—I feel a physical, gnawing pain at his absence. It looks to me today that Henry is going to be a part of my life for many years even if he is only my lover for a few months. A snapshot of him, with his heavy mouth open, moves me. I quickly start thinking about a lamp that will be better for his eyes, become concerned over his vacation. It makes me acutely happy that he has finished rewriting his second book within the last two months, that he is so energetic and productive. And what do I miss? His voice, his hands, his body, his tenderness, his bearishness, his goodness and deviltry. As he says, "June has never been able to discover whether I am a saint or a devil." I don't know either.

At the same time I find plenty of love to give Hugo. I marvel at this, when we are acting like lovers, cursing the twin beds and sleeping in great discomfort in a too small bed, holding hands over the dinner table, kissing in the boat. It is easy to love and there are so many ways to do it.

When I ask Henry what stopped him from reading the rest of my purple journal, he answers: "I don't know any more than you why I stopped reading at a certain point. You may be sure I regret it. I can only say that it was an impersonal sadness, things turning out badly not because of evil or maliciousness but through a sort of inherent fatality. Making even the most cherishable and sacred things seem so illusory, unstable, transitory. If you substituted *X* for a certain character, it would be just the same. As a matter of fact, perhaps I was substituting myself."

No one can help weeping over the destruction of the "ideal marriage." But I don't weep any more. I have exhausted my scruples. Hugo has the most beautiful nature in the world, and I love him, but I also love other men. He lies a yard away from me while I write this, and I feel innocent.

I live in his kingdom. Peace. Simplicity. Tonight we were talking about evil, and I realized that he lives in complete security about me. He cannot ever imagine that . . . whereas I can so easily imagine. Is he more innocent than I am? Or does one trust when one's self is so integral?

The more I read Dostoevsky the more I wonder about June and Henry and whether they are imitations. I recognize the same phrases, the same heightened language, almost the same actions. Are they literary ghosts? Do they have souls of their own?

I remember a moment when I allowed myself to feel petty resentment for Henry. It was a few days after he had told me about being with the whores. He was to meet me at Fraenkel's to talk over the possibility of helping him publish his book. I felt very hard and cynical. I resented being looked upon as the wife of a banker who could protect a writer. I resented my tremendous anxiety, my wakeful nights, turning over ways and means of helping Henry. He suddenly seemed to me a parasite, a tremendously voracious egoist. Before he arrived I talked with Fraenkel, told him it was impossible and why. Fraenkel felt so much pity for Henry; I, none. Then Henry himself appeared. He was so carefully dressed for me, showing me his new suit, new hat and shirt. He was carefully shaved. I don't know why this infuriated me. I did not welcome him very warmly. I went on talking about Fraenkel's work. Henry felt that something was wrong and asked, "Have I come too early?" Finally he mentioned our going to dinner. I said that I couldn't go. Hugo had not left for London as I had expected he would. I had to take the seven-thirty train home. I looked at Henry's face. It gave me pleasure to see he was fearfully disappointed. I left them.

But I was very unhappy immediately afterwards. All my tenderness returned. I was afraid I had hurt him. I wrote him a note. The next day Hugo was gone, and I went to him immediately. That night we were so contented together that, falling asleep, Henry said, "This is heaven!"

## *AUGUST*

When I read Henry's ardent love letters, I am not stirred. I am not impatient to return to him. His defects stand in the foreground. Perhaps I have simply swung back to Hugo. I don't know. I am aware of a tremendous distance between us. And it is difficult for me to write lovingly. I feel insincere. I evade the issue. I write less than I should. I have to force myself to write at all. What has happened?

Hugo is surprised because I am so restless. I smoke, get up, move about. I cannot bear my own company. I have not learned yet to replace introspection by thinking. I could meditate on Spengler, for instance, but in ten minutes I am again devouring myself. As Gide says, introspection falsifies everything. Perhaps it estranges me from Henry. I need his voice and his caresses. He writes a beautiful letter about our last days in Clichy, Henry desiring me, lost without me.

Yet it is impossible for me to desire him in Hugo's presence. Hugo's laughter, Hugo's devotion paralyzes me. Finally I write to him, hinting at all this. But as soon as I have mailed the letter, the artificially pent-up feelings overwhelm me. I write him a mad note.

The next morning I receive an enormous letter from him. The very touch of it moves me. "When you return I am going to give you one literary fuck fest—that means fucking and talking and talking and fucking. Anaïs, I am going to open your very groins. God forgive me if this letter is ever opened by mistake. I can't help it. I want you. I love you. You're food and drink to me, the whole bloody machinery as it were. Lying on top of you is one thing, but getting close to you is another. I feel close to you, one with you, you're mine whether it is acknowledged or not. Every day I wait now is torture. I am counting them slowly, painfully. But make it as soon as you can. I need you. God, I want to see you in Louveciennes, see you in that golden light of the window, in your Nile green dress and your face pale, a frozen pallor as of the night of the concert. I love you as you are. I love your loins, the golden pallor, the slope of your buttocks, the warmth inside you, the juices of you. Anaïs, I love you so much, so much! I am getting tongue-tied. I am sitting here writing you with a tremendous erection. I can feel your soft mouth closing over me, your leg clutching me tight, see you again in the kitchen here lifting your dress and sitting on top of me and the chair riding around over the kitchen floor, going thump, thump."

I answer in the same tone, enclose my mad note, send a telegram. Oh, there is no fighting against Henry's invasion of me.

Hugo is reading. I bend over him and pour out love, a love which is acutely penitent. Hugo gasps, "I swear I could never find such joy in anyone but you. You're everything to me."

I have a sleepless night, with nerve-wracking pain, thinking of Jung's wise words: "Let things happen." The next day I slowly pack, dreaming of Henry. He is food and drink to me. How could I, even for a few days, swing away from him? If Hugo would not laugh like that, like a child, if his warm, furry hands would not reach out constantly for me, if he would not lean over to give chocolate to a black Scotch terrier, if he would not turn that finely chiseled face to me, saying, "Pussywillow, do you love me?"

Meanwhile it is Henry who leaps in my body. I feel the spurt of him, his thumping and pushing. Monday night is intolerably far off.

The length of his letters, twenty and thirty pages, is symbolical of his bigness. His torrent lashes me. I desire to be only a woman. Not to write books, to face the world directly, but to live by literary blood transfusion. To stand behind Henry, feeding him. To rest from self-assertion and creation.

Mountaineers. Smoke. Tea. Beer. The radio. My head floats away from my body, suspended midair in the smoke of Tyrolean pipes. I see frog eyes, straw hair, mouths like open pocketbooks, pig noses, heads like billiard balls, monkey hands with ham-colored palms. I begin to laugh, as if I were drunk, and say Henry words: "cripes," "screw," and Hugo gets angry. I am silent and cold. My head floats back. I cry. Hugo, who has been trying to tune himself to my gaiety, now observes the swift transition and is baffled.

I increasingly experience this monstrous deformation of reality. I spent a day in Paris before leaving for Austria. I rented a room to rest in because I had not slept the night before, a small attic room with dormer windows. As I lay there I had the sensation of all connections breaking, I parted from each being I loved, carefully and completely. I remembered Hugo's last glance from the train, Joaquin's pale face and fraternal kiss, Henry's last milky kiss, his last words—"Is everything all right?" which he says when he is embarrassed and wants to say something deeper.

I parted from them all exactly as I parted from my

grandmother in Barcelona when I was a child. I could have died in a small hotel room, dispossessed of my loves and my belongings, not registered in the hotel book. Yet I knew that if I stayed in that room a few days, living on the money Hugo had given me for my trip, an entirely new life could begin. It was the terror of this new life more than the terror of dying which roused me. I threw myself out of bed and ran away from the room that was growing around me like a web, seizing upon my imagination, gnawing into my memory so that I would forget in five minutes who I was and whom I loved.

It was room number thirty-five, from which I might have awakened the next morning a whore, or a madwoman, or what is worse, perhaps, altogether unchanged.

I am happy with today, so I entertain myself by imagining sorrow. What would I feel if Henry were to die, and I heard, in some corner of Paris, the accordion I used to hear in Clichy? But then, I have wanted to suffer. I cling to Henry for the same reason that June clings to him.

And Allendy?

I need his help again, certainly.

Paris. I needed nobody's help. Only to see Henry again at the station, to kiss him, to eat with him, to hear him talk, in between more kisses.

I wanted to make him jealous, but I am too faithful, so I dug into the past and created a story. I wrote a false letter from John Erskine, tore it up and pasted it together again. When Henry arrived at Louveciennes, the fire was devouring all the rest of John's letters. Later in the evening I showed Henry the fragment which had escaped destruction, supposedly, through its insertion in the journal. Henry was so jealous that on the second page of his new book he had to throw a bomb at John's writing. Childish games. And meanwhile I am as faithful as a slave—in feeling, in thought, in flesh. My lack of a past now seems good. It has preserved my ardor. I have come to Henry like a virgin, fresh, unused, believing, eager.

Henry and I are one, lying soldered for four days. Not with bodies but with flames. God, let me thank somebody. No drug could be more potent. Such a man. He has sucked my life into his body as I have sucked his. This is the apotheosis of my life. Henry, Louveciennes, solitude, summer heat, quivering smells, chanting breezes, and, within us, tornadoes and exquisite calms.

First I dressed up in my Maja costume—flowers, jewelry, make-up, hardness, brilliancy. I was angry, full of hatred. I had arrived from Austria the night before, and we had slept in a hotel room. I thought he had betrayed me. He swears not. It does not matter. I hated him because I loved him as I have never loved anyone.

I stand at the door when he comes in, hands on my hips. I look out of a savage self. Henry approaches, dazed, and does not recognize me until he comes very near and I smile and speak to him. He cannot believe it. He thinks I have gone mad. Then before he has quite awakened I take him to my room. There, on the grate in the fireplace, is a large photograph of John and his letters. They are burning. I smile. Henry sits on the couch. "You frighten me, Anaïs," he says. "You are so different, and so strange. So dramatic." I sit on the floor between his knees. "I hate you, Henry. That story about [Osborn's girl friend] Jeanne . . . You lied to me."

He answers me so gently that I believe him. And if I

do not believe him, it does not matter. All the treacheries in the world do not matter. John is burnt away. The present is magnificent. Henry asks me to undress. Everything is shed but the black lace mantilla. He asks me to keep it on and lies on the bed, watching me. I stand before the mirror, shedding carnations, earrings. He looks through the lace at my body.

The next day I run about the house cooking. Suddenly I love cooking, for Henry. I cook richly, with infinite care. I enjoy seeing him eat, eating with him.

We sit in the garden, in our pajamas, drunk on the air, the caresses of the swaying trees, the songs of birds, attentive dogs licking our hands. Henry's desire is always coursing. I am ploughed, open.

At night, books, talk, passion. As he pours his passion into me I feel that I become beautiful. I show him a hundred faces. He watches me. It all passes like a procession, up to this morning's climax, before he leaves me, when he sees a burnt face, heavy, sensual, Moorish.

There was a storm last night. Marble-sized hail. Sea fury of the trees. Henry sits in an armchair and asks, "Are we going to read Spengler now?" He sits purring like a cat. He has the yawn of a tiger, all the jungle cries of contentment. His voice vibrates in his stomach. I have put my head there and listened, as against an organ. I am lying on the bed. I wear a lace dress, nothing else, because it gives him pleasure to look at me. "Now," he says, "you look like an Ingres." I cannot bear the space between us. I sit on the floor. He caresses my hair. He gives me winged kisses on the eyes. He is all tenderness, thoughtfulness.

Sensuality was exhausted in the afternoon. But he looks

down and shows me his lanced desire again. He himself is surprised: "I love you; I wasn't even thinking of fucking. But your touch alone . . ." I sit on his knees. And then we sink into that drunkenness of sucking. For a long, long time, just tongues, eyes closed. Then the penis and the yielding walls of flesh, clutching, opening, beating. We roll on the floor until I cannot bear any more, and I lie still, saying no. But when he helps me off with my dress and embraces me from behind, I leap up to him, all aflame again. What sleep afterwards, lost, dreamless.

"When it comes to sensuality," Henry says, "you are almost more sensual than June. Because she may be a splendid animal when you hold her in your arms, but afterwards, nothing. She is cold, hard, even. Your sex permeates your mind, runs into your head afterwards. Everything you think is warm. You are constantly warm. The only thing is that you have the body of a girl. But what power you have to keep the illusion. You know how men feel after they have had a woman. They want to kick her off the bed. With you it remains as heightened afterwards as before. I can never get enough of you. I want to marry you and return to New York with you."

We talk about June. I laugh at his efforts to break with her, in his own mind. We are two against her, two in harmony, in love, in profound fusion, yet she is stronger. I know better than he knows. He has admitted so much against her and in favor of me. But I smile with a wisdom rooted in doubt. I want no more than what I have been given these past days, hours so fecund that a lifetime of remembrance could not exhaust them, wear them thin.

"This is no ordinary garden," Henry says at Louveciennes. "It is mysterious, significant. There is mentioned in a Chinese book a celestial garden, a kingdom, suspended between heaven and earth: this is it."

Over all this hangs the joyous probability that his book *Tropic of Cancer* will be published. When I am alone, I hear him talk. Like Lawrence's snake, his thinking comes from the bowels of the earth. Someone has compared him to an artist who was known as the "cunt painter."

He is so much clearer to me. Towards certain women, he shows toughness and hard-boiledness; towards others, a naïve romanticism. At first June appeared like an angel to him, out of her dance-hall background, and he offered her a fool's faith (June asserts that in nine years she has had only two lovers, and until now he has believed that). I see him now as a man who can be enslaved by wonder, a man who can believe anything of woman. I see him sought out by women (this has been true of all the women he has loved seriously). It is the women who take the initiative in sexual contact. It was June who put her head on his shoulder and invited a kiss the first night they met. His toughness is external only. But like all soft people he can commit the most dastardly acts at certain moments, prompted by his own weakness, which makes him a coward. He leaves a woman in the cruelest manner because he cannot face the breaking of the connection.

His sensuality, too, directs actions of the most scoundrelly nature. It is only by understanding the violence of his instincts that one can believe any man could be so ruthless. His life rushes onward in such torrential rhythm that, as he said about June, only angels or devils can catch the tempo of it.

We have been separated for three days. It is unnatural.

We had acquired small habits, sleeping together, awaking together, singing in the bathroom, adjusting our likes and dislikes to fit one another. I am so hungry for the little intimacies. And he?

I feel a powerful sense of life unimaginable to either Hugo or Eduardo. My breasts are swollen. I hold my legs wide apart in love-making instead of, as before, closed. I have enoyed sucking to the point of almost coming to a climax while doing it. I have finally eliminated my childish self.

I push Hugo away from me, exacerbate his desires, his terror of losing me. I talk cynically to him, taunt him, call women to his attention. There is no room in me for sadness or regrets. Men look at me and I look at them, with my being unlocked. No more veils. I want many lovers. I am insatiable now. When I weep, I want to fuck it away.

Henry comes to Louveciennes on a hot summer afternoon and lays me on the table, and then on the black carpet. He sits on the edge of my bed and looks transfigured. The scattered man, easily swayed, now collects himself to talk about his book. At this moment he is a big man. I sit and marvel at him. A moment before, flushed by drink, he was scattering his riches. The moment he crystallizes is beautiful to watch. I was slow in tuning myself to his mood. I could have fucked all afternoon. But then I also loved our transition into big talk. Our talks are wonderful, interplays, not duels but swift illuminations of one another. I can make his tentative thoughts click. He enlarges mine. I fire him. He makes me flow. There is always movement between us. And he is grasping. He takes hold of me like a prey.

Here we lie, putting order in his ideas, deciding on the

place of realistic incidents in his novels. His book swells up inside of me like my very own.

I am fascinated by the activity in his head, the surprises, the curiosity, the gusto, the amorality, the sensibilities, and the rascalities. And I loved his last letter to me: "Don't expect me to be sane any more. Don't let's be sensible. It was a marriage at Louveciennes, you can't dispute it. I came away with a piece of you sticking to me; I am walking about swimming, in an ocean of blood, your Andalusian blood, distilled and poisonous. Everything I do and say and think relates back to our marriage. I saw you as the mistress of your home, a Moor with a heavy face, a Negress with a white body, eyes all over your skin, woman, woman, woman. I can't see how I can go on living away from you—these intermissions are death. How did it seem to you when Hugo came back? Was I still there? I can't picture you moving about with him as you did with me. Legs closed. Frailty. Sweet treacherous acquiescence. Bird docility. You became a woman with me. I was almost terrified by it. You are not just thirty years old—you are a thousand years old.

"Here I am back and still smoldering with passion, like wine smoking. Not a passion any longer for flesh, but a complete hunger for you, a devouring hunger. I read the papers about suicides and murder and I understand it all thoroughly. I feel murderous, suicidal.

"I still hear you singing in the kitchen . . . a sort of inharmonic, monotonous Cuban wail. I know you're happy in the kitchen and the meal you're cooking is the best meal we ever ate together. I know you would scald yourself and not complain. I feel the greatest peace and joy sitting in the dining room listening to your rustling about, your dress like the goddess Indra studded with a thousand eyes. Anaïs, I only thought I loved you before, it was nothing like this certainty that's in me now. Was all this so wonderful because it was brief and stolen? Were we acting for each other, to each other? Was I less I, or more I, and you less or more you? Is it madness to believe that this could go on? When and where would the drab moments begin? I study you so much to discover the possible flaws, the weak points, the danger zones. I don't find them—not any. That means I am in love, blind, blind, blind. To be blind forever!

"I picture you playing the records over and over—Hugo's records. *Parlez moi d'amour.* The double life, double taste, double joy and misery. How you must be furrowed and ploughed by it. I know all that but I can't do anything to prevent it. I wish indeed it were me who had to endure it. I know now your eyes are wide open. Certain things you will never believe any more, certain gestures you will never repeat, certain sorrows, misgivings, you will never again experience. A kind of white criminal fervor in your tenderness and cruelty. Neither remorse nor vengeance, neither sorrow nor guilt. A living it out, with nothing to save you from the abysm but a high hope, a faith, a joy that you tasted, that you can repeat when you will.

"While it thunders and lightnings I lie on the bed and go through wild dreams. We're in Seville, and then in Fez, and then in Capri, and then in Havana. We're journeying constantly, but there is always a machine and books, and your body is always close to me and the look in your eyes never changes. People are saying we will be miserable, we will regret, but we are happy, we are laughing always, we are singing. We are talking Spanish and French and Arabic and Turkish. We are admitted everywhere and they strew our path with flowers. I say this is a wild dream—but it is this dream I want to realize. Life and literature combined; love, the dynamo; you, with your chameleon's soul, giving me a thousand loves, being anchored always in no matter what storm, home wherever we are. In the mornings, continuing where we left off. Resurrection after resurrection. You asserting yourself, getting the rich varied life you desire; and the more you assert yourself the more you want me, need me. Your voice getting hoarser, deeper, your eyes blacker, your blood thicker, your body fuller. A voluptuous servility and tyrannical necessity. More cruel now than before—consciously, wilfully cruel. The insatiable delight of experience . . ."

It is ironical that the deepest experience of my life has come to me when I am famished not for profundity but for pleasure. Sensualism consumes me. What is deep and serious I look at with less intensity, but it is that which fascinates Henry, the depths he has not yet lived out in love.

Is this the high moment? If only June would return now, to leave in Henry and me that taste of the climax, never to be reached again, never to be annihilated.

Henry said, "I want to leave a scar on the world."

I write to him how I feel about his book. Then: "There will never be darkness because in both of us there is always movement, renewal, surprises. I have never known stagnation. Not even introspection has been a still experience. . . . If this is so, then think what I find in you, who are a gold mine. Henry, I love you with a realization, a knowledge of you, which takes in all of you, with the strength of my mind and imagination, besides that of my body. I love you in such a way that June can return, our love can be destroyed, and yet nothing can sever the fusion that has been. . . . I think today of what you said: 'I want to leave a scar on the world.' I will help you. I want to leave the feminine scar."

Today, I would follow Henry to the end of the world. What saves me is only that we are both penniless.

Lucidity: There is in Henry a lack of feeling (not a lack of passion or emotion) that is betrayed by his emphasis on fucking and talking. When he speaks about other women, what he remembers of them are the defects, the sensual characteristics, or the disputes. The rest is either absent or implied. I don't know yet. But feelings are fetters. Henry is not to be worshiped as a human being, but as a genius-monster. He may be soft-hearted but only indiscriminately so. He gave Paulette, out of generosity, the pair of stockings I had left in his drawer, my best pair, while I was wearing mended stockings so I could save to buy gifts for him. The money I sent him from Austria, for a woman, he spent on records for me. Yet he stole 500 francs from Osborn's legacy to his girl friend when Osborn left for America. He gives my dog half his steak, yet he keeps the surplus change given to him by a taxi driver. These sudden acts of callousness, which also appear in June, bewilder me and I expect to suffer from them, though Henry swears he could never act thus with me. And so far I cannot see anything in his treatment of me but the utmost delicacy. He has not hesitated to fling out cruel truths—he is fully aware of my defects—but at the same time he succumbs to the spell, the softness. Why do I trust him so, believe in him, have no fear of him? Perhaps it's as much of a mistake as it is for Hugo to trust me.

I crave Henry, only Henry. I want to live with him, be free with him, suffer with him. Phrases from his letters haunt me. Yet I have doubts about our love. I fear my impetuosity. Everything is in danger. All that I have created. I follow Henry the writer with my writer's soul, I enter into his feelings as he wanders through the streets, I partake of his curiosities, his desires, his whores, I think his thoughts. Everything in us is married.

Henry, you are not lying to me; you are all I feel you are. Don't deceive me. My love is too new, too absolute, too deep.

As Hugo and I walked tonight from the top of the hill I saw Paris lying in a heat haze. Paris. Henry. I did not think of him as a man, but as life.

Perfidiously, I said to Hugo, "It is so fearfully hot. Couldn't we ask Fred and Henry and Paulette for a visit overnight?"

This, because I received this morning the first pages of his new book, stupendous pages. He is doing his best writing now, fevered yet cohesive. Every word now hits the mark. The man is whole, strong, as he never was. I want to breathe his presence for a few hours, feed him, cool him, fill him with that heavy breath of earth and trees which whip his blood. God, this is like living every moment in an orgasm, with only pauses between plunges.

I want Henry to know this: that I can subordinate the jealous grasping of woman to a passionate devotion to the writer. I feel a proud servitude. There is splendor in his writing, a splendor which transfigures everything he touches.

Last night Henry and Hugo talked for each other, admired each other. Hugo's generosity blossomed. When we were in our bedroom, I compensated him. At breakfast, in the garden, he read Henry's latest pages. His enthusiasm flared. I took advantage of it to suggest we open our home to him, the great writer. Holding my hand, weighing my words of reassurance—"Henry interests me as a writer, that's all"—he assented to all I wanted. I go to the gate to see him off. He is happy just to be loved, and I am astonished by my own lies, my acting.

I did not come out unscathed from the inferno of Henry's overnight visit. The development of those two days was intricate. Just as I was beginning to act like June, "capable of worship, devotion, but also of the greatest callousness to obtain what she wants," as Henry had said, he fell into a sentimental mood.

It was after Hugo had gone off to work. Henry said, "He is so sensitive, one ought not to hurt a man like that." This roused a storm in me. I left the table and went to my room. He came to watch me weeping, and he was glad to see me weep, showing the absence of callousness. But I became tense, poisonous.

When Hugo returned in the evening, Henry began again to listen to him attentively, to speak his language, to talk gravely, ponderously. The three of us were sitting in the garden.

Our talk was at first desultory, until Henry began to ask questions on psychology. (Sometime during the day, probably out of jealousy of June, I had said something which had aroused Henry's jealousy of Allendy.) Everything I had read the previous year, all my talks with Allendy, my own broodings on the subject, all this gushed out of me with amazing energy and clarity.

Suddenly Henry stopped me and said, "I don't trust either Allendy's ideas or your thinking, Anaïs. Why, I only saw him once. He is a brutish, sensual man, lethargic, with a fund of fanaticism in the back of his eyes. And you—why, you put things so clearly and beautifully to me—so crystal clear—it looks simple and true. You are so terribly nimble, so clever. I distrust your cleverness. You make a wonderful pattern, everything is in its place, it looks convincingly clear, too clear. And meanwhile, where are you? Not on the clear surface of your ideas, but you have already sunk deeper, into darker regions, so that one only thinks one has been given all your thoughts, one only imagines you have emptied yourself in that clarity. But there are layers and layers—you're bottomless, unfathomable. Your clearness is deceptive. You're the thinker who arouses most confusion in me, most doubt, most disturbance."

This is the outline of his attack. It was set forth with extraordinary irritation and vehemence. Hugo added quietly, "One feels that she gives you a neat pattern and then slips out of it herself and laughs at you."

"Exactly," said Henry.

I laughed. I realized that the sum total of his criticism was flattering, and I was joyful at having irritated and puzzled him, but then I felt raked by bitterness at the idea that he should suddenly fight me. Yes, war was inevitable. He and Hugo continued talking while I was trying to toughen myself. It was too unexpected for me. Henry's admiration of Hugo, too, was puzzling, after all he had said.

I remember thinking, now the two slow-minded ones, the ponderous German and the unflashy Scotchman, have found solidarity against my nimbleness. Well, I will be more nimble and more treacherous. Henry identifies himself with Hugo, the husband, as I identify with June. June and I would have flagellated the two men with pleasure.

What a night! How one can go to sleep poisoned, heavy with tears, with rage still smoking. Go ahead, Henry, pity Hugo, because I am going to deceive him a hundred times. I would deceive the greatest and finest man on earth. The ideal of faithfulness is a joke. Remember what I taught you tonight: psychology tries to reestablish the basis of life not on ideals but on sincerity with one's self. Hit, hit all you want to. I'll hit back.

I went to sleep full of hatred and love for Henry. Hugo awakened me later with caresses and was trying to make love to me. Half asleep, I pushed him away, without feeling. I found excuses for it afterwards.

In the morning I awoke heavy, brittle. Henry sat in the garden. He had stayed on to talk. He was worried about the previous night. I just listened. He told me that he acted in his usual way. He said and did things he did not mean. "Did not mean?" I repeat. Yes, he had been carried away by his intention to dissimulate his love for me. He did not admire Hugo as much as he said, not nearly. The truth was he had been swept off his feet by my tirade. He wanted to embrace me. He had never seen me go to the bottom of a subject like that. Most of my thinking was like shorthand to him. He had fought against a feeling of admiration, jealousy of Allendy, also a perverse hatred of the person who can tell him something new. I had opened worlds to him.

It occurred to me that he might be acting, one comedy following another, that now, for some reason, he was playing with me. I told him so. He said quietly, "So help me God, Anaïs, I never lie to you. I cannot help it if you will not believe me."

His explanation sounded weak. What need to dissimulate? I was taking care of Hugo's blindness. Was it not, rather, that he enjoyed difficulties, that our last week of interpenetration, harmony, confidence, now brought on his usual perverse craving for discord. "No, Anaïs, I don't want war. But I lost my confidence. You said that Allendy . . ." Oh, Allendy. So I had wounded him, started him off. Jealousy inspired him. I said, "I will not deprive you of the pleasure you find in jealousy by answering your questions."

Then he said something which moved me. It began: "What a man wants [what a man wants!] is to believe that a woman can love him so much that no other man can interest her. I know that's impossible. I know that every joy carries its own tragedy." Then we could again have openness? If I were truthful? "Listen," I said awkwardly, "what a man wants is what I have given you to date, with an absolutism you could never imagine."

"That is wonderful," he said, very tenderly, dazed. Our first duel had come to an end.

There was a great deal of insanity in all this, more in his explanations than in his initial actions. Was this really a scene of jealousy or the first expression of his instability in human relationships, his unaccountableness? For once I stand before a nature more complicated than my own. It may be that we have become more interesting to each other at the expense of trust. He is glad to have seen me, like an instrument, giving out all its range of sounds. Humanly, I have lost something. Faith, perhaps. In place of that blind openness to him, I summon my cleverness.

Later, when he weeps while telling me his father is starving, I sit paralyzed and my pity does not flow. I would give anything to know if he has sent his father some of the money I have given him, starving himself to do so. All I need to know is: Can he lie to me? I have been able to both love him and lie to him. I see myself wrapped in lies, which do not seem to penetrate my soul, as if they are not really a part of me. They are like costumes. When I loved Henry, as I did those four days, I loved him with a naked body that had shed its costumes and forgotten its lies. Perhaps it is not so with Henry. But love, in all this, trembles like a spear in a sand dune. To lie, of course, is to engender insanity. The minute I step into the cavern of my lies I drop into darkness.

I have had no time to write down the lies. I want to begin. I suppose I have not wanted to look at them. If unity is impossible to the writer who is a "sea of spiritual protoplasm, capable of flowing in all directions, of engulfing every object in its path, of trickling into every crevice, of filling every mold," as Aldous Huxley said in *Point Counter Point*, at least truth is possible, or sincerity about one's insincerities. It is true, as Allendy said, that what my mind engenders fictionally I enrich with true feeling, and I am taken in, in good faith, by my own inventions. He called me *"le plus sympathique"* of the insincere ones. Yes, I am the noblest of the hypocrites. My motives, psychoanalysis reveals, possess the smallest degree of malevolence. It is not to hurt anyone that I let my lover sleep in my husband's bed. It is because I have no sense of sacredness. If Henry himself were more courageous, I would have given Hugo a sleeping potion during Henry's visit so I could have gone and slept with him. He was too timid, however, to steal a kiss. Only when Hugo had left did he throw me on the ivy leaves, in the back of the garden.

I once spent four days with a passionate human lover. That day I was fucked by a cannibal. I lay exhaling human feelings, and I knew at that precise moment he was nonhuman. The writer is clothed in his humanity, but it is only a disguise.

My talk the night before about sincerity, about dependence on one another, about the flow of confidence such as one cannot have even with the being one loves, had hit the mark.

Perhaps my desire to preserve the magnificence of those four days with Henry is a wasted effort. Perhaps, like Proust, I am incapable of movement. I choose a point in space and revolve around it, as I revolved for two years around John. Henry's movement is a constant hammering to draw sparks, unconcerned about the mutilations involved.

I later asked him, "When your feeling for June comes back, does it, even for a moment, alter our relationship? Does our connection break? Do your feelings flow back to a source love or flow into two directions?" Henry said it was a double flow. That he had been carrying in his head a letter to June: "I want you back, but you must know that I love Anaïs. You must accept that."

The estrangement between Hugo's body and mine will drive me mad. His constant caresses are intolerable to me. Up to now I could steel myself, find a tender pleasure in his closeness. But today I might be living with a stranger. I hate it when he sits near me, running his hands up my legs and around my breasts. This morning when he touched me, I jumped away angrily. He was terribly taken aback. I can't bear his desire. I want to run away. My body is dead to his. What is my life going to be now? How can I go on pretending? My excuses are so futile, so feeble—bad health, bad moods. They are transparent lies. I will hurt him. How I crave my liberty!

During our siesta Hugo tried to possess me again. I closed my eyes and let go, but without pleasure. If it is true that this year I have reached new peaks of joy, it is also true that I have never reached such black depths. Tonight I am afraid of myself. I could leave Hugo this minute and become a derelict. I would sell myself, take drugs, die with voluptuous pleasure.

I said to Hugo, who was boasting of being a little drunk, "Well, tell me something about yourself that I do not know, tell me something new. You have nothing to confess? And you couldn't invent something?"

He did not get my meaning. Nor did he get my meaning when I jumped away from his caresses. Sweet faith. To be laughed at, made use of. Why aren't you cleverer, less believing? Why don't you hit back, why have you no aberrations, no passions, no comedies to play, no cruelty?

As I was working today I realized that I had given away to Henry many of my ideas on June and that he is using them. I feel impoverished, and he knows it, because he writes me that he feels like a crook. What was left for me to do? To write as a woman and as a woman only. I worked all morning, and I still felt rich.

What Henry has asked of me is intolerable. I not only have to thrive on a half love but I have to nourish his conception of June and feed his book. As each page of it reaches me, in which he does more and more justice to her, I feel it is my vision he has borrowed. Certainly no woman was ever asked as much. Henry would not ask this of primitive June. He is testing my courage to the full. How can I extricate myself from this nightmare?

Henry has watched me for my first weakness, for the first flash of jealousy, and he has caught it, reveled in it.

Because I am a woman who understands, I am asked to understand everything, to accept everything. I will demand my dues. I want a million days like those four days with Henry, and I am going to have them even if they are not from him. I'll give Henry and June back to each other, wash my hands of all superhuman roles.

One does not learn to suffer less but to dodge pain. I began to think of Allendy as an escape. His ideas have been underlying many of my acts. It is he who has taught me that more than one man can understand me, that to cling is a weakness, that to suffer is unnecessary. I think my feeling for him crystallized when Henry described him in the garden that night. He spoke of him as a sensual man. I have a sharp recollection of how he looked on our last day. I was too full of Henry then to notice. The other day I wrote Allendy a very grateful letter and I ended by enclosing a partial copy of one of Henry's letters to me. It fitted in logically with what I was saying and gave proof of what, psychoanalytically, he could consider a successful piece of work. But the truth is, I hoped to make him jealous.

What I have found in Henry is unique; it cannot be repeated. But there are other experiences to be had. Yet, tonight I was planning how to improve his latest book, how to fortify him, reassure him.

But he has also fortified me, so that I now feel strength enough to do without him, if I must. I am not the slave of a childhood curse. The myth that I have sought to relive the tragedy of my childhood is now annihilated. I want a complete and equal love. I am going to run away from Henry as actively as I can.

He came yesterday. A serious, tired Henry. He had to come, he said. He had not slept for several nights, keyed up by his book. I have forgotten my sorrows. Henry is tired. He and his book must be nurtured. "What do you want, Henry? Lie on my couch. Have some wine. Yes, this is the room I have been working in. Don't kiss me just now. We'll have lunch in the garden. Yes, I have a lot to tell you, but it must all wait. I am deliberately postponing everything which might disturb the breathing of your book. It can all wait."

And then Henry, pale, intense, eyes very blue, said, "I came to tell you that while I worked on my book I realized everything between June and me had died three or four years ago. That what we lived out together the last time she was here was only an automatic continuation, like a habit, like the prolongation of an impetus which cannot come to a dead stop. Of course, it was a tremendous experience, the greatest upheaval. That is why I can write so frenziedly about it. But this is the swan song I am writing now. You must be able to differentiate between the writer's evocation of the past and his present feelings. I tell you, I love you. I want you to come away with me to Spain, on any pretext, for a few months. I dream of our working together. I want you close to me. Until things work out in such a way that I can completely protect you. I have learned a bitter lesson with June. You and June are women of such personalities that you cannot thrive on drabness, hardships. It is not your element. You are both too important. I won't ask that of you."

I sat dazed. "Certainly," he added, "I had to live through all that, but precisely because I have lived it through, I am finished with it and I can experience a new kind of love. I feel stronger than June, yet if June comes back things might start again out of a kind of fatal necessity. What I feel is that I want you to save me from June. I do not want to be diminished, humiliated, destroyed by her again. I know enough to know I want to break with her. I dread her return, the destruction of my work. I was thinking how I have absorbed your time and attention, worried you, hurt you, even; how other people's troubles are poured on you, too; how you are asked to solve problems, to help. And meanwhile there is your writing, deeper and better than anybody's, which nobody gives a goddamn about and nobody helps you to do."

At this I laughed. "But, Henry, you do give a goddamn, and besides I can wait. It is you who are behind time and must be given a chance to catch up."

I told him a little of the storm I had been through in the past days. I felt like someone condemned to die and then suddenly paroled. It didn't seem to matter any more how often June might take Henry back. At this moment he and I were indissolubly married. The fusion of our bodies that followed was almost extraneous—for the first time, only a symbol, a gesture. A fusion so swift that it seemed to take place in space, and the movements of the body followed at a slower pace.

I have written thirty pages about June in an intense and wholly imaginative manner, the best I have done so far. It is good to see all the laboratory experiments culminate in a lyrical outburst.

Last night I deeply enjoyed myself at the Grand Guignol: the convulsions of a woman tempted by passion, lying naked on a black velvet couch. A lusty woman takes her pajamas down. I felt tremendous sexual excitement.

Hugo and I visited another house, where the women were uglier than those at 32 rue Blondel. The room was lined with mirrors. The women moved like a herd of passive animals, two by two, turning to the phonograph music. Beforehand, I had been roused to high expectations. I could not believe the ugliness of the women as they came in. In my head, the dance of the naked women was still a beautiful and voluptuous orgy. As I saw the sagging breasts with their large brown leather tips, the bluish legs, the protruding stomachs, smiles with teeth missing, and that brutish mass of flesh turning lifelessly, like wooden horses of a merry-go-round, my feelings collapsed. Not even pity. Just cool observation. Again we see monotonous poses, and in between, when most uncalled for, the women kissed each other dispassionately, sexlessly. Hips, valleyed buttocks, the mysterious darkness between the legs—all exposed so meaninglessly that it took Hugo and me two days to separate the association of my body, my legs, my breasts from that troupe of turning animals. What I would like is to join them for one night, to walk naked into the room with them, to look at the men and women sitting there and to see their reaction when I appear, I and my halo of illusion.

Cruelty to Eduardo. When he has elaborated a plan of intellectual domination of his pain, I sit very near him on the couch and make him read Henry's writing, which he hates. He says I am breeding a little giant. I see him looking at my more aggressive breasts. I see him turn pale and rush away on an earlier train.

Today I almost lost my mind craving Henry. I cannot

live three days without him. Joyful, terrible slavery. Oh, to be a man, capable of satisfying one's self so easily, so indiscriminately.

I have returned, by very devious roads, to Allendy's simple statement that love excludes passion and passion love. The only time Hugo's love and mine turned to passion was during our desperate quarrels after our return from New York, and in the same way June has given Henry the maximum of passion. I could give him the maximum of love. But I refuse to because at the moment passion seems of greater value. Perhaps I am blind just now to deeper values. There was danger in my reconciliation with Henry the other day, the danger of falling in love. I should not only have let him be jealous of Allendy, but I should have deceived him with Allendy. That would have raised our love to passion. Even Henry's vocabulary changes when he writes to me or about me; his tone is less extravagant, more profound. And I am opposed to this treatment, because I myself am whipped up to a paroxysm. Nothing less than passion can satisfy me now. Yet I cannot act according to my ravings. Allendy has made me afraid of premeditated acts. My instincts lead me to love over and over again.

After a long weekend, Henry telephones that he will not come to see me until Wednesday. I had been expecting him all day. I told him I couldn't see him until Thursday, that I was working for Allendy. I wanted to hurt him. And when I mentioned our plans for Spain, he said, "Under the circumstances it is better not to go."

I knew then that he loved me only to console himself for his loss of June, to help himself to live, only for the happiness I could give him. Even the trip to Spain was planned to save himself from June, not to be with me. As soon as Allendy returns, I will give myself to him.

Hugo reads my thirty pages on June and exclaims they are good. Again I wonder if he is only half alive or simply inarticulate. I ask him this and hurt him. He makes a remarkable statement: "If this is your real self, the one you are asserting, I say it is a very hard self."

Yes. This assertion is the beginning of June, of another volcano. I have been sweetly asleep for a few centuries, and I am erupting without warning. The hardness in me, an inexhaustible amount, has slowly accumulated through the efforts I made to subdue the voraciousness of my ego. Henry is going to suffer, too. I asked him to come today.

He came immediately, on his bicycle, soft and anxious. I let him read over a long letter I wrote, containing all the things I told my journal. He did not protest. He laughed, half sadly. Then he sat on the couch, completely absorbed by the terror of knowing how easily everything could crumble. I waited, baffled by his brooding. Finally he awoke to say, "I am only what you imagine me to be." I don't know what else we said. I realized both the extent and the limits of Henry's love, of his being possessed by June against his will, just as I am, and of his loving me deeply, as I do him. When he said to me, in torment, "I need to know what you want," I told him, "Nothing more than this closeness. When all is right between us I can bear my life."

He said, "I realized that a holiday in Spain for a few months is no solution. And I know that if we took it, you would never return to Hugo. I would not let you return." I answered, "And I cannot think any further than a holiday because of Hugo." We looked at one another and knew how much each of us was paying for his weakness: he, for his slavery to passion, and I, for my slavery to pity.

The days that followed were unique, resplendent. Talk and passion, work and passion. What I need to keep, to hold warmly against my breast, are the hours in that top-floor room. Henry could not leave me. He stayed two days, which culminated in such a burst of sexual frenzy that I was left burning for long afterwards.

I have ceased worrying. I lie back and just love him, and I get such love from him as would justify my whole existence. I stutter when I mention his name. Each day he is a new man, with new depths and new sensibilities.

I received a photograph of him today. It was a strange feeling to see so clearly the full mouth, the bestial nose, the pale, Faustian eyes—that mixture of delicacy and animalism, of toughness and sensibility. I feel that I have loved the most remarkable man of our age.

Most of my life has been spent in enriching as well as I could the long, long waiting for the great events which fill me now so deeply that I am overwhelmed. Now I understand the terrific restlessness, the tragic sense of failure, the deep discontent. I was waiting. This is the hour of expansion, of true living. All the rest was a preparation. Thirty years of anguished watchfulness. And now these are the days I lived for. And to be aware of this, so fully aware, that is what is almost humanly unbearable. Human beings cannot bear the knowledge of the future. To me, the knowledge of the present is just as dazzling. To be so acutely rich *and to know it*!

Last night Hugo put his head on my knees. As I looked at him tenderly I said to myself, "How can I ever reveal to him that I no longer love him?" And what is more, I realize that I am not wholly wrapped up in Henry, that Allendy preoccupies me, that the other night I was sentimentally stirred by Eduardo's presence. The truth is that I am capricious, with sensual stirrings in many directions. I see Allendy on Thursday. I am very keen on this meeting. In imagination I have been out with him to the Russian restaurant, and he has visited me here in Louveciennes. Henry can well be jealous of Allendy. Allendy himself has freed me of the sense of guilt.

Henry was mystified by my new pages. Was it more than brocade, he asked, more than beautiful language? I was upset that he did not understand. I began to explain. Then he said, as everybody else has said, "Well, you should give a clue, you should lead up to it; we are thrown into the strangeness unexpectedly. This must be read a hundred times."

"Who is going to read it a hundred times?" I said sadly. But then I thought of *Ulysses* and the studies which accompany it. But Henry, with his characteristic thoroughness, would not stop there. He walked about and raved that I must become human and tell a human story. Here, I faced my lifelong problem. I wanted to go on in that abstract, intense way, but could anyone bear it? Hugo understood it, nonintellectually, as poetry; Eduardo, as symbolism. But for me there was meaning in those brocaded phrases.

The more I talked about my ideas, the more excited Henry became, until he began to shout that I should continue exactly in that same tone, that I was doing something unique. People would have to struggle to decipher me. He always knew I would do something unique. Besides, he said,

I owed it to the world. If I didn't do something good I should be hung; after nurturing this work with a lifetime of journal writing, the orange squeezer, where all the seeds and rinds are left behind.

He stood by the window saying, "How can I go back to Clichy now? It is like returning to a prison. This is the place where one grows, expands, deepens. How I love this solitude. How rich it is." And I stood behind him, clinging to him, saying, "Stay, stay."

And when he is here, Louveciennes is rich for me, alive. My body and mind vibrate continuously. I am not only more woman, but more writer, more thinker, more reader, more everything. My love for him creates an ambiance in which he is resplendent. He becomes ensorcelled and cannot leave until Fred telephones that there are people asking for him and mail to be read.

How extraordinarily our thinking leaps along with opposition of themes, contrasts, and fundamental accord. He mistrusts my swiftness, slows down my rhythm, and I plunge into his creativeness as into unlimited wealth. Our work is interrelated, interdependent, married. My work is the wife of his work.

Often Henry stands in the middle of my bedroom and says, "I feel as if I were the husband here. Hugo is just a charming young man whom we are very fond of."

More and more I realize that his life with June was a dangerous, shattering adventure. I understand it when he wants me to save him from June. When he begins to talk about renting a place like Louveciennes somewhere and I say, "When your book comes out, you'll send for June and do all that," he smiles sorrowfully and tells me that is not what he wants. I know it, or, rather, I know he wishes a life like mine and Hugo's were possible with June.

Last night because Henry was tired and looked for a moment less lusty, less truculent, such a tenderness for him welled in me that I almost walked over to him in front of Hugo and Mother to embrace him, to ask him to come downstairs to our big soft bed and rest. How I wanted to care for him. He was almost crying as he talked about women loving each other in the movie *Jeunes filles en uniforme*.

Then he said, in front of Mother, "I must talk to you a few minutes. I have corrected your manuscript." We went downstairs and sat on my bed. I was so moved by the work he had done. We began kissing. Tongues, hands, moisture. I bit my fingers so as not to scream.

I went upstairs, still throbbing, and talked to Mother. Henry followed, looking like a saint, creamy voiced. And I felt his presence down to my toes.

Hugo is playing and singing as he used to play and sing in Richmond Hill, fumbling, hesitating. His fingers are not skillful, and his voice wavers. The sadness I experience as I listen to him shows how deeply his songs and sweetness have receded for me, into a past linked to the present hour only by the continuity of memories. Memories alone hold Hugo and me together; and my journal preserves them. Oh, to be able to leap forward without this web around me.

## *SEPTEMBER*

I look into Allendy's face with newborn power, I see his intensely blue, fanatic eyes melt, and I hear the eagerness in his voice when he asks me to return soon. We kiss more warmly than the last time. Henry is still between me and a full tasting of Allendy, but the deviltry in me is stronger. I repeat our kiss in space, holding my head up to it as I walk through the streets, my mouth open to new drink.

All evening his eyes, his mouth, and the ruggedness of his beard stay with me.

I torment Eduardo and arouse his jealousy by awakening the admiration of a young Cuban doctor, whose eyes linger on the lines of my body. We have gone dancing, Hugo, Eduardo, and I. Eduardo wants to draw me back to him, to destroy my exuberance. He is cold, withdrawn, malevolent. He fights against the sinuosity of my body during our dance, the brushing of my cheek, the purring voice in his ears. He kills my joy with his green-eyed fury, and when he has killed it he is unhappy. I see the veins swelling on his temples. He ends the evening with: "What you did to me a few months ago!"

Allendy points out that I abandon myself to the consuming cruelty of life with Henry. Pain has become the ultimate joy. For every cry of joy in Henry's arms, there is a lash of expiation: June and Hugo, Hugo and June. How fervently Allendy now talks against Henry, but I know he is not only discoursing on my plan for self-destruction but that he is moved by his own jealousy. At the end of the analysis I see that he is profoundly disturbed. I have been exaggerating purposely. Henry is the softest, kindest man alive, softer even than I am, though in appearance we are both terrorizers and amoralists. But I enjoy Allendy's concern for me. The power he has nurtured in me is dangerous, more dangerous than my former timidity. He must protect me now by the deftness of his analysis and the strength of his arms and his mouth.

I do not believe men ever had, in one woman, such a potential enemy and such an actual friend. I am full of inexhaustible love for Hugo, Eduardo, Henry, and Allendy. Eduardo's jealousy last night was also my jealousy, my pain. I accompanied him the short distance he wanted to walk, to clear his head, he said. My eyes were blank, my hands cold. I have such a knowledge of pain that I cannot inflict it. Later, at home, Hugo almost threw himself on me, and I opened my legs passively, like a prostitute, empty of feeling. Yet I know that he alone loves generously and selflessly.

Yesterday I told Allendy that I would love to have a dangerous life with Henry and to enter a more difficult, more precarious world; to be heroic and make enormous sacrifices like June, knowing full well that, with my fragility, I would end up in a sanatorium.

Allendy said, "You love Henry out of excessive gratitude, because he has made you woman. You are too grateful for the love given you. It is your due."

I recall the sacrilegious communions during my childhood at which I received my father in place of God, closing my eyes and swallowing the white bread with blissful tremors, embracing my father, communing with him, in a confusion of religious ecstasy and incestuous passion. Everything was for him. I wanted to send him my journal. Mother dissuaded me because it might have gotten lost on the way. Oh, the hypocrisy of my lowered eyes, the hidden bursts of tears at night, the voluptuous secret obsession with him. What I remember best of him at this moment is not paternal protection or tenderness, but an expression of intensity, animal vigor, which I recognize in myself, an affinity of temperament which I recognized with a child's innocent intuition. A volcanic life hunger—that is what I remember and still participate in, secretly admiring a sensual potency that automatically negates my mother's values.

I have remained the woman who loves incest. I still practice the most incestuous crimes with a sacred religious fervor. I am the most corrupt of all women, for I seek a refinement in my incest, the accompaniment of beautiful chants, music, so that everyone believes in my soul. With a madonna face, I still swallow God and sperm, and my orgasm resembles a mystical climax. The men I love, Hugo loves, and I let them act like brothers. Eduardo confesses his love to Allendy. Allendy is going to be my lover. Now I send Hugo to Allendy so that Allendy will teach him to be less dependent on me for his happiness.

When I immolated my childhood to my mother, when I give away all I own, when I help, understand, serve, what tremendous crimes I am expiating—strange, insidious joys, like my love for Eduardo, my own blood; for Hugo's spiritual father, John; for June, a woman; for June's husband; for Eduardo's spiritual father, Allendy, who is now Hugo's guide. It only remains for me now to go to my own father and enjoy to the full the experience of our sensual sameness, to hear from his lips the obscenities, the brutal language I have never formulated, but which I love in Henry.

Am I hypnotized, fascinated by evil because I have none in me? Or is there in me the greatest secret evil?

My analysis was really over when Allendy kissed me the last time and I felt the nascence of a personal relationship. I took great pleasure in his kiss, and an hour later I was in Henry's arms. Henry is asleep now in my writing room, and I sit a few yards away writing about Allendy's kiss. I loved Allendy's bigness, his mouth and his hand at my throat. Henry was waiting for me at the station afterwards. I know I love him and that with Allendy it is coquetry, a pleasant game I am learning to play.

Allendy says that if I were to give Hugo several shocks, like my desire for John, I would rouse him, but I cannot do this, and I prefer to put him in Allendy's hands. To awaken him through pain—here is my limitation, my failure. And secretly, I have a fear of plumbing his limitations. I am afraid to find a fund of deep feeling and nothing else. How much mind, how much imagination, how much sensuality is there in him? Can he ever be resuscitated, or am I to continue this course from man to man? Now that I am moving, I am afraid. Where am I going?

I see what I do not like in Allendy—a certain conventionality, a veneer of conservatism; he is a lightweight being, when what I love are tragic, heavy-souled men, just as Henry said he loved romantic women.

Today Allendy tried not to acknowledge that I am well. He wants me to need him. His analysis was less perfect insofar as there is now a personal element in it. I could see the crumbling of his objectivity. I marvel that this man, who knows the worst about me, is so strongly attracted. I am his creation.

Henry reads Hugo's journal and finds it to be that of a cripple. He begins to suspect I was also a cripple when I married him.

When Henry said this, I brought out my journal of that period, when I was nineteen, and read it to him. He was startled, jubilant, too. He wanted to read more, and to read the novel I wrote at twenty-one.

Hugo was away on a business trip, and for five days

Henry and I lived here together, never going to Paris, working, reading, walking. One afternoon I asked Eduardo to come. They discussed astrology, but secretly they fought each other. Henry told Eduardo he was dead, a fixed star, while he himself was a planet always revolving, always in movement. Eduardo remained composed, superior through his coolness, deftness, courtesy. Henry became confused and lost. Eduardo looked at once faunesque and clever. Henry was slow and Germanic, offering a smile to me, so infinitely moving.

I was glad it was Henry who was staying at Louveciennes—warm, soft, human Henry. He was in such a chastened, helpless mood. We sat in the garden. He said he wanted to be buried there, never to be sent away, to be metamorphosed into a bear who would come in through my bedroom window when anyone was making love to me. He became child, lulled by my tenderness. I had never seen him so small and frail. There is the weirdest contrast between his drunkenness, when he sits flushed, combative, destructive, sensual, all instinct, a man whose animal vitality lures and subjugates women; and his soberness, when he can sit before a woman and read to her from books, talk to her in an almost religious tone, become wistful, pale, holy. It is an amazing transformation. He can sit in the garden like a gentle Eduardo of fifteen years ago, and then a few hours later, bite with great ferocity and utter the most obscene words while we lie convulsed with pleasure.

Yet great tenderness wells up in me when Hugo returns. I want to give him joy, I force myself, and I begin to sincerely respond to his passion. I remember that one evening when Henry and I were lying on the couch in my studio, a string of Hugo's guitar snapped, the deepest string, resonant like his voice. It terrorized me, a foreboding of a finality I do not desire.

I went to Allendy Monday, and I refused to be analyzed because, I said, I had begun to lie to him. So we sat and talked, and he was aware of my hostility. When I first came in I evaded his kiss. What I felt was that he was destroying my relationship with Henry; he was making fissures in it. I resented his strong influence, his domination of me. He answered wisely. Suddenly I again wanted to obey him. I said I was ready for analysis, that I would not lie any more, that I had exaggerated the dangers of my flight with Henry only to see how concerned he was about my life. His strange blue eyes fascinated me. I got up and walked around in my usual way, arms raised behind my head. He stretched out his arms.

He has a big, overwhelming body, like John's. He holds me so tightly I almost suffocate. His mouth is not as voluptuous as Henry's, and we don't understand each other. But I stay in his arms. He says, "I will teach you to play, not to take love so tragically, not to pay such a heavy price for it. You have made it too dramatic and intense a thing. This will be pleasant. I have such a strong desire for you." Detestable wisdom. Oh, I hate him. While he talks I bow my head and smile. He shakes me, wanting to know what I am thinking. I really want to weep. I had aspired to this sort of relationship, and now I have it. Allendy is poised, powerful, but I have upset him. I have got him to love me first, to betray his love. If this is joy, I don't want it. He is aware of my reaction. "This seems tame to you?" There is only his body to fascinate me. He is the unknown.

Eduardo, to whom I pour out this story, is glad I am moving towards Allendy. Both of them hate Henry.

Still, I want Henry tonight, my love, my husband, whom I am going to betray soon with as much sorrow as I felt when I betrayed Hugo. I crave to love wholly, to be faithful. I love the groove in which my love for Henry has been running. Yet I am driven by diabolical forces outside of all grooves.

Hugo is being greatly helped and strengthened by Allendy. He is beginning to love him, because there is in him a certain element of homosexuality.

Allendy is now a devil god directing all our lives. Last night as Hugo talked I could observe Allendy's deft and beautiful influence. I laughed riotously when Hugo said Allendy had told him I needed to be dominated. Hugo answered, "Yes, but that is easy. Anaïs is Latin and so pliable." Allendy must have smiled. Then Hugo comes home and throws himself on me with a new savagery, and I enjoy myself, oh, I enjoy myself. It seems to me that at this moment I am blessed with three wonderful men and quite able to love all three.

I suppose only a scruple keeps me from enjoying them. I wish Allendy were more forceful. He submits to women. He liked my aggressivity in our sexual games. His first sexual experience was a passive one when he was sixteen and an older woman made love to him.

I went back to see him with great impatience, trembling now with cold, now with fever. We have discarded analysis. We talked about Eduardo, Hugo, astrology. I asked him to come and see me, but he feels he cannot yet because of his analysis of Hugo. We laughed together about the domination question. I like the way he caresses me. He makes none of Henry's obscene gestures, yet I feel the man whose planetary symbol is the Bull. I like it when we kiss standing up and I am made to feel small in his arms. He knows me better than I know him. I am baffled by his enigmatic character. I told him that I trusted him blindly, that we should just let things happen. I refused to analyze. This, he understood.

From his house I went to a café on the corner, where I had asked Henry to meet me. Before I saw Allendy, I talked with Eduardo. And at eight-thirty I agreed to meet Hugo. When I saw Henry, I felt estranged from him. I hated my capriciousness.

Now I must keep secrets from Henry, and I can no longer confide everything to Allendy because we are man and woman with passion growing between us. I have lost a father! I cannot tell him I still love Henry. Shall I try to be altogether truthful with Henry?

Hugo plays his guitar tonight while I write and draws me to him with a new violence, roused by analysis. He has been writing profusely in his journal and talking expansively, and, at last, interestingly.

Eduardo does not believe my confidences about Allendy. He thinks we have planned to save him by arousing his jealousy—my beloved pathological child, Eduardo, whom I will love in a certain way eternally. The only time we are happy together is when we retrogress to a magical sphere of beauty. He has wiped our sexual hours from his memory, but not my offense. He dreams that I will one day go to him and crawl on my knees, so that he can make me suffer for flaunting Henry before him.

He fights me blindly, furiously, reproaching me for the night we went out to dance, for my trying to force him to be alive. At the same time his jealousy is obvious, and he shows Allendy a note in which I tell him I love him and will always love him, in a strange, mystical fashion.

I rush to Allendy for help, because my apparent desire for Eduardo was expressed merely to efface the offense he cannot bear. I wanted him to have the last word, to feel that he had refused me, because he needs to feel his strength. But when Allendy shows me the tenderest, most protective love, I rebel against it. He wants to postpone personal intimacy for the sake of the analysis he feels I still need. As I fight off analysis, I betray exactly what he suspects: that I require extravagant, passionate demonstrations of love, not tenderness or protection. He has sensed that I want his love as a trophy, not for his very own self. Yet as soon as I write these words, I know they are not entirely true.

I leave him completely shattered. And today I receive my true love, Henry, with great joy, and ardent commingling. How we flash! And then I realize I can only love fully when I have confidence. I am sure of Henry's love, and so I abandon myself.

Then Henry tells me, because he has been jealous and worried, that he has read about those hysterical women who are capable of loving two or three men profoundly at the same time. Is this what I am?

The only thing psychoanalysis achieves is to make one more conscious of one's misfortunes. I have gained a clearer and more terrifying knowledge of the dangers in my course. It has not taught me to laugh. I sit here tonight as somberly as I sat when I was a child. Henry alone, the most alive of all men, has the power to make me blissful.

I had a stupendous scene with Allendy. I brought him two pages of "explanations," which at first bewildered him. I stressed two moments which made me withdraw from him: one, when he said, "And what is to become of poor Hugo if I let myself go? If he finds out I have betrayed him, his cure will be impossible." Scruples. Like John's scruples. They are unbearable to me, because I have suffered too much from scruples, and so I love Henry's unscrupulousness. June's. They create a balance which puts me at ease. But, as Allendy points out, balance is not to be sought by association with others; it must exist within one's self. I should be free enough of scruples not to need to be swept off my feet by the unscrupulousness of another.

The second complaint: Allendy's great tenderness, aroused by a reading of my childhood journal. I hate all semblance of tenderness, because it reminds me of Eduardo's and Hugo's treatment of me, which nearly wrecked me. Here, Allendy was angry because he misinterpreted my words. Was I comparing him to Eduardo and Hugo? But I had enough presence of mind, although I was weeping, to say how aware I was that my reaction deformed the true sense of tenderness, that there was no weakness in him but, rather, an abnormal craving for aggressiveness and reassurance in me. He talked softly then, explaining how a separation of the erotic and the sentimental was no solution, that although my experience with love, before Henry, had been a failure, I would get no happiness from a purely erotic connection.

At first he wandered in the maze of ramifications I had created. I wanted to confuse him, to elude the exact truth. To my great surprise he suddenly discarded everything I had been saying and said, "You were under the impression last time, because I talked quietly about Hugo and my work, that I loved you less. And immediately you withdrew from me, in order not to suffer. You hardened yourself. It is your childhood tragedy repeating itself. If, when you were a child, you had been made to realize that your father had to live his own life, that he was forced to abandon you, that in spite of this he loved you, you would not have suffered so terribly. And it is always the same. If Hugo is busy in the bank, you feel he is neglecting you. If I talk about work, you are hurt. Believe me, you are deeply mistaken. I love you in a way which is far deeper and more true than what you seek. I sensed that you still needed an analyst, that you were not well. I was determined that no attraction to you should interfere with my care of you. If I were wildly impatient merely to possess you, you would soon realize what a meager gift I was making you. I want more than that. I want to do away with this conflict which causes you so much pain."

"You cannot do any more for me," I said. "Since I have begun to depend on you I feel weaker than ever before. I have disappointed you by acting neurotically at the very moment when I should have shown the wisdom of your guidance. I don't want to ever come back to you. I feel that I must go and work and live and forget about all this."

"That is no solution. This time you must face the whole thing with me. I will help you. I must lay aside all personal desire for the moment, and you must give up this doubt completely today. It always ruins your happiness. If you can accept what I tell you this time—that I love you, that we must wait, that you must realize how entangled I am with Hugo and Eduardo, that I must, first of all, finish my task as a doctor before I take any pleasure in our personal relationship—then we may conquer your reaction for good."

He talked so fervently, so justly. I lay back in my chair, weeping silently, realizing how right he was, racked with pain, not only because of my struggle to win him but because of the accumulated bitterness of all my unhappy relationships.

When I left him, I felt dazed. I almost fell asleep in the train.

To Henry: "Do you remember the time I told you I was in great revolt against Allendy and analysis? He had made me reach a point where, by great effort of logic on his part, he had resolved my chaos, established a pattern. I was furious to think I could be made to fit within one of those 'few fundamental patterns.'

"For me, it became a question of upsetting the pattern. I set out to do this with the most ingenious lies, the most elaborate piece of acting I have ever done in my life. I used all my talent for analysis and logic, which he admitted I had to a great degree, my own ease at giving explanations. As I hinted to you, I did not hesitate to play with his own personal feelings, every bit of power I had I used, to create a drama, to elude his theory, to complicate and throw veils. I lied and lied more carefully, more calculatingly than June, with all the strength of my mind. I wish I could tell you how and why. . . . Anyway, I did it all without endangering our love: it was a battle of wits in which I have taken the utmost delight. And do you know what? Allendy has beaten us, Allendy has found the truth, he has analyzed all of it right, has detected the lies, has sailed (I won't say blithely) through all my tortuousness, and finally proved today again the truth of those damned 'fundamental patterns' which explain the behavior of all human beings. I tell you this: I would never let June go to him, for June would simply cease to exist, since June is all ramifications of neuroses. It would be a crime to explain her away. . . . And tomorrow I go to Allendy and we start another drama, or I start another drama, with a lie or a phrase, a drama of another kind, the struggle to explain, which is in itself deeply dramatic (are not our talks about June sometimes as dramatic as the event we are discussing?). I find that I do not know what to believe, that I have not decided yet whether analysis simplifies and undramatizes our existence or whether it is the most subtle, the most insidious, the most magnificent way of making dramas more terrible, more maddening. . . . All I know is that drama is by no means dead in the so-called laboratory. This is as passionate a game as it has been for you to live with June. And then when you see the analyst himself caught in the currents, then you are ready to believe there is drama everywhere. . . ."

My letter to Henry reveals my lies to him, necessary lies, mostly lies meant to heighten my confidence.

## *OCTOBER*

I spend a night with my beloved. I ask only that he does not return to America with June, which reveals to him how much I care. And he makes me swear that whatever happens when June comes I must believe in him and in his love. It is a difficult thing for me to do, but Allendy has taught me to believe, so I promise. Then Henry asks, "If I had the means today and I asked you to come away with me for good, would you do it?"

"Because of Hugo and June I would not, could not.

But if there were no June and no Hugo, I would go away with you, even if we had no means."

He is surprised. "Sometimes I wondered if it was a game for you." But he sees my face and is moved to silence. A night of clear, calm talk, when sensuality is almost superfluous.

Allendy is watching over my life. He has hypnotized me into a trusting somnolescence. He wants me to be lulled by my happiness, to rest on his love. We decide, for Hugo's sake (Hugo has become jealous of him), that I should not come to see him for ten or twelve days. It is also like a test of my confidence. Suddenly I relax my fevered desire for him and accept his nobility, his seriousness, his self-sacrifice, his concern for my happiness, and I feel humble. What makes me humble is that he believes I love him, and I feel that I am lying. It moves me to think I can lie to this great, sincere man. I wonder whether he knows better than I whom I love or whether I am deceiving him, as I have deceived them all. In 1921, when I was still corresponding with Eduardo, I was already in love with Hugo. If Hugo knew that in Havana, while we were exchanging love letters, I was stirred by Ramiro Collazo. If Henry knew that I love Allendy's kisses, and if Allendy knew how deeply I want to live with Henry . . .

Allendy believes my life with Henry, my low life, is not true or real or lasting, whereas I know I belong to it. He says, "You have traversed shady experiences, but I feel that you have remained pure. They are temporary curiosities, a hunger for experience." Whatever experience I enter I come out unscathed. Everyone believes in my sincerity and purity, even Henry.

Allendy wants me to see my love for Henry as a literary or dramatic excursion and my love for him as an expression of my true self, whereas I believe it is exactly the opposite. Henry has me, mind and womb; Allendy is my "experience."

There is continuous music from our new radio. Hugo listens while he beatifically contemplates the benefits of Allendy's help. The announcer talks in a strange language from Budapest. I think about my lies to Allendy and wonder why I lie. For example, I have worried inordinately about Henry's troubles with his eyes. If he should become as blind as Joyce, what would become of him? I say to myself, "I ought to give up everything and go and live with him and take care of him." When I tell Allendy about my fear, I exaggerate the danger Henry is in.

Lies are a sign of weakness. It seems to me that I do not have the courage to tell Allendy openly I do not love him, and so, instead, I want him to see what I am ready to do for Henry.

An afternoon with Henry. He begins by telling me that our conversation the other night was the deepest and closest we have had, that it has changed him, given him strength. "To run away from June, I feel now, is no solution. I have always run away from women. Today I feel that I want to face June and the problem she represents. I want to test my own strength. Anaïs, you have spoiled me, and now I cannot be satisfied with a marriage based on passion alone. What you have given me I never imagined I could find in a woman. The way we talk and work together, the way you adapt yourself, the way we fit together like hand and glove. With you, I have found myself. I used to live with Fred and listen to him, but nothing that he said really hit me until I lived with you those few days during Hugo's trip. I realize how insidiously you have affected me. I had scarcely felt it, yet suddenly I realize the extent of your influence. You made everything click."

I said, "I will accept June as a devastating tornado while our love remains deeply rooted."

"Oh, if you could do that! Do you know my greatest anguish has been that you might begin to battle with June, that I would be caught between you, not knowing what to do for you, because June paralyzes me with her savagery. If you could understand and wait. It may be a tornado, but I will take my stand once and forever against what June represents. I need to fight this battle out. It is the great issue of my whole life."

"I will understand. I will not make it more terrible for you."

And here we are, Henry and I, talking in such a way that the end of the afternoon finds us rich, eager to write, to live. When we lie down together, I am in such a frenzy that I cannot wait for our unison.

Later we sit in the dim light of the iridescent aquarium, bowed with turmoil. Henry gets up and walks about the room. "I cannot go away, Anaïs. I should be here. I am your husband." I want to cling to him, to hold him, to imprison him. "If I stay another minute," he continues, "I will do something mad."

"Go away quickly," I say. "I can't bear this." As we go down the stairs he smells the dinner cooking. I bring his hands to my face. "Stay, Henry, stay."

"What you desire," said Allendy, "is of lesser value than what you have found."

Because of him, tonight I even understand how John loved me in his own way. I believe in Henry's love. I believe that even if June wins, Henry will love me forever. What tempts me strongly is to face June with Henry, to let her torture us both, to love her, to win her love and Henry's. I plan to use the courage Allendy gives me in greater schemes of self-torture and self-destruction.

No wonder Henry and I shake our heads over our similarities: we hate happiness.

Hugo talks about his session with Allendy. He tells him that love is now like a hunger to him, that he feels the desire to eat me, to bite into me (at last!). And that he has done so. Allendy begins to laugh heartily and asks, "Did she like it?" "It's strange," said Hugo, "but she seems to." Whereupon Allendy laughs even more. And for some queer reason this arouses Hugo's jealousy of Allendy. He had the impression that Allendy took delight in this talk and would have liked to have a bite at me himself.

At this, it is I who laugh madly. Hugo continues seriously, "This psychoanalysis is a tremendous thing, but what a still more terrific thing it must be when the feelings get involved. What if, for instance, Allendy took an interest in you."

Here I get so hysterical that Hugo is almost angry. "What do you find so funny about all this?"

"Your smartness," I said. "Psychoanalysis certainly puts new and amusing ideas into your head."

I realize it is nothing but coquetry with Allendy, coquetry and little feeling. He is a man I want to make suffer, I want to make him wander, to give *him* an adventure! Born of men who sailed the seas, this big healthy man is now imprisoned in his book-lined cave. I like to see him standing at the door of his house, eyes glowing like the blue Mallorcan sea.

"To proceed from the dream outward . . ." When I first heard these words of Jung's, they fired me. I used the idea in my pages on June. Today as I repeated the words to Henry they affected him strongly. He has been writing down his dreams for me, and then antecedents and associations. What an afternoon. It was so cold in Henry's place that we got into bed to warm each other. Then talk, mountains of manuscripts, hills of books, and rivulets of wine. (Hugo comes over while I write this, bends down and kisses me. I had just time enough to turn the page.) I am in a great fever, frantically pulling at the bars of my prison. Henry smiled sadly when I had to leave, at eight-thirty. He realizes now that his not knowing he was a man of great value almost led to his self-destruction. Will I be given time to place him on his throne? "Are you really quite warm enough?" he asks, closing my coat around me. The other night he was stumbling against obstacles on the dark road, his weak eyes blinded by automobile lights. In danger.

At the same time I lead Hugo to Allendy, who not only saves him humanly but awakens in him an enthusiasm for psychology, which makes him interesting.

As I look at Henry talking I realize again that it is his sensuality I love. I want to go deeper into it, I want to wallow in it, to taste it as profoundly as he has, as June has. I feel this with a kind of desperation, a secret resentment, as if Hugo and Allendy and even Henry himself all wanted to stop me, whereas I know that it is I who stop myself. I am terribly in love with Henry, so why doesn't restlessness, fever, curiosity become attenuated? I am steaming with energy, with desires for long voyages (I want to go to Bali), and last night during a concert I felt like Mary Rose in Barrie's play, who hears music while visiting an island, walks away and disappears for twenty years. I felt that I could walk out of my house like a somnambulist, forgetting utterly, as in that hotel room, all my connections and go forth into a new life. Each day there are more demands from me that deprive me of the liberty I need, Hugo's growing demands of my body, Allendy's demands on the noblest in me, Henry's love, which makes me a submissive and faithful wife—all this, against the adventure I must constantly renounce and sublimate. When I am most deeply rooted, I feel the wildest desire to uproot myself.

Hugo's reading of Allendy's books has convinced him that I do not love Allendy, nor he me. It is simply a mutual attraction born of the analysis, the intimacy, certain strong currents of sympathy.

I spend an hour in a café with Henry, who has been reading my journal of 1920, when I was seventeen, and sobbing over it. He was reading about the period when Eduardo did not write to me because he was going through a homosexual experience. Henry said he wanted to write me a letter for each day of disappointment, answer all my expectations, make up to me for every gift denied to me before. I told him it was precisely this he had been doing.

Later, he wrote about my love at seventeen: "And so she exclaims: 'All my heart is singing with my longing for love.' She is in love with love, but not as a mere adolescent, not as a girl of seventeen, but as the embryonic artist that she is, the one who will fecundate the world with her love, the one who will cause suffering and strife because she loves too much. . . .

"In the hands of an ordinary individual the journal may be regarded as a mere refuge, as an escape from reality, as the pool of another Narcissus, but Anaïs refuses to let it sink into this mold. . . ."

The man who understood this, who wrote these lines, at one blow accepts the challenge of my love and shatters the idea of narcissism.

I lay on the couch rereading Henry's letter many times, with acute pleasure, as if he were lying over me, possessing me. No longer do I have to fear loving too much.

After drinking a bottle of Anjou last night, Henry talked about his difficulty in passing from a gentle treatment of women to courtship. He either conversed with them or threw himself on them and ran amuck. He had his first sexual experience at sixteen in a whorehouse and caught a disease. Then came the older woman whom he dared not fuck. He was surprised when it happened and promised himself not to do it again. But it happened, and he went on fearing it was not right. He wrote down the number of times, with dates, like the record of so many conquests. Tremendous physical exuberance, games, stunts, roughhousing.

He told me about his talk with a whore the other night. He was at a café reading Keyserling. The woman approached him, and because she was unattractive, he at first repulsed her. But he let her sit down and talk to him. "I have a hard time attracting men, but when they get to know me they realize I'm better than most whores, because I enjoy going with a man. What I want now is to put my hand in your pants and take it out and suck it."

Henry was affected by the directness of her words, the image she left with him, but he ran away from her. He could not understand why he should have been so susceptible when he was in another world a moment before and when he didn't even like the woman. He prefers aggressivity in women. Was this a weakness? he asked. I didn't know, but I had to learn to be aggressive, to please him.

After he had talked thus, flushed, exultant, dancing before me, illustrating his raving and biting a woman's ass, he was suddenly quiet, thoughtful, and a great change came over his face. "I have outgrown all this," he said. And I, who was clapping at his show, was tempted to say, "I have not outgrown it. I have yet to run amuck."

I look at Hugo's tormented face (a period of torment and jealousy in his analysis) and experience great effusions of tenderness. And Henry says, "When you and I get married, we will take Emilia with us." As we climb the stairs to my "cave" he puts his hands between my legs.

I am rushing again into June's chaos. It is June I want and not Allendy's wisdom, not even Henry's love of aggressivity. I want eroticism, I want those moist dreams I dream at night, four more days like those summer days with Henry when he was constantly throwing me down on the bed, the carpet, or the ivy. I want to wallow in sexuality until I outgrow it or become as sated as Henry.

I arrive at Clichy for dinner, drunk and feverish. Henry has been writing about my writing. The last page is still in the typewriter. And I read these extraordinary lines: "It was presumptuous of me to want to alter her language. If it is not English, it is a language nevertheless and the farther one goes along with it the more vital and necessary it seems.

It is a violation of language that corresponds with the violation of thought and feeling. It could not have been written in an English which every capable writer can employ. . . . Above all it is the language of modernity, the language of nerves, repressions, larval thoughts, unconscious processes, images not entirely divorced from their dream content; it is the language of the neurotic, the perverted, 'marbled and veined with verdigris,' as Gautier put it, in referring to the style of decadence. . . .

"When I try to think to whom it is you are indebted for this style I am frustrated—I do not recall anyone to whom you bear the slightest resemblance. You remind me only of yourself. . . ."

I rejoiced because it seemed to me Henry had written the male counterpart to my work. I sat with him at the kitchen table, drunk and stuttering: "It's wonderful, what you've written!" We got ourselves more drunk, we fucked deliriously. Later, in the taxi, he takes my hand as if we have been lovers only a few days. I come home with two of his phrases engraved on my mind: "surcharged with life" and "saturated with sex." And I will give him greater and more terrifying riddles to unravel than June's lies!

There is in our relationship both humanness and monstrosity. Our work, our literary imagination, is monstrous. Our love is human. I sense when he is cold, I am anxious about his eyesight. I get him glasses, a special lamp, blankets. But when we talk and write, a wonderful deformation takes place, whereby we heighten, exaggerate, color, distend. There are satanic joys known to writers only. His muscular style and my enameled one wrestle and copulate independently. But when I touch him, the human miracle is accomplished. He is the man I would scrub floors for, I would do the humblest and the most magnificent things for. He is thinking of our marriage, which I feel will never be, but he is the only man I *would* marry. We are greater together. After Henry, there will never again be this polarity. A future without him is darkness. I cannot even imagine it.

Allendy admits to Hugo that there is danger in my literary friendships because I play with experience like a child and take my games seriously, that my literary adventures carry me to milieus where I don't belong. Big, compassionate Allendy and faithful and jealous Hugo, anxious over the child who has such a dangerous need of love.

Allendy has not taken my literary-creative side seriously, and I have resented his simplification of my nature to pure woman. He has refused to cloud his vision with a consideration of my imagination.

The absolute sincerity of men like Allendy and Hugo is beautiful but uninteresting to me. It does not fascinate me as much as Henry's insincerities, dramatics, literary escapades, experiments, rascalities. When Henry and I are lying in each other's arms, all games cease, and for the moment we find our basic wholeness. When we take up our work again, we instill our imagination into our lives. We believe in living not only as human beings but as creators, adventurers.

That side of me which Allendy discards, the disturbed, dangerous, erotic side, is precisely the side Henry seizes and responds to, the one he fulfills and expands.

Allendy is right about my need of love. I cannot live without love. Love is at the root of my being.

He talks to ease Hugo's burning jealousy, perhaps to

ease his own doubts. His passion is protective, compassionate, so he underlines my frailty, my naïveté; whereas I, with a deeper instinct, choose a man who compels my strength, who makes enormous demands on me, who does not doubt my courage or my toughness, who does not believe me naïve or innocent, who has the courage to treat me like a woman.

JUNE ARRIVED LAST NIGHT.

Fred telephoned the news. I was stunned, although I had so often imagined the scene. I have been aware all day that June is in Clichy. I choke over work and food, remembering Henry's pleading words: to wait. But the period of waiting is unbearable. I swallow large doses of sleeping medicine. I jump when the telephone rings. I call up Allendy. I'm like a person drowning.

Henry telephoned me yesterday and again today, grave, bewildered. "June has come in a decent mood. She is subdued and reasonable." He is disarmed. Will this last? How long will June stay? What must I do? I cannot wait, here, in this room, face to face with my work.

I go to sleep with pain oppressing me. When I awake in the morning, it lies at the back of my head like a stone. Hugo's love, at this moment, is tremendous, superhuman. And Allendy's. They are fighting for me. I almost died, as a child, to win my father's love, and I let myself die psychically for the same reason, to torment and tyrannize those I love, to obtain their care. This realization has whipped me. I am fighting now to help myself.

I should not give up Henry simply because June is reasonable. Yet I must give him up temporarily, and to do this I must fill the immense vacancy his absence creates in my life.

June telephoned me, and I felt no pang at the sound of her voice, no bliss, none of the excitement I expected to feel. She is coming to Louveciennes tomorrow night.

Hugo drove me to Allendy's. I had planned a trip to London, where I would meet new people and find salvation, sanity. By the time I saw Allendy, I had control of myself. He was so happy to have saved me from masochism. He imagined the end of my subjection to Henry and June. While he kissed my hands continuously he talked eloquently and humanly. The jealous Allendy versus Henry. He is so deft. I happened to say that Henry's great need of woman was due to his being such a man, a hundred-percent man; glory be to the pagan gods that there was no femininity in him. But Allendy said it is precisely the sexually mature man who contains tender and intuitive feminine qualities. The true male has strong protective instincts, which Henry does not have. Allendy is a sage except where Henry is concerned. He, the great analyst, is so jealous that he made the insane statement that perhaps Henry is a German spy.

He wants me to be liberated of the need of love so that I can love him of my own volition. He does not want the need of love to push me into his arms. He does not want to use his influence over me to possess me, as he could. He wants me, first, to stand on my own feet.

He said that Henry enjoyed the power of a love such as I gave him, that he would never again possess such a precious gift in his life, that this happened only because I had no sense of my own value. He hoped, for my sake, that it was over.

I accepted all this rationally. I trust Allendy, and I am drawn to him. (Particularly today, when I saw the sensual modulation of his mouth, the possibility of savagery.) But underneath, I felt, like all women, a strong, protective love for Henry—the more imperfect, the more to be loved.

I grow strong. I telephone Eduardo to help him, to sustain him. I give up my trip to London. I do not need it. I can face Henry and June. The suffocating knot of pain is gone. I do not need to lean on external changes, on new friends.

All this is nothing but a fierce defense against the loss of the lover I will never forget. What is going to become of his work, his happiness.? What will June do to him?—my love, Henry, whom I filled with strength and self-knowledge; my child, my creation, soft and yielding in women's hands. Allendy says he will never again have a love like mine, but I know that I will always be there for him, that the day June hurts him I will be there to love him again.

Midnight. June. June and madness. June and I standing at the station and kissing while the train rushes by us. I am seeing her off. My arm is around her waist. She is trembling. "Anaïs, I'm happy with you." It is she who offers her mouth.

During our evening together she talked about Henry, about his book, about herself. She was truthful, or I am the greatest dupe who ever existed. I can only believe in our ecstasy. I don't want to know, I only want to love her. I have one great fear, that Henry will show her my letter to him and hurt her, kill her.

She compared me to the teacher in *Jeunes filles en uniforme*, and herself to the worshipful girl Manuela. The teacher had beautiful eyes, full of pity, but she was strong. Why does June want to think me strong and herself a passionate child beloved by the teacher?

She wants protectiveness, a refuge from pain, from a life which is too terrible for her. She looks in me for an intact image of herself. So she tells me the whole story of herself and Henry, the other face of the story. She loved and trusted Henry until he betrayed her. He not only betrayed her with women but he distorted her personality. He created a cruel person, which she was not, wounding her tenderest, weakest self. She felt an absence of confidence, a gigantic need of love, of fidelity. She took refuge in Jean, in Jean's loyalty, faith, understanding. And now she has set up a barrage of self-protecting lies. She wants to protect herself against Henry, create a new self inaccessible to him, invulnerable. She draws strength from my faith, my love.

"Henry is not imaginative enough," she says. "He is false. He is not simple enough either. It is he who has made me complex, who has devitalized me, killed me. He has introduced a fictitious personage who could make him suffer torments, whom he could hate; he has to whip himself by hatred in order to create. I do not believe in him as a writer. He has human moments, of course, but he is a trickster. He is all that he accuses me of being. It is he who is a liar, insincere, buffoonish, an actor. It is he who seeks dramas and creates monstrosities. He does not want simplicity. He is an intellectual. He seeks simplicity and then begins to distort it, to invent monsters. It is all false, false."

I am stunned. I sense a new truth. I am not vacillating

between Henry and June, between their contradictory versions of themselves, but between two truths I see with clarity. I believe in Henry's humanness, although I am fully aware of the literary monster. I believe in June, although I am aware of her innocent destructive power and her comedies.

At first she had wanted to fight me. She feared that I believed Henry's version of her. She wanted to arrive in London instead of Paris and ask me to join her there. At the first sight of my eyes she trusted me again.

She talked beautifully, coherently last night. She brought Henry's weaknesses into cruel relief. She shattered his sincerity, his wholeness. She shattered my protection of him. I had achieved nothing, according to her. "Henry only pretends to understand, so he can then turn around and attack, destroy."

I will only know the truth through my own experience with each one. Hasn't Henry been more human with me, and June more sincere? I, who partake of the nature of both, will I fail to destroy their poses, to seize their true essence?

Allendy has deprived me of my opium; he has made me lucid and sane, and I am suffering cruelly from the loss of my imaginary life.

June, too, has become sane. She is no longer hysterical or confused. When I realized this change in her today, I was dismayed. Her sanity, her humanness, that is what Henry wanted, and that is what he is being given. They can talk together. I have changed him, mellowed him, and he understands her better.

Then she and I sit together, knees touching, and look

at each other. The only madness is the fever between us. We say, "Let us be sane with Henry, but together let us be mad."

I walk into the chaos of June and Henry and find them becoming clearer to themselves and to each other. And I? I suffer from the insanity they are leaving behind. Because I pick up their tangles, their insincerities, their complexities. I relive them in my imagination. I can see June again depriving Henry of faith in himself, confusing him. She is destroying his book. Through her love of me, she is seeking to remove my influence on Henry, to win me away from him, to dominate him again, only to leave him dispossessed and reduced; for this, she will even love me. She advises him strongly against publication of his book by the route I have opened. She resents his having lost faith in her capacity to help him. I see her using my means now—reasonableness, calm—to accomplish the same destruction.

I am in her arms in a taxi. She holds me tightly and says, "You are giving me life, you are giving me what Henry has taken away from me." And I hear myself answering in fevered words. This scene in the taxi—knees touching, hands locked, cheek against cheek—is going on while we are aware of our fundamental enmity. We are at cross-purposes. Yet I can do nothing for Henry. He is too weak while she is there, as he is weak in my hands. While I tell her I love her I am thinking of how I can save Henry, the child, no longer the lover to me, because his feebleness has made him a child. My body remembers a man who has died.

But what a superb game the three of us are playing. Who is the demon? Who the liar? Who the human being? Who the cleverest? Who the strongest? Who loves the most? Are we three immense egos fighting for domination or for love, or are these things mixed? I feel protective about both

Henry and June. I feed them, work for them, sacrifice for them. I also must give life to them, because they destroy each other. Henry worries about my walking back from the station at midnight after seeing June off, and June says, "I am afraid of your perfection, of your acuity," and nestles in my arms, to make herself small.

And then a beautiful letter from Henry, his sincerest, because of its simplicity: "Anaïs, thanks to you I am not being crushed this time. . . . Don't lose faith in me, I beg you. I love you more than ever, truly, truly. I hate to put in writing what I wish to tell you about the first two nights with June, but when I see you and tell you, you will realize the absolute sincerity of my words. At the same time, oddly enough, I am not quarreling with June. It is as though I had more patience, more understanding and sympathy than ever before. . . . I have missed you greatly and I have been thinking of you at moments when, God help me, no sane, normal man ought to. . . . And please, dear, dear Anaïs, don't say cruel things to me as you did over the telephone—that you are happy for me. What does that mean? I am not happy nor am I greatly unhappy; I have a sad, wistful feeling which I can't quite explain. I want you. If you desert me now I am lost. You must believe in me no matter how difficult it may seem sometimes. You ask about going to England. Anaïs, what shall I say? What would I like? To go there with you—to be with you always. I am telling you this when June has come to me in her very best guise, when there should be more hope than ever, if I wanted hope. But like you with Hugo, I see it all coming too late. I have passed on. And now, no doubt, I must live some sad beautiful lie with her for a while, and it causes you anguish and that pains me terribly.

"And perhaps you will be seeing more in June than

ever, which would be right and you may hate or despise me but what can I do? Take June for what she is—she may mean a great deal to you—but don't let her come between us. What you two have to give each other is none of my affair. I love you, just remember that. And please don't punish me by avoiding me."

Last night I wept. I wept because the process by which I have become woman was painful. I wept because I was no longer a child with a child's blind faith. I wept because my eyes were opened to reality—to Henry's selfishness, June's love of power, my insatiable creativity which must concern itself with others and cannot be sufficient to itself. I wept because I could not believe anymore and I love to believe. I can still love passionately without believing. That means I love humanly. I wept because from now on I will weep less. I wept because I have lost my pain and I am not yet accustomed to its absence.

So Henry is coming this afternoon, and tomorrow I am going out with June.